FLORIDA PLACE NAMES

ALACHUA TO ZOLFO SPRINGS

First store and ferry landing at Alva, about 1900.

FLORIDA
PLACE NAMES

BY ALLEN MORRIS

JOAN PERRY MORRIS
PHOTO EDITOR

PINEAPPLE PRESS, INC.
Sarasota, Florida

FOR DAVID, WITH LOVE AND GRATITUDE

Inquiries should be addressed to:
PINEAPPLE PRESS, INC.
P.O.Box 3899
Sarasota, Florida 34230

LIBRARY OF CONGRESS
CATALOGING IN PUBLICATION DATA

Morris, Allen Covington, 1909-
      Florida place names : Alachua to Zolfo Springs / Allen Morris ; Joan Perry Morris, photo editor.
            p.   cm.
      Includes bibliographical references and index.
      Originally published: Coral Gables, Fla., University of Miami Press, 1974.
      ISBN 1-56164-084-0: (Hb : alk. paper)
      1. Names, Geographical—Florida.   2. Florida—History, Local.   I. Title.
F309.M673 1995
975.9'003—dc20   95-294
                                                                    CIP

First Edition
10 9 8 7 6 5 4 3 2 1

Design by Carol Tornatore
Printed and bound by Quebecor/Fairfield in Fairfield, Pennsylvania

As City Editor of the *Tampa Morning Tribune* in 1900, and newly arrived in Florida, E. D. Lambright already was fascinated by Florida place names. He was inspired to write what he entitled "The Names of Florida."

THE NAMES OF FLORIDA

He had traveled over Florida, and
    the map had been impressed
On his many mental tablets—
    Pensacola to Key West—
And you couldn't doubt his knowledge
    for he surely had the hunch
On the names of all the places from
    Yulee to Saddle Bunch.

But he stuck to it so constantly and
    he toured the State so long,
That he strained his cerebellum and
    his tired brain went wrong;

From early dawn till late at night, he
    tragically yells:

Alafia, Micanopy, Panasoffkee,
    Bonifay,
Sarasota, Wacahoota, Ocoee,
    Fenholloway
Palma Sola, Umatilla, Cisco and
    Estero Bay.

Tallahassee, Kanapaha, Ochlockonee,
    Manatee,
Pasadena, Panasoffkee, Picolata,
    Mokalee;
All aboard for Okahumpka,
    Withlacoochee, Nocatee.

We'll just take a trip to Joppa,
    Miccosukee and Quintette,
Visit Ichetucknee, Chuluota, Rye and
    don't forget

To see Juno sigh to Jupiter, Romeo
    to Juliette.
Interlachen, Hypoluxo, Econfina and
    Lanark,
Homasassa, Isagora, Early Bird and
    Orange Park,
Take in Jacksonville by daylight and
    Ocala after dark.

Astatula, Istachatta, Osowaw and
    Carrabelle,
Laparita, Manavista, Cassadaga,
    Citronelle,
Gasparilla, Aventina, Boca Grande and
    Sanibel.

Okahumpka, Okeelanta, Okeechobee
    and Osteen,
Ojus, Olga, Ona, Oldsmar, Owanita,
    Tangerine,
Estiffanulga, Islamorada, Osprey,
    Bowling Green.

Change cars here for Eucheeanna,
    stranger have you ever been
To Lacoochee, Ocklawaha, Injunhamoc,
    New Berlin,
To Thonotosassa, Ybor, Wewahitchka or
    to Lynne?

Then there's Largo and Narcoossee,
    Tampa, home of the cigar,
Arredondo, Cerro Gordo, Stillepica,
    Malabar,
And so on, ad infinitum, till you don't
    know where you are.

Now I caught this rhyme infernal as I
    heard this madman rant,
And I thought I would add to it, but
    regret to say I can't—
For Sopchoppy and Eau Gallie were the
    next names on the list
Then Ocheesee and Ochlochnee—
    please excuse me—I desist.

PREFACE

"**L**et's go down to St. Marks for a seafood dinner tonight," or "I'm going to run over to Five Points—anything you want me to get?"

These expressions and variations of them are heard in virtually all households. What they have in common is the use of a place name.

Everyday communication demands that places be consistently identified by a given name. So it is easy to believe the rule of thumb of place name specialists: a place name for every square mile. Florida then would have 54,136 place names.

This compilation obviously does not attempt to list all Florida place names. The foundation for this book is the federal census, the highway map of the State Department of Transportation, and the sectional map of the State Department of Agriculture. To the names of communities have been added the names of counties, present and past, and place names of special historical interest.

I have included ghost towns, even though Florida has very few towns that remain after the people are gone. My personal view is that no community ever passes totally out of existence as long as we remember that people once lived there. In Magnolia, for example, history still lives even if all that remains is a cemetery.

This compilation began in 1946 when I drew together information on the origin of county names for the first edition of *The Florida Handbook*. Subsequently, for the fifth biennial edition, an effort was made to account for the names of all incorporated cities. This updating was followed through the 14th *Handbook* edition. Incidentally, some idea of how fast Florida has produced cities may be gained from these figures: In 1930 Florida had 110 cities whereas in 1993 there were 393. At the time of the 1990 federal census, there were 295 communities of 1,000 or more inhabitants.

The collection of county histories and other Florida materials in the Florida State Library has been a basic source for information. An unpublished survey of Florida places names, compiled in the 1930s by the Works Progress Administration, was an extremely helpful beginning, particularly for the smaller communities. Another source of information was the responses to a 1953 questionnaire I prepared and the Florida State Advertising Commission mailed to postmasters and other officials.

Compiling this book has been fascinating and frustrating. It has been interesting to see the vignettes of community life revealed from my research. The author of a county history commented that one central Florida town had a 19-piece brass band. What more need be said of that town's spirit! What an image that sentence creates of families gathered around a bandstand on a Saturday or Sunday afternoon.

My research has been informative in disclosing anew that those making a choice between Flagler and Miami as the name for the new Dade County community thought Miami meant "sweet water." Of what real importance, then, is all the hair-splitting over what *miami* may have meant to this or that Indian tribe?

And there have been frustrations, too. I invested much time in trying to determine the origin of Bunker Hill, a name that appears with some prominence on maps of Collier County. For no special reason except curiosity, I wanted to know if those who named Florida's Bunker Hill had in mind the American Revolution's misnamed Battle of Bunker Hill. The search went unrewarded, although I talked with seven authorities on the area and read several regional histories. Incidentally, there had been an earlier Bunker Hill in Jefferson County, the source of its name also lost to history, at least for this moment.

Finally, it should be remembered that this book gathers together the knowledge and beliefs of many people. Sources disagree. The most often cited source in the Works Progress Administration's unpublished *Florida Place Names* is "local tradition." What is a compiler to do when there is a conflict of traditions? Here it has been resolved usually by relating all versions or picking the one which seems, on the basis of other evidence, to be more logical. Readers who either disagree or possess other facts are invited to write me at 2015 East Randolph Circle, Tallahassee, FL 32312-3323.

I hope readers will find this book as entertaining and informative to read as I have found it to compile.

Allen Morris

INTRODUCTION

F lorida was the first European name given to a place on this continent. And Florida it has remained, although the land has been Spanish, French, English, and American. Only the pronunciation has changed: the Spanish emphasizing the second syllable, the English the first.

The tradition that it was named Florida in 1513 by Spanish explorer Juan Ponce de León comes from the Spanish historian Antonio Herrera. He wrote that de León sailed along its coast for four days and "believing that land to be an island, they named it Florida, because it appeared very delightful, having many pleasant groves and it was all level. Also because they discovered it at Easter, which as has been said, the Spanish called *Pasqua de Flores*, or Florida."

The shape has changed, too. Not the peninsula: That has remained Florida since de León. But ancient maps show various versions of Florida extending from Cape Hatteras to the Mississippi. Once there were even two Floridas: East and West. And some folks say that Florida is in fact many Floridas. Probably that is so.

Just the name Florida evokes various images, sometimes fantastic, in the minds of people around the globe. What is true of Florida is also true of the many exotic names of places in Florida: Caloosahatchee, Okeechobee, Loxahatchee, Miami, Everglades, Key West. The names of Florida's places are the names of Florida's people, their dreams, fears, hopes, and humor. That is the subject of this book. When the first edition appeared almost two decades ago, I thought it was pretty complete. As the years went by, however, a number of oversights came to my attention. New to this edition are: Tate's Hell Swamp, Devil's Garden, and many others. And how did I overlook one of my favorite places, Ybor City?

Any history of place names in America might properly begin with Indian names, since the Indians were here first and had already named many places. Ironically, almost all of the aboriginal names vanished with the original inhabitants. The many Indian names that survive today came with the relative newcomers who arrived in the 17th and 18th centuries. These newcomers, who came to be known as Seminoles, were Yamasee, from the Carolinas, and Oconee and Creeks, from Georgia.

The Indian names in Florida, as elsewhere in this country, described places in terms useful to the Indians; for example, "cow ford," "bloody creek," "rabbit creek," "sunning turtles," and "fallen tree." So, beware of Indian names that have been translated, as was *Itchepackesassa*, in such idyllic terms as "where the moon put the colors of the rainbow into the earth and the sun draws them out in the flowers." In Creek, *Itchepackesassa*, pronounced itch-e-puck-ah-sas´-sa, simply meant "tobacco field."

Indian names were signposts distinguishing places within a relatively small area from one another (Stewart, 1970). A big river seldom had the same name throughout its course because, as Stewart wrote, a tribe often had no idea from where its rivers came or where they went.

There was no universal Indian language. "To say that a name is Indian is even less than to say that it is European, for among the tribes the languages differed much more than English from French, Dutch, or Russian," said Stewart. The native Florida tribes that were numerous and powerful for a century and a half after the discovery of America contributed little to the catalog of Florida names. These early tribes disappeared long ago, and with the exception of the Timucua, little or nothing is known of their languages.

According to the standard work for this state, *Florida Place-Names of Indian Derivation* by J. Clarence Simpson, published by the Florida Geological Survey in 1956:

> We are immediately impressed by the observation that most of the surviving Indian place-names are derived from the language of those immigrant bands from the North who moved into Florida after the decline and disappearance of the native Floridians. The newcomers were principally speakers of Hitchiti and Creek, or of other tribes whose language indicated affiliation with the basic Muskogean linguistic stock.

Simpson cautions us to remember that none of the old Indian languages had a written form with either an original alphabet of any description or an established orthography. The various Europeans who heard the Indian words spoken and attempted to express them in writing followed the usages of their own European languages.

Other authoritative books in the field of Indian names are Professor William A. Read's *Florida Place-Names of Indian Origin and Seminole Personal Names* and Minnie Moore-Willson's *The Seminoles of Florida*.

In the early days of settlement after Florida passed into American possession, names were chosen to honor postmasters and early landowners or to honor railroad officials. For example, Jacksonville gained its name from the first American governor of Florida, Andrew

Jackson, and Bradenton from a pioneer sugar grower, Dr. Joseph Braden. Plant City was named for Henry B. Plant of the Atlantic Coast Line Railroad, and the name of Flagler County came from Henry M. Flagler of the Florida East Coast Railway. In later years, Floridians sought names for cities that were intended to create the image of a good place to live. Interestingly, when settlers named the 7,712 lakes in Florida, however, they broke away from these patterns of name-choosing and usually said what they thought.

Cockroach Creek in Hillsborough County is an example of some now-forgotten incident that resulted in a place name. It is easy to guess what precipitated the naming of the two Baptizing Ponds in Washington County and the Baptizing Hole in Sumter County.

Sunday picnics come to mind with the names of the six lakes or ponds called Dinner. Booze Lake in Madison County well could commemorate a pioneer family of that name rather than something alcoholic. There is Beer Can Pond in Leon County, Polecat Lake in Polk County, Starvation Lake in Hillsborough County, Yankee Lake in Seminole County, Stealing Lake in Walton County, Up and Down Lake in Putnam County, Squaw Pond in Marion County, Lake Confusion in Polk County, and River Styx Lake in Alachua County. Other interesting names are the five lakes called Hiawatha and Kitchen Cow House Pond in Levy County, Camel Pond in Liberty County, Lake Hellen Blazes in Brevard, and, wonder of wonders, Lake Morality in Franklin County.

Repetitive names include: 37 variations of Sand Lake, including Sand Mountain Pond in Washington County; 59 names prefaced by Little, including Little Hell Lake in Suwannee County; 29 Long Lakes or Ponds; 27 versions of Mud Lake or Pond; 20 Silver Lakes; 17 Black Lakes; 15 Crystal Lakes; 14 Buck Lakes; 12 Duck Ponds; 12 Horseshoe Lakes; five Rattlesnake Lakes or Ponds; and three Red Bug Lakes.

Sentiment likely dictated the frequent use of the names of women to identify lakes. The roll call of these include: Ada, Adelaide, Alice, Alma, Amelia, Ann, Anna Maria, Annette, Annie, Bess, Bessie, Blanche, Caroline, Carrie, Catharine or Catherine, Cathy, Charlotte, Cindy, Clara, Claire, Cloe, Cora Lee, Daisy, Dora, Effie, Elizabeth, Ella, Ellen, Erin, Fanny, Florence, Frances, Gertrude, Grace, Helen, Hettie, Hilda, Ida, Idamere, Irene, Jane, Jennie, Jessie, Jewel, Josephine, Katherine, Kathryn, Kitty, Lou, Lena, Lenore, Lillian, Lily, Lizzie, Louisa, Louise, Lucie, Lucy, Lulu, Mable, Margaret, Maria, Marie, Martha, Mary, Mary Ann, Mary Jane, Miranda, Minnie, Molly, Myrtle, Nan, Nellie, Nona, Ola, Opal, Sara, Sarah, Stella, Susan, Susannah, Sylvia, Victoria, Virginia, Violet, Violetta, Wilma, and Yvonne.

Anyone not yet honored has plenty of opportunity for this to be done. The census taken in 1969 by the State Department of Conservation, now the Department of Environmental Protection, showed literally hundreds of unnamed lakes in Florida.

Another historical influence on Florida place names has been the unusually large number of forts built here. Florida often has been called the nation's most fortified state. Even many of those who use the term do not realize just how true it is. Counting the Spanish, French, and British forts for which we have recorded history, more than 300 forts, batteries, redoubts, and named camps existed in Florida from earliest settlement to 1903, according to the meticulous research of Francis B. Heitman, compiler of the *Historical Register and Dictionary of the United States Army.*

The great forts—Clinch at Fernandina Beach, Castillo de San Marcos at St. Augustine, Jefferson in the Dry Tortugas, and Pickens and Barrancas at Pensacola—are the exceptions among the hundreds of Florida forts. Virtually all American forts of the Seminole wars were simple defensive works, usually a combination of ditches and embankments of earth and trees to protect relatively small military units for short periods of time. Their temporary nature means that all but traces of them have disappeared.

Although Spanish, French, and British forts usually were named for saints or members of royal families, American forts generally were named after officers of the local command. Of the surviving towns, therefore, Fort Lauderdale was named for Maj. William Lauderdale, Fort Meade for Lt. George Gordon Meade (later Gen. Meade of Gettysburg), Fort Myers for Lt. Abraham Charles Myers (afterward Gen. Myers), and Fort Pierce for Lt. Col. Benjamin Kendrick Pierce. But there were the usual exceptions, that is, Fort Pleasant and Camp Lang Syne.

Six incorporated cities retain today the names of forts: Fort Lauderdale, Fort Meade, Fort Myers, Fort Pierce, Fort Walton, and Fort White.

A number of forts survive in communities that have dropped Fort from their name: Maitland once was Fort Maitland, Jupiter once was Fort Jupiter, and Dade City once was Fort Dade. Still others are known now by different names: Miami was Fort Dallas, Jacksonville was founded across the river from the old site of Fort San Nicholas, and Tampa grew up on the fringe of Fort Brooke.

Finally, I would like to mention that no place names are more important to the typical man or woman than those of the streets on which he or she lives and works. Unfortunately, this book does not have room for the inclusion of all the names of interest. By mentioning a few in these final paragraphs, however, I would like to encourage each of my readers to appreciate the sense of history that surrounds us if we will but notice it.

I reside on land within the Lafayette grant, and my office window overlooks a columned face of Florida's 1902 Capitol. I have no problem identifying with Florida's history because I am so near to it. You may not be as fortunate, but history has touched everywhere in our state. The names of streets of many communities recall significant events in Florida's life. Miami's Flagler Street, Pensacola's Palafox Street, Jacksonville's Bay Street, and Tampa's Lafayette Street are among those streets of memories. As Malcolm Johnson, editor of the *Tallahassee Democrat,* once wrote: "The street names of an old city . . . provide an index to its history." Let us take the capital, for example: Tallahassee's main street, Monroe, was named for President James Monroe, who was in office when Florida was acquired from Spain. Paralleling Monroe is Adams Street, named for John Quincy Adams, Monroe's secretary of state who succeeded him in the presidency. DuVal Street was named for William P. DuVal, the first territorial governor. Other Tallahassee street names recall persons whose identification with Florida may be found elsewhere in this book: Gadsden, Lafayette, Gaines, and Call.

There is a street name in Tallahassee that evidences the love of liberty that existed when the nation was young and also how place names are corrupted through the passage of time. Boulevard started out as Bolivar, named for the South American liberator Simón Bolívar, who was a hero of the hemisphere when Tallahassee was established. Eventually some French people settled on Boulevard. "Bolívar sounds very much like Boulevard, as the French pronounce it, so gradually that's the way it came to be spelled," explained Johnson. But that was not the end of Bolívar/Boulevard: in 1980 the street became Martin Luther King, Jr., Boulevard.

Another of Tallahassee's streets gained its present name in an interesting way. McCarthy Street, so named in 1845, became Park Avenue because a prominent Tallahassee woman felt McCarthy was too plebeian a name to appear on her daughter's wedding invitations. Park Avenue, to her thinking, had the right sound, so McCarthy became Park.

Alachua's Atlantic Coast Line Railroad depot, 1975.

Zolfo Springs' main street in the 1920s.

ABERDEEN • *Jackson County*
Recognized as a post office in 1889 and named for the Scottish county and seaport on the North Sea.

ABE'S **S**PRINGS • *Calhoun County*
Abe has been perpetuated in the name of this community. If only someone would come forward with his last name! The community is an old one, a post office having been established here in October 1850. Once the seat of Calhoun County, the name appears also as Abe Springs Bluff and Abe's Springs Bluff.

ABINES **P**OINT • *Franklin County*
Known also as Light House Point, it is the eastern extremity of St. James Island, the western limit of the entrance to Apalachee Bay. Simpson (1956) says this word resembles the Chocktaw *abina*, "an outdoor camp or lodging," and "this may have been its meaning in the Apalachean tongue."

ACHACKWEITHLE **B**LUFF • *Franklin County*
Better known now as Prospect Bluff, this is a low rise on the east bank of the Apalachicola River not far above its mouth. A British fort was built here in 1814. Simpson (1956) finds the word likely was corrupted from the Creek *ahechka*, "view or prospect," and *huethle*, "standing up."

ACHAN • *Polk County*
All that remains now is the reclaimed area of an early phosphate digging, reported Homer Hooks of the Florida Phosphate Council in 1973. A source suggests Achan was named for the Israelite who sinned by stealing gold and silver of Babylon (*Joshua 7:19-26.*) This seems unlikely. Hooks opined the railway, as often was the case, bestowed the name of a right-of-way engineer or some other person or place. Hooks suggested it could have been a corruption of Aachen, the German city known to the French as Aix-la-Chappelle.

ACLINE • *Charlotte County*
From 1910; signifies "without inclination," "horizontal," literally "a flat place."

ACOSTA **B**RIDGE • *Duval County*
Dedicated July 1, 1921, as the first motor vehicular bridge across the St. Johns River at Jacksonville. Named for St. Elmo W. (Chic) Acosta, who had served Duval County as a state representative and county commissioner.

ACRON • *Lake County*
Now known as Paisley and formerly as Lightwood, Acron may have derived its name from the Greek *acro*, meaning "topmost or highest."

ACTON • *Polk County*
Established by a group of Englishmen in 1884 and named after the British author Lord Acton. The community lasted until 1894, when its residents scattered after a great freeze. During its decade of existence, Acton had about 200 inhabitants, a hotel, a sawmill, stores, and a church. Its atmosphere, dress, and customs were typically English, with polo, fox hunting, and cricket a part of life. Lakeland has absorbed the site of Acton.

ADAM • *Alachua County*
Adam, in Alachua County, and Eve, in Levy County, were separated by a few miles, but linked by a railroad. At the turn of the century, sawmills, turpentine stills, and phosphate mines were served by the railroad, and it was railroad officials who named Adam and Eve. Adam remains on the sectional map of the Florida Department of Agriculture, but Eve has disappeared. Unlike Adam, Eve had a post office between 1899 and 1909.

ADAMSVILLE • *Sumter County*
Retains a place in history for a negative reason: It was from Adamsville that the Lee family in the 1860s spread out into neighboring lands, finally to establish the city known as Leesburg. Adamsville was the seat of Sumter County in the 1850s. Known first as Okahumpka, the community became Adamsville in 1852, taking the name of Postmaster John Adams.

AERONAUTIC • *Escambia County*
The name used for three years, beginning in 1914, for the post office at the Navy's flying school at Pensacola.

AGRICOLA • *Polk County*
A Latin name which signifies agriculturist. The natural fertility of the soil and the fact that this is the greatest citrus-producing county in Florida probably prompted the name.

ALACHUA • *Alachua County*
Can be traced back to the first half of the eighteenth century, and appears to have had the same name since that time. It is a derivative of the Seminole-Creek Indian word *luchuwa*, meaning "jug," apparently given when the place was first settled by Creeks who came down from Oconee in Georgia. The "jug" was a large chasm in the earth about two and a half miles southeast of the present site of Gainesville. The name, with slight variations in spelling, is used to indicate a Creek settlement on maps of 1715, 1720, and 1733. When the town became a center of white population following the British acquisition of Florida in 1763, the name was left unchanged and later applied to the county formed there, whose seat is at Gainesville.

ALACHUA COUNTY
The ninth county, established December 29, 1824.

ALADDIN CITY • *Dade County*
Developed during the boom of 1925. It was built so rapidly in the rich farmland of South Dade County that it was named for the lad in *Arabian Nights* who acquired the magic lamp. Later, the land reverted for a time to its agricultural use. It is west of Goulds and south of Richmond on the Seaboard Railroad.

ALAFIA • *Polk and Hillsborough counties*
A river in Polk and Hillsborough counties and a community in Hillsborough county. The river appears by that name on an 1839 map, and the community on an 1855 postal list, although the area has been continuously settled at least since 1836. The name likely derives from the Spanish *alafia*, a species of the dogbane family known in Florida as oleander and periwinkle.

An 1890s Gainesville Bicycle club in front of the Alachua County Courthouse.

ALAMANA • *Volusia County*
Established in 1910 and named for a settler, J. A. Alaman.

ALAPAHA RIVER • *Hamilton County*
A stream traversing Hamilton County to discharge into the Suwannee River. This appears to be the Muscogee or Creek word *halpata*, "alligator," as these saurians were formerly abundant in the stream.

ALAQUA CREEK • *Walton County*
A corruption of Seminole-Creek *hilukwa*, "a sweet gum."

ALBERT • *Lake County*
Captain D. J. Westbrook, prominent among those who reestablished the citrus industry in Lake County after the big freeze of 1885, probably named this community, located on the Palatlakawha River near Lake Susan, for one of his sons.

ALBION • *Levy County*
From Albion, a poetical name for England. The community gained post office recognition in 1878.

ALDERMANS FORD • *Hillsborough County*
For years the traditional place for state and county candidates to begin political campaigns in Hillsborough County.

ALDRICH LAKE • *Orange County*
From the first settlers, of Scottish origin, who homesteaded here.

ALFORD • *Jackson County*
Named for S. A. and Chauncey Alford, who were pioneer naval stores operators in the vicinity during the early part of the century.

ALIMACANI • *Duval County*
The Timucuan name of both the present Fort George Island and of a village on the island. Here also was later a Spanish mission known as San Juan del Puerto, from the location near the mouth of the St. Johns River.

ALLANDALE • *Volusia County*
Once known as Halifax City, the place later was known for two brothers, Thomas and William Allen, who settled here in the 1880s. At that time there already was an Allendale, in Osceola County; hence, Allandale.

ALLANTON • *Bay County*
For Andrew Allen, who was postmaster in 1902. Again, the number of Allens and variations among Florida post offices may have resulted in this post office being spelled with an "a" instead of an "e."

ALLAPATTAH • *Dade County*
A community center in Miami. From the Seminole-Creek *halpata*, "alligator."

ALLENHURST • *Brevard County*
Formerly known as Haulover, where travelers transferred from the St. Johns River to the Indian River. Established by Captain D. Dummitt in 1852. Commodore J. H. Allen and associates formed a hunting club here in the early 1900s and the change of name followed.

ALLIANCE • *Jackson County*
For the Farmers' Alliance, organized in 1886 at nearby Chipley as a political action arm of agriculturists-populists. Fielding a candidate for governor in 1892, this group polled 14,000 votes to the winning Democratic nominee's 22,000 and thereby earned political recognition.

ALLIGATOR • *Columbia County*
Originally called *Alpata Telophka*, or Alligator Town, this site was a Seminole village ruled by the powerful Chief Alligator, an instigator of the Dade Massacre, which began the Seminole War of 1835. Following the cessation of hostilities, a settlement sprang up on the site of the old Seminole village and became known simply as Alligator. As time passed, some citizens found Alligator distasteful as the name of the seat of Columbia County. They caused the 1858 Senate to pass a bill changing its name to Lake City. In the House, a puckish member moved to amend by substituting "Crocodile" for "Lake." Fortunately for the Lake City boosters, the amendment failed.

Alligator town was ruled by the powerful Seminole chief, Alligator.

Picnic at Alligator, former name of Lake City, circa middle 1880s.

ALLIGATOR (CREEK, LAKE, REEF, BAY, POINT) •

A peculiarity of this common creature—pointed out by the master of American place names, George R. Stewart—is that its name rarely was transferred from natural features to places of human habitation. Perhaps the reason is that people usually give to places of residence names which convey some measure of warmth: warmth often in the sense of personal identification or warmth in the sense of promotional attractiveness. Like Rattlesnake, Alligator has an image of unpleasantness that caused few if any to want the name applied to a home site. A possible exception is Alligator Point, a spit of land in Franklin County jutting into Apalachee Bay which has become the summer home of many families from the Big Bend of Florida and neighboring Georgia and Alabama. But in this instance, the name of the place came before the general settlement. Too, there is at least one instance of the name not being repugnant to residents because it was used in a corruption of the Seminole-Creek version *halpata* or, as Miamians know it, Allapattah, for the community in the northwest section of that city.

ALLIGATOR ALLEY • *Collier and Broward counties*

An 84-mile cross-state tollway through the Big Cypress Swamp and the Everglades, commencing near Naples on the west coast and ending at Andytown, 16 miles west of Fort Lauderdale on the East Coast. The road was to have been known as the Everglades Parkway but Alligator Alley, first used disparagingly ("only alligators would use that road," scoffed one opponent to its construction), has gained official acceptance.

ALMARANTE • *Walton County*

An area of the Euchee Valley first settled by Scots in 1823.

Waiting for the train at the Altamonte Springs depot, about 1885.

ALPINE • *Highlands County*
Gained its name from the location in the scenic highlands.

ALPINE HEIGHTS • *Walton County*
This name derives from the fact that Florida's highest known natural point, a hill of 345 feet, is nearby in northeast Walton County.

ALSACE • *Manatee County*
For the French province, possibly named by immigrants during the period when the province was a part of Germany.

ALTAMONTE SPRINGS • *Seminole County*
In 1882, a group of Boston businessmen bought 1,200 acres of high, lake-dotted land and formed the Altamonte Land, Hotel and Navigation Company. The original seat of their operation, reports Mary Ann Campbell, was called simply Altamonte and was about three miles northwest of the present Altamonte Springs, which originally was called Snow's Station. Springs followed as a name to call attention to the small spring and its therapeutic value.

ALTHA • *Calhoun County*
The post office at Altha was established in 1901, and the postmaster, Lula M. Richards, chose the name. Mrs. Richards studied a postal guide containing 5,000 names and chose Altha because there was only one other office with that name and it was far away. Old maps show an Indian village called *Hyhappo* or Savannah near this place.

ALTON • *Lafayette County*
When Gov. George F. Drew, who in 1865 built Florida's largest sawmill at Ellaville on the Suwannee River, extended his operations into Lafayette County, he named a sawmill site here after his birthplace: Alton, N. H.

ALTOONA • *Lake County*
Either Thomas J. Hinson, a pioneer lumberer, or Augustus Gottschee, an early merchant, named this town in the 1880s for his former home in Altoona, Penn.

ALTURAS • *Polk County*
In the scenic highlands of central Florida. The name is of Spanish origin and means "high land." The community had its beginning in 1913.

ALVA • *Lee County*
The founder of the community in the 1880s was Capt. Peter Nelson, a Dane, who conferred the name because of a small white flower he had found growing there. Alva derives from the Latin *alba*, signifying "white."

AMELIA (CITY, ISLAND, RIVER) • *Nassau County*
In establishing the colony of Georgia, Gen. James Oglethorpe put a garrison on the island to prevent an attack, and in 1734 named the island Amelia to honor Princess Amelia, daughter of King George II of England.

AMERICAN BEACH • *Nassau County*
Before integration of Florida's improved beaches, blacks had few ocean or gulf bathing facilities. *Florida: A Guide to the Southernmost State* says employees of the Afro-American Life Insurance Company of Jacksonville established American Beach in the 1930s to meet this need. A seaside tract of some 20 acres, American Beach offered summer cottages and year-round homes.

AMHERST • *Brevard County*
Whether commemorating Amherst College; Amherst, Mass.; Amherst, Ohio; Amherst County, Va.; Amherst Glacier, Alaska; or some individual, the name surely derives from Baron Jeffrey Amherst, who was, as the song goes, a soldier of the king and came from a far "countree." Lord Amherst was governor-general of British North America, 1760-1763. Amherst, Fla., dates from the 1950s.

A. L. Lewis first had the idea of acquiring a beach resort and influenced the naming of American Beach streets.

ANACAPE • *Volusia County*
Indians of the Surruque tribe had a settlement called Anacape just north of the Tomoka River. In 1655, a mission known as San Antonio de Anacape was built. By 1680, the Surruque Indians had disappeared, having been displaced by Yamasees from Georgia.

ANASTASIA • *St. Johns County*
Said to be a corruption of the Spanish *Santa Estacia* and said to have been named by Pedro Menéndez, who landed here on this saint's day in 1565. At one time during the English period, it was known as Fish Island, named for Jesse Fish, one of the most influential inhabitants of the province.

ANCLOTE (COMMUNITY, KEY, RIVER) • *Pinellas and Pasco counties*
Spanish for "safe anchorage." This was applied to the basin or bay inside the keys.

Anclote light, at Tarpon Springs, in the 1910s.

ANDALUSIA • *Flagler County*
For a region in southern Spain, bordering on the Atlantic Ocean and the Mediterranean Sea.

ANDREWS • *Nassau County*
A post office for ten years beginning in 1910. The community likely bore a family name.

ANDYTOWN • *Broward County*
Andy Poulus, then a linen service operator in Philadelphia, stopped in 1947 at a small cafe at the junction of U.S. 27 and S.R. 84 for a cup of coffee. He returned the next day and bought ten acres at the junction for $50,000. Poulus retired to south Florida and the junction developed into a sizable community. Poulus died in 1972 during a visit to his native Greece, a place he left at the age of ten. Andytown was demolished in 1979 to make way for expansion of Alligator Alley, the section of Interstate 75 that crosses the Everglades.

ANGEL CITY • *Brevard County*
State Rep. Jane W. Robinson reported in 1973 that Angel City was named for an early settler, John Angel. The community had a post office between 1927 and 1932.

ANGLEVILLE • *St. Lucie County*
Appears to have been the predecessor name of the present Angle Road community. The name may have been derived from a byway to the main road.

ANHAICA • *Leon County*
The village, near the present city of Tallahassee, where Hernando De Soto established winter quarters in 1539 after leading his army on a circuitous march from Tampa Bay, harassed by Indians and passing near the present sites of Manatee, Ruskin, Dade City, Inverness, Ocala, and across the Suwannee River. It was at Anhaica that the first Christmas mass in the United States probably was celebrated, since 12 priests accompanied De Soto's army.

ANKONA • *St. Lucie County*
Founded in the 1880s, this community is distinguished for having been the birthplace of a chief justice of the Florida Supreme Court, Elwyn Thomas.

ANNA MARIA ISLAND • *Manatee County*
Tradition (and the Manatee County Historical Society) says that Ponce de León visited this island in 1513 and gave it the name of the queen of his sponsor, King Charles II. Indians of the Timucua tribe lived here, and their burial mounds have been the source of artifacts for archaeologists seeking to learn about the Timucua. Pronunciation of the island's name is a matter for dispute: Anna Mar-EYE-a has been the favorite of many old-timers, but islanders nowadays are said to prefer Anna Mar-EE-a.

ANNUTTELGIA • *Citrus, Hernando, and Pasco counties*
The name applied to a hammock in Citrus, Hernando, and Pasco counties. For an obvious reason, it is better known as Big Hammock. Simpson (1956) believes the ancient name was derived from the Creek *nuchka*, "sleep," and *laiki*, "site," which with the vocative prefix 'A' would indicate a sleeping or lying down place.

ANONA • *Pinellas County*
A variation of *Annona reticulata*, the custard apple, which is the fruit of a small West Indian tree growing along the Florida west coast. This fruit—with soft, rather insipid, edible, yellowish-green pulp—is also known as the sweetsop. The community dates from the 1880s.

ANTHONY • *Marion County*
First called Anoty Place. Named for Col. E. C. Anthony, who in 1882 was one of a group which established the community as a center for citrus, cattle, lumbering, and sheep-raising.

ANTIOCH • *Hillsborough County*
Thought to have been named for the capital of Syria, the starting point of Paul's first missionary journey (*Acts 6.5*). Antioch supported a post office in 1892.

APALACHEE • *Jefferson, Leon, and Wakulla counties*
A name originally applied to the territory between the Aucilla and Ochlockonee rivers and to its aboriginal inhabitants. Most likely from the Choctaw *apelichi*, "the place in which to rule, preside, or govern."

APALACHICOLA • *Franklin County*
One of the most musical names to be found on the map of Florida, and asso-

ciated in the minds of most people with a most excellent and delicious oyster. According to some authorities, *apalachicola* is a Hitchiti Indian word which means simply, "the people on the other side." Simpson (1956), however, says *apalachi* is a Choctaw word signifying "allies." The settlement of the present site of the town dates back to the times of the Creek Indians, and since it is located at the tip of a considerable peninsula, just west of the mouth of a river, the first version explains how the word might have become the designation of those who lived there. It later was applied to the river and the bay into which it empties. Apalachicola is the county seat of Franklin County.

APALACHICOLA BAY • *Franklin County*
Off the coast of Franklin County. Called *Inlet of Tanaquachile* by Bishop Don Gabriel Díasvara Calderón.

APALACHICOLA RIVER
Formed by the convergence of the Chattahoochee and Flint rivers, at the north border line of Florida, the Apalachicola flows south through the state, forming boundary lines for a number of counties before emptying into Apalachicola Bay. Cotton is believed to have been first shipped in 1822 down the Apalachicola River, destined for New York. By 1836, 43 three-story brick cotton warehouses and brokerages lined the city of Apalachicola's waterfront. Their granite-columned facades caused Apalachicola to be known as The City of Granite Fronts. By 1840, 130,000 bales of cotton left Apalachicola annually after being fed into the port by riverboats. Foreign and domestic shipments amounted to between $6 million and $8 million a year. Apalachicola was the third-largest cotton port in the United States. Between 1828 and 1928, some 200 sidewheelers and sternwheelers plied this waterway. Corresponding amounts of merchandise were received for transportation into the interior.

APOLLO BEACH • *Hillsborough County*
Named by its developers in the 1950s for the Greek and Roman god of light because of the pleasing suggestion of a sunlit beach.

APOPKA • *Orange County*
Authorities seem to agree that the Indian word from which this town derives its name has something to do with eating, but just what was eaten is uncertain. One source gives two Creek words, *aha*, "potato," and *papka*, "eating place," and asserts that the original spelling was Ahapopka. Another ascribes the name to the word *tsalopopkohatchee*, "catfish-eating creek." Still another gives *tsala apopka* as meaning "trout-eating-place." Of this we can be certain: the town shares its name with Lake Apopka.

APOXSEE • *Osceola County*
From the Seminole-Creek *apaksi*, "tomorrow." The name was bestowed on the place in the 1920s by J. E. Ingraham, vice president of the Florida East Coast Railway and president of its subsidiary Model Land Company.

APPLE CREEK • *Columbia County*
From the crabapple trees here.

Arcadia before the 1904 fire.

AQUILLA (LAKE AND SWAMP) • *Alachua and Bradford counties*
What we know today as Santa Fe Swamp and the adjacent Big and Little Santa Fe lakes once were called Aquilla. Simpson (1956) finds the name derived from the Timucuan *aquilla*, which means "reed or vine."

ARCADIA • *DeSoto County*
First called Waldron's Homestead, then Tater Hill Landing, and finally Arcadia. Local tradition denies that the name has anything to do with Arcadia in Greece or Arcadia in Louisiana or the French-Canadian Acadia, also in Louisiana. Instead, say the old-timers, the town was named by the Rev. James (Boss) Hendry, who built a sawmill here on July 23, 1884, his 45th birthday. The day before, Arcadia Albritton, daughter of pioneer settlers at Lilly on Horse Creek, had baked him a birthday cake.

ARCH CREEK • *Dade County*
One of the satellite communities gathered into Miami in the 1920s. The name derives from a stream flowing beneath a natural bridge of oölitic rock. The old Dixie Highway, the first road down the east coast to Miami, passed over the bridge. More than a century earlier it was part of the Capron Trail, over which United States soldiers marched in their campaign to blockade the Seminoles from their source of supplies in Cuba. At the south end of the bridge was Luis the half-breed's stone house and mill, where Seminoles and federal troops fought a bitter battle. Luis, part Indian and part Cuban, was killed, his house and mill demolished, and the Indians retreated into the Everglades.

Trains at the Archer depot in the 1890s.

ARCHER • *Alachua County*
Established in 1852 by the Florida Land Company of Fernandina, and at first called Deer Hammock. Later it was renamed in honor of Brig. Gen. James J. Archer of the Army of the Confederacy. Archer had fought in the Mexican War, where he was brevetted in the field following the Battle of Chapultepec. In the Civil War he fought at Seven Days, Cedar Mountain, Second Manassas, Antietam, Fredericksburg, Chancellorsville, and Gettysburg. He was captured by the federal forces and held prisoner for a year, dying soon after his release in 1864. Early settlers were drawn to this section for the planting of orange groves. A company of Quaker settlers from Indiana and Ohio planted oaks throughout the vicinity to act as windbreaks.

ARGYLE • *Walton County*
Established in 1883. Thought to be named after Argyll, a county in West Scotland, perhaps at the suggestion of one of the many Scots who settled in the Euchee Valley beginning in 1823.

ARIEL • *Volusia County*
Named for Lake Ariel in Pennsylvania by settlers in the early 1900s.

ARIPEKA • *Pasco County*
Read (1934) says Sam Jones, a famous Miccosukee chief, went by the name of *Aripeka* or *Arpeika*. The name is possibly corrupted from Creek *abihka*, "pile at the base," "heap at the root," an ancient Creek town near the upper Coosa River. The name was conferred on the town because "in the contest for supremacy its warriors heaped up a pile of scalps, covering the base of the war-pole."

Arran railroad depot, 1906.

ARLINGTON • *Citrus County*
Thought to be named in the 1880s for Arlington, Va., the home of Gen. Robert E. Lee.

ARLINGTON • *Duval County*
A community within the present Jacksonville. Likely, another reminder of Gen. Lee's Arlington. A part of present-day Arlington was originally known as Matthews, but the name was changed to Arlington in 1912.

ARNO • *Alachua County*
Said to be a slightly misspelled tribute to George Arnow, editor of the newspaper *The Cotton States* during the Civil War.

ARRAN • *Wakulla County*
Established in the 1890s and believed to have been named for the Scottish island in the Firth of Clyde.

ARREDONDO • *Alachua County*
The name is that of Don Fernando de la Maza Arredondo, who received a grant of 290,000 acres of land in this vicinity from the Spanish government just prior to the ceding of Florida to the United States.

ARTA HATCHEE • *Okeechobee County*
Read (1934) finds *arta* is probably a corruption of Creek *oto*, "chestnut," or Creek *ata*, "lizard." Hatchee is Creek *hachi*, "creek."

ARTESIA • *Brevard County*
From the fact that the water supply was from artesian wells. Named by Mrs. J. H. Hogan, a homesteader, in 1898.

ASHMORE COVE • *Wakulla County*
For the county's Ashmore family of educators and other professional men and for their spouses.

ASHTON • *Osceola County*
Formerly called Ashton Station on what was then the Sugar Belt Railroad. Named for an English family, the first settlers.

ASHVILLE • *Jefferson County*
Once known as Rhodes Store, the town gained its present name in 1894.

ASPALAGA • *Liberty County*
Read (1934) says the spelling Aspalaga occurs in 1680 as the name of a Spanish mission in the country of the Apalachee Indians, the full name of the mission being San José de Ospalaga. On the Popple map of 1733, the Apalachee settlement is recorded as Asapalaga. He doubts whether it is possible to interpret the name Aspalaga.

ASTATULA • *Lake County*
Local legend says *astatula* means either "lake of sunbeams" or "lake of sparkling moonbeams." These are fancifully pleasant, but Read (1934) suggests another meaning: Seminole-Creek *isti*, "people," and *italwa*, "tribes"— "people of different tribes." Still another authority points out that *atula* is the Timucuan word for "arrow." The use of the name goes back to around 1880.

ASTOR • *Lake County*
First named Fort Butler for Lt. P. M. Butler, the officer in charge of the erection of the fort. The fort was occupied by Union troops during the Civil War and was captured in 1864 by Confederate Capt. J. J. Dickison, whose calvary exploits caused north central Florida to be known as Dixie's Land. The name was changed to Astor for New York financier William Astor. Astor, in the 1870s, purchased the grant which Moses Levy, a Portuguese Jew, had obtained in hopes of establishing a colony of oppressed European Jews. Astor bought a railroad and built hotels and a telegraph line. When steamboat traffic on the St. Johns declined, however, the resort almost disappeared.

ATHENA • *Taylor County*
Settled in the 1890s and named for Athene, the Greek goddess of wisdom.

ATLANTIC BEACH • *Duval County*
Three seaside communities on the Atlantic Ocean, now called (from north to south) Atlantic Beach, Neptune Beach, and Jacksonville Beach, lie contiguous to one another about 18 miles southeast of Jacksonville. Formerly, the territory of all three was included in what was called Pablo Beach, after the Spanish form of Paul. Pablo Beach was first named Ruby Beach. The Pablo was derived from names of Pablo Creek and Point, both of which date from Spanish days. A post office was established here in October 1884. Pablo Beach was incorporated May 22, 1907, and a paved highway leading from Jacksonville was built in 1910. In 1925, when the present town of Jacksonville Beach was incorporated, Atlantic Beach and Neptune Beach broke away and established themselves separately.

ATLANTIS • *Palm Beach County*
Chartered in 1959, Atlantis suggests by its name proximity to the Atlantic Ocean.

ATSEENAHOOFA SWAMP • *Collier, Hendry, and Monroe counties*
This Seminole name, which persisted until the mid-nineteenth century, has given way to Big Cypress Swamp. Simpson (1956) says the name derived from the Creek *achenaho*, "cypress," and *taphe*, "broad or big."

AUBURN • *Bay and Okaloosa counties*
For the location of Alabama Polytechnic Institute (now Auburn University), which a founder had attended. In turn, Auburn suggests the name from Goldsmith's poem. *See also* Auburndale. The Bay County community had its beginnings around 1910.

AUBURNDALE • *Polk County*
It all began when Oliver Goldsmith disguised his native village, Lishoy, under the name of Auburn in *The Deserted Village*, and began with the lines:

> *Sweet Auburn! loveliest village of the plain,*
> *Where health and plenty cheer'd the laboring swain.*

That the poem went on to tell of the destruction of this village by feudalistic wealth did not deter Americans from naming towns after it; today there are Auburns in ten states and Auburndales in Massachusetts and Florida. Florida's was established in 1882, first under the name of Sanatoria, from a hotel erected there by early settlers. The site was shifted when the railroad came through, and some citizens from Auburndale, Mass., suggested that it be rechristened after that town. The most influential of these seems to have been Mrs. Ralph Pulsifer, wife of the publisher of the *Boston Herald.*

Auburndale All American Store was a self-serve grocery.

AUCILLA • *Jefferson County*
An ancient community of many names: Aucilla, Ocello, Ocilla, Ocillo, Williamsburgh, and Station Four. The first post office appears to have been established under the name Ocello in 1834. Eight Walker brothers were among the early inhabitants, and their progeny still live there. In the mid-1800s Aucilla was an overnight stop on the Salt Road, the trail followed by wagons carrying salt from Florida's gulf coast to Georgia and beyond. Later, when the railroad went through, the stop was known as Station Four, since it was the fourth station east from Tallahassee. *Aucilla* is a Timucuan Indian word of unknown meaning.

AUDUBON • *Brevard County*
Honors the naturalist, John James Audubon, who traveled in Florida in 1832 studying bird and animal life.

Naturalist John James Audubon and his 1832 flamingo drawing.

AURANTIA • *Brevard County*
Established by The Bliss Company of New York in 1882 for citrus cultivation. The name is the plural of the botanical designation for a fruit of the orange species.

AVALON BEACH • *Santa Rosa County*
Beside the waters of Escambia Bay, this place gained its name from the song "Avalon," popular in the 1920s.

AVOCA • *Hamilton County*
This could be for Thomas Moore's poem which has the line "sweet vale of Avoca." And it may have been transplanted from Avoca, Pa. The year was 1890.

AVON-BY-THE-SEA • *Brevard County*
Now in space country, Avon-by-the-Sea gained its name from the pleasing imagery of Shakespeare, the bard of Avon, and of the English river called Avon.

AVON PARK • *Highlands County*
The site of this town was selected around 1885 by O. M. Crosby, of Danbury, Conn., president of the Florida Development Company. Shortly thereafter, Crosby visited England, where he recruited many settlers for his new town. Among these were a Mr. and Mrs. William King, who came from Stratford-on-Avon, and gave the Florida town its name.

AYERS • *Hernando County*
From a family name. John Law Ayers, of the family, represented Hernando County in the Florida House of Representatives for five terms commencing in 1956. Previously he had served as a member of the Hernando County Commission for 20 years.

AZALEA PARK • *Orange County*
Named for the species of the rhododendron family, with its handsome, many-colored flowers, Azalea Park gained postal recognition in 1955 as a branch of Orlando.

AZUCAR • *Palm Beach County*
The Spanish word for sugar was the name given in 1930 to this community amidst the cane fields of the Everglades.

AZZA CREEK • *Duval County*
In 1792, 640 acres were surveyed for Francis Goodwin on Azza Creek. It well may have been that Goodwin lent part of his name to the subsequent designation of Azza Creek; first, in 1805, as Goodman's Lake, then Goodby's Lake and Goodby's Creek.

BABSON PARK •

Polk County
Formerly known as Crooked Lake, being situated on the northeast end of the lake by that name. In 1923, Roger W. Babson, an economic forecaster of national reputation, purchased 400 acres of land which included the town site, and in 1925 the name was changed to Babson Park.

First post office building at Crooked Lake, now Babson Park.

BAGDAD • *Santa Rosa County*
For the Bagdad Land and Lumber Company's port on the Blackwater River from which, beginning in 1850, millions of feet of pine and cypress were shipped. There is a belief that the company took its name from the Bagdad of the *Arabian Nights*. Bagdad, the queen city of Mesopotamia, lies between two rivers, as does Florida's Bagdad, on a grassy, pine-covered peninsula between the Escambia and Blackwater rivers. The area once was known as Simpson's Mill, for an earlier timberman.

BAHIA DEL ESPIRITU SANTO • *Pinellas, Hillsborough, and Manatee counties*

Spanish for "Bay of the Holy Spirit." The Final Report of the U.S. De Soto Commission (1939) concluded, "We regard it as established that the Bahia del Espiritu Santo in which (Hernando) De Soto landed was Tampa Bay . . . . " The date of the landing was, depending upon source, May 30 or June 1, 1539. The bay was variously known also as the Bay of Culata (Timucua), Bay of the Cross (Narváez), Bahia de Tocobaga (Lopez de Velasco), Tampe or Spirito Santo (Romans), and Bay of San Fernando (Maria Celi) before the name finally was settled in English days as Tampa Bay. The west fork was called Old Tampa Bay and the east, Hillsboro Bay, for the Earl of Hillsborough, Great Britain's colonial secretary.

BAHIA HONDA KEY • *Monroe County*
From the Spanish "deep bay." Bahia Honda Key marks the geologic transition from the upper to the lower keys. Since about 1870, botanists from all over the world have been visiting Bahia Honda Key to study the plants brought here by the birds, the hurricane winds, and the ocean waves from all the islands of the West Indies and the Carribbean Sea. Very rare plants growing as native plants only on Bahia Honda Key are the West Indies satinwood, or yellowwood tree (*Zanthoxylum flavum*); the *Catesbaea parviflora;* Jamaica morning-glory (*Jaquemontia jamaicensis*); and wild dilly (*Minusops*).

BAILEY • *Madison County*
During the 1830s, Gen. William A. Bailey owned a large plantation, with many slaves, and was considered one of the most successful men in northwest Florida. When the South Georgia and West Coast Railroad was constructed, about 1903, the line passed through part of the old Bailey property. As a sawmill was in operation there, a siding was put in for the convenience of the mill, with a small country store and later a post office. The place was given the name of Bailey in honor of the general.

BAKER • *Baker County*
The thirty-eighth county, established February 8, 1861. Named for James NcNair Baker (1822-1892), Confederate States senator and judge of the Fourth Judicial District in Florida.

BAKERS MILL • *Hamilton County*
For a George Baker, who started a sawmill here in 1887.

The Baker County
Courthouse in
MacClenny, July 14,
1950.

Trolley passengers arriving at Ballast Point Park, 1910.

BALDWIN • *Duval County*
First called Thigpen, but in 1860 renamed to honor Dr. A. S. Baldwin, who had played a leading role in securing the building of the first railroad into Jacksonville. The town had sprung up at the point where the road from the west branches to Jacksonville and to Fernandina. Dr. Baldwin had served in the Florida Legislature in 1852, and during the the Civil War was a prominent surgeon in the Army of the Confederacy.

BAL HARBOUR • *Dade County*
A residential community lapped by the waters of Biscayne Bay; coined for the desirable images the words create in many minds.

BALLAST POINT • *Hillsborough County*
Situated on a cape jutting into Tampa Bay. During pioneer days shipping vessels discharged their ballast or rock at this point, and sometimes outbound vessels in need of ballast took on rock.

B A M B O O • *Sumter County*
Established in 1883 by B. E. Chapman of South Carolina. Probably named for the bamboo growing nearby.

B A N A N A R I V E R • *Brevard County*
So called since 1860, because of the many banana trees that grew along its banks.

B A N Y A N • *Brevard County*
For the East Indian banyan tree, which grows in the area.

B A R B E R V I L L E • *Volusia County*
Named for J. D. Barber when the post office was opened in 1884. Barber had settled there two years earlier. This was not pioneer land, however, for the Rev. J. J. Baker, a physician and Methodist minister, had homesteaded in the area prior to the Civil War.

A 1930s exhibit of Barberville products at a Volusia County fair.

B A R E B E A C H • *Palm Beach County*
With its neighbor, Little Bare Beach, this name was given to a stretch of shore on Lake Okeechobee because of a sandy gap in the lake-encircling swamp, according to Will (1964).

B A R R I N E A U P A R K • *Escambia County*
Established in 1911. Named for W. C. Barrineau, a pioneer.

B A R R O N R I V E R • *Collier County*
Derived its name from Barron G. Collier, developer in the 1920s of the county which also bears his name, according to *The Miami Herald* on February 11, 1973. On the Barron River at Everglades City is the Rod and Gun Club, visited by three U.S. presidents and countless other celebrities. The club's picturesque building, survivor of a fire in 1973 which destroyed its next-door motel, grew out of an Indian trading post established in the 1870s.

BARTH • *Escambia County*
Established in 1910. Named for the Barth family.

BARTOW • *Polk County*
Seems to have had two previous names before acquiring its present one. The first was Peas Creek. Later, when Redding Blount came with Jacob Summerlin to pioneer the raising of cattle in Florida, the town was renamed Fort Blount. In 1867, its name was changed again, this time to honor Confederate Gen. Francis F. Bartow, the first general officer of either side to fall in the Civil War. Nowadays, Bartow likes to be spoken of as "The City of Oaks."

BASCOM • *Jackson County*
Established in 1890 by the Bevis family, and named for a member of that family.

BASINGER • *Okeechobee County*
Takes its name from neighboring Fort Basinger, in Highlands County, another of the numerous Florida places whose names are reminders of the Seminole Wars. In most instances, the forts were earthworks or palisades named for an army officer associated with the operation. Fort Basinger, established in 1837, was named for Lt. William E. Basinger, killed in the Dade massacre.

BAY COUNTY •
The forty-ninth county, established April 24, 1913. Named for St. Andrews Bay, on which the county borders.

BAYARD • *Duval County*
Named by Henry M. Flagler, of the Florida East Coast Railway, for his friend, Thomas Francis Bayard, a member of President Cleveland's cabinet in Cleveland's 1885-1889 administration and later ambassador to the Court of St. James during Cleveland's 1893-1897 term.

BAY HARBOR • *Bay County*
Located on the shores of St. Andrews Bay, this town takes its name from the bay.

BAY HARBOR ISLANDS • *Dade County*
As might be guessed, this community derives its name and fame from Biscayne Bay. Stepping down in 1973 after 26 years as the community's first mayor, Shepard Broad said he had been "elected unanimously by 750 empty lots" in 1946, a year after the developer acquired two low-lying, sand-covered islands off Miami Beach in the bay.

BAYHEAD • *Bay County*
So called because it is located at the head of West Bay. Once this was the terminus of the stage line from Chipley and a trading center for this section of the country.

BAY LAKE • *Orange County*
One of the twin cities—Lake Buena Vista being the other—whose legislatively-conferred municipal powers are used to administer a fairyland, Disney World.

BAYOU GEORGE • *Bay County*
Established in the 1920s by a family named George.

BAY PINES • *Pinellas County*
Likely named for the pines of this sub-peninsula of Boca Ciega Bay.

BAY POINT • *Santa Rosa County*
This community on East Pensacola Bay dates from the 1870s.

BAY RIDGE • *Orange County*
The conjunction of two agreeable natural situations—a bay and a ridge—produced this name.

BAYSHORE • *Lee County*
Known twice as Samville and once as Woodrow before the present name was settled upon in 1925.

BAY SPRINGS • *Escambia County*
Named in 1925 by J. E. MacCaskill.

BAY VIEW • *Bay, Pinellas, and Walton counties*
The names suggested themselves, for Bay County's Bay View overlooks the confluence of North Bay and West Bay; Walton County's, a view of Choctawhatchee; and Pinellas County's, Old Tampa Bay.

BAYWOOD • *Putnam County*
The combination of bay and wood conjured the image for someone of a pleasant place to live.

BEACON HILL • *Gulf County*
A hill with a lighthouse served as a landmark for vessels entering St. Joseph's Bay.

Beacon Hill light before it was moved to the Mexico Beach area in the late 1950s.

BEAN CITY • *Palm Beach County*
Named for the vegetable grown so prolifically in the surrounding Everglades.

BEAN'S POINT • *Manatee County*
Anna Maria Island's first modern-day pioneer, George Emerson Bean, claimed the island's entire north point as homestead land in May 1895. In 1913, Bean's son, George W., founded the Anna Maria Development Company, which opened the island to seasonal visitors and year-round homeowners.

BEAR CREEK • *Gadsden County*
Likely named because of bears in this vicinity.

BEARDALL • *Seminole County*
A loading station named for a family who settled here in 1886.

BEAR HEAD • *Walton County*
Refers to a nearby swamp or hammock in which bears were abundant.

BEAUTIFUL NEW RIVER • *Broward County*
There is a Seminole Indian legend that Beautiful New River appeared suddenly one night. This is where, according to Bill Raymond, marine geologist, the river originally raced its course through tropical jungle and pine forest. The Indians called the river Himmarshee, the New Water, which later residents called New River.

BEE RIDGE • *Sarasota County*
A Baptist preacher named Isaac Redd came this way and settled here. The story goes that "most every hollow tree had a bee hive." Because of this and the ridge terrain, the Rev. Mr. Redd named it Bee Ridge.

BEL AIR (OR BELLAIR) • *Leon County*
Just two miles south of Tallahassee, it was in the mid-1800s a place of nearby refuge from the summer heat of the capital for well-to-do families.

BELL • *Gilchrist County*
Incorporated in 1903, shortly after a branch of the Seaboard Air Line Railroad had been built through. The name was selected by means of a beauty contest, in which the winner's name was to be given to the new station and post office. The one who received the most votes for queen was Bell Fletcher, the daughter of Daniel E. Fletcher, a native of Florida and a successful farmer of Alachua County. Bell later married G. W. Everett and lived in the Bell community until her death in 1919.

BELLAMY • *Alachua County*
Believed to have been named for John Bellamy, of South Carolina, who was contractor for the St. Johns–Ochlockonee rivers segment of the Territorial Road from Pensacola to St. Augustine. The Bellamy Road, as it was known, was used until the beginning of the Civil War. Bellamy, who accepted land when the Florida government ran out of money, also built a plantation home in a grove of hickory and live oaks near Monticello. The family cemetery remains.

BELLAMY ROAD, THE

The 1824 Congress authorized the opening of a public road between St. Augustine and Pensacola, the capitals of the territories of East and West Florida. It was directed that the road between St. Augustine and the present area of Tallahassee should follow as nearly as practicable the old Spanish Mission Trail. Congress appropriated $20,000 for construction and authorized the use of troops stationed in Florida. Contracts were awarded John Bellamy, a South Carolinian who had moved to Jefferson County, for sections extending from the St. Johns River (St. Augustine) to the Ochlockonee River (Tallahassee). The western half of the project finally was undertaken and completed by troops. While the act of Congress authorizing the St. Augustine–Pensacola road stated a width of 25 feet, the specifications given in the advertisements by the territorial government for the eastern half required only 16 feet. Bellamy regarded his task as completed by May 19, 1826. Critics complained about the width of the road, that stumps had been left standing to a height that impeded the passage of wheeled vehicles, that the bridges were flimsy, and that the causeways over swampy areas were inadequate and unstable. Bellamy's defenders argued that the stumps did not bar the passage of carriages and wagons, and declared it was impractical to cut a wide roadway, because too much sunlight and air would promote the growth of underbrush and scrub oak. The Bellamy Road was used until the beginning of the Civil War. Traces may be seen today. *See also* Trails, El Camino Real, *and* King's Road.

BELLEAIR • *Pinellas County*

The name, to indicate the excellence of the air in these parts, was given by Henry B. Plant in 1896, when he purchased most of the land now included in the town and built his Belleview Hotel. The town was incorporated in 1925. The soothing name of the older community has been appropriated for three nearby Pinellas County cities: Belleair Beach, Belleair Bluffs, and Belleair Shore.

The Belleview Biltmore Hotel at Bellair, in the late 1890s.

BELLE GLADE • *Palm Beach County*
Until 1921, this community on the south shore of Lake Okeechobee was known as the Hillsborough Canal Settlement. In that year a post office was sought, and a prerequisite to this was a more euphonious name. F. M. Myer, proprietor of the Pioneer Hotel, placed a blackboard in his lobby and solicited suggestions. One day a group of tourists came down the canal from West Palm Beach and stayed at the hotel after making a trip through the Everglades. One of them remarked that the Hillsborough Canal Settlement was the belle of the Glades. Mrs. Elsie Myer, wife of the hotel proprietor, quickly added Belle Glade to the list of names on the blackboard, and when an informal poll was later taken, it was voted the favorite. The town was incorporated in 1928. Bellglade Camp, nearby, takes its name from the larger community.

BELLEISLE • *Bay County*
Mrs. W. H. Covington, whose husband operated a turpentine still at this location, named the place. The name in a book appealed to her.

BELLE ISLE • *Orange County*
Combines the French "beautiful" with the poetic English "island" to evoke a mental image of a desirable place to live.

BELLE MEADE • *Collier County*
For beautiful meadow.

BELLEVIEW • *Escambia, Marion, and Pinellas counties*
The name simply means beautiful view.

BELL SHOALS • *Hillsborough County*
Louis Bell settled here on the Alafia River in 1846, and operated a cattle ferry much in use during the annual transporting of cattle to Gulf ports. The place then was known as Bell's Ford. *Florida: A Guide to the Southernmost State* reports Bell was harassed by Indians and often took refuge in a small log fort he had built. Once his six-year-old son was captured and returned only after Bell gave up all the family's blanket

Bell Shoals gained worldwide fame as the locale of Jules Verne's fantastic novel *From the Earth to the Moon* (1865). Here the 900-foot cannon was supposed to have been cast and erected. In the first edition of the novel, the man-bearing projectile was not properly aimed and remained whirling in a vast orbit around the moon. Readers objected so strenuously to this tragic ending that in later editions Verne brought the adventurers back to earth unharmed. For 60 years a semi-buried piece of machinery on the banks of the river was believed by some to be a fragment of the gigantic cannon. On being unearthed, it was found to be a ten-foot steel shaft with vanes attached at the ends. Although the origin and use of the shaft is unknown, it probably was a part of an old water-driven grist mill that served pioneers in this region.

BELLVILLE • *Hamilton County*
Named for the Bell brothers, Col. James E. and Daniel, who came here from the Carolinas in 1824.

BENOTIS • *Taylor County*
Legend says this lost town's name was derived by reversing from the Latin phrase *nota bene*, meaning "note well."

BENTON • *A former county*
Displaced Hernando as the name of the twenty-second county from March 6, 1844, until December 24, 1850, when the former name was restored. Benton was named for Thomas Hart Benton (1782-1853), U.S. senator from Missouri for 30 years (1821-51). His vociferous opposition to paper money and a national bank earned him the nickname "Old Bullion." Florida's recognition was the result of Benton's sponsorship of the Armed Occupation Act of 1842, which opened central Florida to settlers.

BERESFORD • *Volusia County*
Established in 1874 by A. H. Alexander. Named for the lake, which English settlers possibly named for John Beresford, an Irish statesman of renown during the British occupation of Florida. Beresford descendants were among the British nobility—Hillsborough and Grenville were two—whose claims to land along the Halifax and St. Johns rivers were denied by Congress in 1830. Neither Hillsborough nor Grenville ever saw his claimed Florida possessions. *See also* Hillsborough.

BERLIN • *Duval, Manatee, and Marion counties*
Once there was a Berlin in each of the three counties, but none now appears in the index to the State Department of Agriculture's sectional map. The date given—January 31, 1917—for discontinuance of the post office of Marion County's Berlin suggests this name may have been a casualty of World War I.

BETHEL • *Okaloosa County*
Given its name for the Bible's *bethel*, "house of God" in Hebrew.

BETTS • *Bay County*
A lumberman, J. S. Betts, of Ashburn, Ga., was one of the first settlers in this part of the country. The place was named for him in 1912.

BEVERLY BEACH • *Flagler County*
Claude Varn, a St. Augustine attorney, named the area for his granddaughter Beverly. The name was retained when the town was incorporated.

BIG CYPRESS • *Collier and Hendry counties*
Big Cypress is the name of (1) a Seminole Indian reservation in Hendry County, (2) stands of cypress trees, mainly in Collier and Hendry counties, and (3) the Big Cypress National Freshwater Reserve, together with contiguous land and water areas ecologically linked with the Everglades National Park, estuarine fisheries and the freshwater aquifer of south Florida in Collier, Hendry, Dade, and Monroe counties. The name Big Cypress seems to refer to the size of the original trees concentrated in the area. These grew as tall as 100 feet. Many of the trees remaining are as old as any cut, but their stunted nature saved them from timbering. The Big Cypress known to hunters has spawned its own place names, among them Devil's Garden, Dark Strand, Lost Dog Prairie, Airplane Prairie, Lard Can Slough, and Thompson's Pine Island.

BIG PINE • *Monroe County*
On Big Pine Key; named for the large pine trees growing on this key.

BISCAYNE (Bay, Key Biscayne, Biscayne Park) • *Dade County*
Marjory Stoneman Douglas, in *Florida: The Long Frontier*, tells how Juan Ponce de León, sailing southward in 1513 from his landing near St. Augustine, found "the bright nameless great bay and fresh springs." He called it Chequescha. The bay we know as Biscayne, but there are several stories about where the bay got its name. Most assume it is merely a variant on the Bay of Biscay, in the Atlantic Ocean north of Spain and west of France. Fontaneda says it was named because of the wreck there of a ship belonging to a man called El Biscaino (the Biscayan, from the Spanish province of Biscaya). Mrs. Douglas accepts this, and Helen Muir, in *Miami U.S.A.*, adds that on one of the islands in the bay lived Don Pedro el Biscaino, who, upon his return to Spain, became keeper of the swans at the Spanish court. The name Vizcaino appears on the de la Puente map of 1765. Vizcaino is said to have been the name of a prosperous Spanish merchant in Manila, who set out from Mexico to colonize lower California. Interestingly, the bay was called Sandwich Gulf on J. L. Williams' map of 1837.

BITHLO • *Orange County*
From *pilo*, the Seminole-Creek word for "canoe." In transliterating this language, the voiceless "i" was often written "thl." The town was established in 1822.

BLACK CAESAR'S ROCK • *Dade County*
A tiny island between Old Rhodes and Elliott keys, in the island chain separating the Atlantic Ocean and Biscayne Bay, this once was the headquarters of the legendary pirate Black Caesar. *Florida: A Guide to the Southernmost State* says that there are many different and conflicting tales told of Black Caesar, but it is agreed generally that he was a Negro who escaped from a wrecked slave ship. After a successful career as a single-handed wrecker, Black Caesar became a lieutenant of the notorious Teach, better known as Blackbeard. *Florida* reports: "Flying the skull and crossbones, their ship, the *Queen Ann's Revenge*, was captured by Lieutenant Robert Maynard in 1718. Teach was killed during the battle, sustaining 25 wounds before he fell dead. Caesar attempted to blow up the ship and all on board by dropping a match into the powder magazine, but one of the men prevented him. Taken to Virginia, Black Caesar was hanged."

BLACK CREEK • *Clay County*
Corrupted from the Spanish *rio blanco*, "white river."

BLACK POINT • *Dade County*
Established in the early 1900s. It is said that early settlers, viewing from a distance an exceptionally dense growth of trees, found the point of land blackish in hue.

BLACK POINT • *Duval County*
A point of land on the St. Johns River in Duval County. Known as Punta

Negra during the Spanish reign; hence, the name. Near here a federal gunboat was torpedoed and sunk during the Civil War. In 1917, Camp Joseph E. Johnston was established on this point, named in honor of Gen. Joseph E. Johnston. Later the name was changed to Camp Foster, honoring the Florida Guard's Adj. Gen. J. Clifford R. Foster.

BLACK POINT • *Flagler County*
Established about 1910-12, it derives its name from the fact that two rivers form a point here. The soil is rich and almost black.

BLACKWATER RIVER • *Santa Rosa County*
Called *Weikasupka* or Cold Water on Purcell's map of 1778.

BLAKE • *Volusia County*
About 1877, D. O. Balcom purchased the Sequi Hammock on the Halifax River front for a town site. Blake is a name conferred by Mrs. Balcom for a community near Boston, Mass.

BLANTON • *Pasco County*
Established in the mid-1880s and named for a prominent south Florida family.

BLITCHTON • *Marion County*
For a pioneer family, among whose distinctions was that of having two brothers serving simultaneously in the state senate.

BLITCHVILLE • *Gilchrist County*
Likely named for an offshoot of the same family that gave its name to Blitchton.

BLOOMFIELD • *Lake County*
Established in 1882 by William D. Mandonhall who, as postmaster, sought to convey the image of blooming trees and plants.

BLOUNTSTOWN • *Calhoun County*
John Blount, after whom this county seat is named, was a Seminole Indian and the distinguished chief of the Indians who occupied the reservation which once lay just east of here. Blount had been given this Anglo-American name because it was said that he had many traits in common with William Blount of North Carolina, whom President Washington appointed superintendent of Indian affairs in 1790. When the Florida reservation was ceded to the United States by a treaty made at Tallahassee, October 11, 1832, John Blount led a delegation of Seminoles to explore the new reservation west of the Mississippi. Later he led the Seminole band to take up the new territory. The first white settlers named the town after the great Seminole.

BLOXHAM • *Almost a county*
William Dunningham Bloxham was in the forefront of Florida Democratic party activities during the last 40 years of the nineteenth century. A planter-lawyer, he served in the 1861 House of Representatives from Leon County, organized and commanded an infantry company during the Civil War, lost the election as lieutenant governor in 1870, and was defeated for governor in 1872, appointed secretary of state in 1877, and elected governor in 1880.

Looking north on Highway 71 through Blountstown, in 1948.

Afterwards, he declined appointment in 1885 as American minister to Bolivia but served as U. S. surveyor for Florida. He was appointed comptroller in 1890 and was elected comptroller and reelected. He then was reelected governor in 1896. He died in 1911. In 1915, the legislature voted to establish Bloxham County, with Williston as the temporary seat, subject to ratification by voters in the affected areas of Levy and Marion counties. The voters rejected the new county. Bloxham thus is remembered on the map only by a Leon County community better known for having given its name to a stretch of road called the Bloxham Cut-off.

BLUE SPRINGS • *Marion, Taylor, and Hamilton counties*
The name Blue refers to the color of the springs here. The Indians called the Marion spring *Wikaiwa* and the Spaniards *Las Aguas Azules* or "blue water."

BLUFF SPRINGS • *Escambia County*
Established in 1819. This place first was known as the Old Pringle Mill after Abraham Pringle. The formal name, which came later, was suggestive of the bluffs and springs in the locality.

BOARDMAN • *Marion County*
Established in 1863 and named for a Mr. Boardman, thought to have been an early settler.

BOCA CHICA • *Monroe County*
From the Spanish "little mouth," which originally referred to a narrow channel at this point.

BOCA CIEGA • *Pinellas County*
Named for Boca Ciega Bay, southwest of St. Petersburg. The Spanish word *boca* means "mouth," while *ciega* means "blind." In this use, however, the words mean "obstructed or closed passage"—a reference, probably, to what looked like the entrance to a river but proved impassable, either because there was no river or because of dense vegetation.

BOCA GRANDE • *Lee County*
On Gasparilla Island. A Spanish name which means "big mouth" or "large entrance." Refers to a passage from the Gulf. The island is historically famous as the home of the Spanish pirate Gasparilla. As with Black Caesar, Gasparilla has become a person of controversy and legend. *Florida: A Guide to the Southernmost State* identifies him as José Gaspar, who later was known as Gasparilla (Spanish for "little Gaspar"). The book says he was a Spaniard who fell from favor at the king's court, stole a ship of the Spanish navy, gathered a band of cutthroats, and established a base on the Florida island from which he preyed upon the rich shipping rounding the keys between the Atlantic Ocean and the Gulf of Mexico. Captiva Island is identified by *Florida* as the place where Gasparilla turned over to his fellow pirates the 11 beautiful Mexican girls who were accompanying the Spanish princess Maria Louise on a ship captured in 1801. "The band," concludes *Florida*, "was broken up in 1822 when Gasparilla gave chase to what appeared to be a large British merchantman; upon being overtaken, the vessel lowered the English flag, ran up the Stars and Stripes, and uncovered a masked battery. With his ship riddled, Gasparilla wrapped an anchor chain about his waist and leaped into the sea."

A Charlotte Harbor and Northern train at the Boca Grande railroad depot.

A Boca Raton bus at the development's Miami office, in 1925.

BOCA RATON • *Palm Beach County*
Established in 1924 and named for Boca Raton Sound. The Spanish words *boca de raton* mean "rat's mouth," a term used by seamen to describe a hidden rock that gnaws or frets a ship's cables.

BOK TOWER—IRON MOUNTAIN • *Polk County*
Embracing 58 acres overlooking some 300 lakes, the Mountain Lake Sanctuary in Polk County was established as "a retreat for man, a refuge for birds and a sylvan setting for the Singing Tower" by Edward William Bok, journalist, editor, and winner of the Pulitzer Prize in 1920. Known as the Singing Tower because the 230-foot tower houses a carillon of 71 bells.

BONAVENTURE • *Broward County*
In the beginning, one of the attractions of this development west of Fort Lauderdale was a golf course with a waterfall hazard. More than 13,000 gallons pour over the falls every minute. The 60-foot waterfront guards a par-three hole, reports *The Miami Herald.* Bonaventure means, in French, "good" and "adventure," which could have appeal for those entering here upon a new life.

BOND • *Madison County*
In 1897, William J. Bond operated a country store here, and the government established a post office in his store. As Bond was the first postmaster, the place was named for him.

BONE VALLEY
Bone Valley occupies a roughly circular area in Hillsborough, Polk, Hardee, and Manatee counties, and is the source of huge land-pebble phosphate deposits. In this subsurface area, once perhaps a large delta or estuary before the sea receded, are to be found fossils of much of the rich and bizarre animal life which roved what now is Florida.

BONIFAY • *Holmes County*
This county seat of Holmes County was established in 1882, and named for a prominent old family of that vicinity.

BONITA SPRINGS • *Lee County*
Bonita is derived from the Spanish "pretty."

BOTHAMLEY • *Seminole County*
Named for the owner of a turpentine camp in this area in the 1880s.

BOTTS • *Santa Rosa County*
Established in 1890. Named for the Botts family.

BOULOGNE • *Nassau County*
Probably named for the city in France. Established in 1880 by Andrew Price.

BOWLEGS CREEK • *Polk County*
Doubtless named for the Indian Billy Bowlegs, known among the Seminoles as *holatter micco*, or "alligator chief."

BOWLES • *Volusia County*
Compilers of the unpublished listing of Florida place names by the Federal Writers' Project accepted "local tradition" that Bowles derived its name from William Augustus Bowles, frontier adventurer. Bowles first came to Florida at the age of 15 as an ensign in the Maryland regiment of British soldiers defending Pensacola. He went to live among the Indians and married a chief's daughter. Later, with Florida again Spanish, Bowles recruited money and men in the Bahamas to harass Spanish stores at Lake George and Saint Marks. He was captured at Saint Marks, and imprisoned in Havana, Madrid, and Manila. He escaped and raised more money to return to Florida, again was captured, and died at Morro Castle in Havana in 1806.

William Augustus Bowles married an Indian princess and tried to break Spain's hold on east and west Florida.

BOWLING GREEN • *Hardee County*
Known as Utica until the late 1890s, when a number of farmers from Bowling Green, Ky., purchased large holdings in the district and renamed the town after their former home.

BOYD • *Taylor County*
Named for J. B. Boyd in 1891.

BOYETTE • *Hillsborough County*
Once known as Fishhawk, the place was named for Thomas Boyett in 1902.

B O Y N T O N   B E A C H • *Palm Beach County*
Founded in 1896, this town was first called Boynton, after Maj. N. S. Boynton
of Port Huron, Mich., who erected a hotel on the beach. In 1925, the name
was changed to Boynton Beach.

B R A D E N T O N • *Manatee County*
In 1854, Dr. Joseph Braden, a pioneer sugar planter, built his home close to
the point where Hernando De Soto had first landed on the Florida peninsula in 1539. When a post office was established in 1878, the spelling was given
as Braidentown by error. The "i" was later dropped, and in 1924 the "w" was
eliminated to make the present spelling. Bradenton is the county seat of
Manatee County.

B R A D F O R D   C O U N T Y •
The thirty-sixth county, established December 21, 1858, as New River
County. Capt. Richard Bradford, whose name this county bears, was the first
Florida officer killed in the Civil War. He died in the Battle of Santa Rosa
Island, October 9, 1861, and the county was given his name on December 6,
1861.

B R A D L E Y   J U N C T I O N • *Marion County*
Established in 1910 and incorporated April 25, 1912, as Bradley. It is not clear
when the "Junction" was added.

B R A N C H T O N • *Hillsborough County*
Named around 1888 for an early resident, James Branch.

B R A N D O N • *Hillsborough County*
Named by John Brandon, who with his family and possessions moved to
Florida from Alabama in 1857. He lived in several places in Florida before he
homesteaded in 1874, 12 miles east of Tampa, and named the place for his
family.

B R A N D Y   B R A N C H • *Nassau County*
Known also as Brandy Creek, this community lost its alcoholic connotation in
1886 with a change of name to
Bryceville. Brandy Branch
was so called because of the
color of the water entering
the St. Marys River. *See
also* Bryceville.

*Old Ivey House
Hotel at Branford in
the early 1900s.*

B R A N F O R D •
Suwannee County
Henry B. Plant, the great
Florida developer and
president of the Savanah,
Florida and Western
Railroad, now the Atlan-tic
Coast Line, named
this town after Branford,

Conn., where he had formerly lived. The Connecticut town, it is said, was named by variation after the town of Brentford in England. The Spanish mission of Ajoica stood a few miles northeast of the present site of Branford.

BRENT • *Escambia County*
Established about 1870. Named for F. C. Brent, who built a summer home here because of its healthful location among pine woods. Formerly called Brentwood.

BREVARD COUNTY •
The twenty-fifth county, established March 14, 1844. This county honors Theodore Washington Brevard (1804-1877), a North Carolinian who came to Florida in 1847 and later became state comptroller (1853-1861). The county was originally named St. Lucie, the name being changed to Brevard on January 6, 1855. St. Lucie was restored to the map in 1905 when another county was created and given the name.

BREWSTER • *Polk County*
Named for the chemical company, which had phosphate operations in the area.

BRICKTON • *Escambia County*
Named for a large number of brick kilns which were used to take advantage of the red clay in the vicinity.

BRIGHTON • *Highlands County*
Despite its English sound, Brighton was named not for the seaside resort but for James H. Bright, who had a cattle ranch here. Bright was a partner of Glenn H. Curtiss in the founding of Hialeah, a community that survived the collapse of the land boom in the 1920s to become one of the state's larger cities.

BRINY BREEZES • *Palm Beach County*
A community of mobile homes, 568 occupying 45 acres in 1990. Once this was Miller's Farm, where a trailer park grew. When Mr. Miller decided to sell, the mobile homers bought, incorporated, and gave their community a name which the location suggested to them.

BRISTOL • *Liberty County*
Established as Riddeysville in 1850, this town changed its name several years later.

BROADBRANCH • *Calhoun County*
Likely named for a nearby waterway, Broadbranch twice enjoyed recognition as a post office: in 1911-1915 and 1919-1933.

BRONSON • *Levy County*
At first called Chunky Pond, through a mistaken transliteration of an Indian word meaning "dance," this town was established during the Civil War. By 1882, the town had been named Bronson to honor an early settler of great popularity and that is the name under which it was incorporated in 1884. It is the seat of Levy County.

BROOKER • *Bradford County*
In 1892, Thomas R. Collins, a native of nearby Columbia County, bought a piece of property about a mile southwest of the present site of Brooker. His petition for a post office was granted in August of 1894, he was named postmaster, and he named the post office after the old Brooker Bridge across the Santa Fe River. The bridge had been named after Ed Brooker, a farmer in that area. A settlement had been established in this vicinity in 1838.

BROOKSVILLE • *Hernando County*
This county seat of Hernando County is said to have been named for Congressman Preston Brooks of South Carolina. On May 20, 1856, during the debate on the Kansas-Nebraska Bill, Sen. Charles Sumner of Massachusetts denounced Sen. A. P. Butler of South Carolina, who was then absent from the chamber and who was an uncle of Preston Brooks. The latter, hearing of the verbal attack on his relative, found Sumner in the Senate chamber after adjournment that day, broke a gutta percha cane over his head and left him insensible on the floor. Sumner reportedly never recovered fully from the assault. A move to expel Brooks from the House of Representatives failed, but he resigned and was promptly reelected by his constituents. He was the recipient of a number of gold-headed canes and gold-handled whips. Congressman Anson Burlingame of Massachusetts, on the other hand, publicly denounced Brooks as a coward. Brooks challenged Burlingame to a duel; the latter accepted, and named the Canadian side of Niagara Falls as the place. Brooks said he could not make his way with safety through the northern states to this site, and refused to go. He died about a year later.

A 1949 interior view of the Florida Cafe in Brooksville.

BROWARD COUNTY •

The fifty-first county, established April 30, 1915. Named for Napoleon B. Broward, who, as governor of Florida, 1905-1909, played a leading part in the draining of the Everglades. Earlier, he was the owner of a steam tug, *The Three Friends,* which he commanded in eluding both United States and Spanish authorities to supply war materials to Cuban revolutionists. He had a stormy political career.

BROWARD'S NECK • *Duval County*

The grandfather of Gov. Napoleon B. Broward settled near where the Broward River, formerly Cedar Creek, enters the St. Johns River and forms a neck (an isthmus or cape). Broward's Neck entered history in its own right when the "Ladies of Broward's Neck" petitioned the state government on November 6, 1860, to withdraw Florida from the Union. On December 28, 1860, two weeks before Florida's secession, Miss Helen Broward presented Gov. Madison Starke Perry with a new state flag, the handiwork of the Ladies of Broward's Neck. Gov. Perry, in acknowledging the gift, described the flag thus: ". . . a bright and effulgent star . . . on a field of azure. . . ."

BROWN • *Holmes County*

Settled by Joe Brown, head of the county's Farmers' Alliance in the 1880s.

BROWN'S FARM • *Palm Beach County*

Gained prominence in Florida and nationally for a number of years in the 1930s and 1940s as one of the first to report election returns. A precinct with a handful of voters, Brown's Farm could complete its poll while most Florida voters were still at breakfast. Alas, good roads and larger precincts destroyed the claim to fame of Brown's Farm.

BROWNSVILLE • *Escambia County*

Named for L. S. Brown, who was known as "Clean-Sweep Brown" after he and all his chosen candidates were elected to the first city council when the municipal government was formed.

BRYANT • *Palm Beach County*

This settlement in the sugar cane country of the Everglades first was known as *azucar,* Spanish for "sugar."

BRYCEVILLE • *Nassau County*

Founded and named in 1886 by George W. Bryce, at one time the largest landowner in the county. *See also* Brandy Branch.

BUCKHORN • *Gulf County*

A landmark on the Chipola River once used by riverboats. Named because of a tree near the river that resembled the horns of a deer. Later known as Scott's Ferry.

BUCKINGHAM • *Lee County*

Formerly called Twelve Mile Creek. Edward M. Williams, formerly of Bucks County, Pa., served as first postmaster, and it was he who suggested the name when the government objected to the former name. It may honor

Buckingham Smith, nineteenth-century historian and federal reclamation commissioner for Florida, Mr. Williams' former home, or both.

BUENA VISTA • *Dade County*
This community of "beautiful view" antedated Miami as a municipality, having been established in 1892, but was among the adjacent towns consolidated with Miami in 1925. Blackman (1921) reported Buena Vista was given its name by Charles Crowley, an early settler.

BULOW • *Volusia County*
The plantation established by James Russell in 1812. Remains still exist. The plantation was purchased by Charles Bulow in 1821 and a sugar mill was erected on the plantation in 1830-1831. The plantation served as headquarters for Maj. Putnam during the Seminole Indian War of 1835, but was destroyed by Indians after the troops were withdrawn.

BUMPNOSE • *Jackson County*
Whose nose was bumped? The surviving reference is in *A Chronology of Florida Post Offices*, a monumental undertaking by Alford G. Bradbury and E. Story Hallock. Bumpnose was a post office from November 11, 1896, until March 2, 1899, when its postal functions were absorbed by Marianna.

BUNCHE PARK • *Dade County*
This community near Opa-Locka first took shape in 1960 and was named for Dr. Ralph Bunche, the African-American peacemaker who negotiated an armistice for the United Nations in the Arab-Israeli War of 1948, earning world acclaim and the Nobel Peace Prize.

BUNKER HILL • *Jefferson and Collier counties*
This name of renown in American Revolutionary history identified two Florida places at opposite ends of the peninsula. Bunker Hill, in Jefferson County, lasted long enough to have a post office from October 18, 1829, to August 24, 1842, then passed out of existence.

In Collier County, Bunker Hill was established in 1920 as a lumber camp on the Atlantic Coast Line Railroad, and remained in existence on highway maps in the 1990s. Bunker Hill has remained in the Collier family, and was used primarily as farmland after the logging operations became obsolete. While the Collier County Museum did considerable research at the behest of State Rep. Mary Ellen Hawkins, it could not be ascertained how the name Bunker Hill was chosen.

BUNNELL • *Flagler County*
The county seat of Flagler County, this town was founded in 1880 by Alva A. Bunnell. At first it was only a sawmill site, but as the soil in the area proved to be especially fertile, it became a great farming center, of which the principal product now is potatoes.

BURBANK • *Marion County*
Thought to honor Luther Burbank, the renowned American horticulturist who joined Henry Ford and Thomas A. Edison in south Florida outdoor trips in the 1920s.

BURNETT'S LAKE • *Alachua County*
Named for Samuel W. Burnett, the builder of the first courthouse in Alachua County (in old Newnansville) about 1823.

BURNT MILL CREEK • *Bay County*
Derives its name from the fact that a sawmill located on its banks was destroyed by fire.

BUSHNELL • *Sumter County*
First settled in the 1870s, this site did not receive a name until 1884, when it was named to honor the young chief engineer of the surveying crew which laid out the railroad right-of-way. Now the county seat of Sumter County.

BUTLER • *Jackson County*
Established in 1892. Named for C. J. Butler, who owned the land.

CADILLAC • *Alachua County*
On the Seaboard Coast Line Railroad between Alachua and Newberry, this community had a post office for five years starting in 1900. The name may be a transplant from the Michigan city named after Antoine de la Mothe Cadillac, who established a fort on the Detroit River in 1701.

CA d'ZAN (Ringling residence) • *Sarasota County*
In the 1920s, John Ringling, the circus magnate, built a palatial home on Sarasota Bay. Under his supervision, Ca d' Zan (which means House of John) arose from a tropically landscaped estate near the Gulf of Mexico.

John Ringling said he would be satisfied with "just a little bit of a place," but Mable Ringling wanted something more magnificent that would remind her of Venice—the city beside the sea both loved most of all.

Architect Dwight James Baum fashioned a $1.5 million Venetian gothic palazzo, combining rather freely elements from two of Mrs. Ringling's favorite buildings, the facade of the Doge's palace in Venice and the tower of the old Madison Square Garden in New York.

Today the House of John is surrounded by the Ringling Museum of Baroque Art of incalculable value; the 18th-century Asolo Theater, an architectural jewel which once occupied the great hall castle in the hill town of Asolo, 20-odd miles from Venice, Italy; a circus museum; and the Asolo Center for the Performing Arts, built in 1990.

CALHOUN • *Calhoun County*
Named not for the southern statesman honored by the county's name but for the Calhoun brothers, who operated a large farm and sawmill here. The Calhouns settled here shortly after the Civil War.

CALHOUN COUNTY •
The twentieth county, established January 26, 1838. Named for John C. Calhoun, the South Carolina senator who was the foremost proponent of the doctrine of states' rights.

Ca d' Zan, the Ringling residence in Sarasota, and Willy Pogany's whimsical portrait of John and Mable in a mural on the ceiling of the "rumpus room."

CALL • *Not quite a county*

The Territorial Council passed an act on November 23, 1828, providing for the creation of a county to be known as Call, but Gov. William P. DuVal vetoed the act, so Call County never was established. Call apparently was to have been situated where parts of Leon, Gadsden, and Jefferson counties now exist, because a description in the laws bounded Leon County, in part, "on the north and east by the County of Call." The county obviously was to honor Richard Keith Call, who first came to Florida with Andrew Jackson in 1814 as a soldier and personal aide and returned with him to Pensacola in 1821 to set up the American government for the new territory. DuVal likely vetoed the act creating Call County because of political differences. However, Call had the satisfaction of twice serving as territorial governor. His stately mansion, The Grove, stands today in Tallahassee, overlooking the home of Florida's present governor across the street. It was on the steps of The Grove that Call stood in January 1861, and was taunted by secessionists upon Florida's leaving the Union. A slaveholder but a Unionist, Call responded: "Well, gentlemen, all I wish to say to you is that you have just opened the gates of hell." A descendant lives in The Grove now: Mary Call Darby Collins, wife of the late LeRoy Collins, twice governor.

CALLAHAN • *Nassau County*

Settled in 1860, this community was named for one of the contractors engaged in the construction of the old Transit Railway.

CALLAWAY • *Bay County*

Named for a sawmill operator, Callaway gained the recognition of having a post office of its own in 1903.

CALOOSA • *Lee County*
See Caloosahatchee River.

CALOOSAHATCHEE RIVER • *Lee, Hendry, and Glades counties*
The name of a river entering the Gulf of Mexico at the south end of Charlotte Harbor, after traversing Lee, Hendry, and Glades counties. Simpson (1956), says this river was named after the Calusa, a powerful tribe of native Florida Indians who, at the first arrival of Europeans, inhabited or controlled all of Florida south of Tampa Bay. The Muscogee ending *hatchee* suggests that the name was accepted and applied to the river by the Creek or some other branch of the Muscogees. Fontaneda, a one-time captive among them, said that *calusa* means "a fierce people."

CAMPBELL • *Osceola County*
Albert S. Campbell moved to this site just after the Civil War, of which he was a veteran. About the time the railroad came through in the 1880s, Campbell gave land for the right-of-way. He operated a general store, had an orange grove, and was the first postmaster. The settlement was named Campbell Station by the railroad, and retained that name through the 1930s. After the turn of the century, the great timber stands in the area were cut, principally by George Singletary. In the 1920s, another large lumber mill was operated here by William Candler of Atlanta.

CAMPBELLTON • *Jackson County*
Established in 1840 or earlier and named for Judge R. L. Campbell.

CAMP BLANDING • *Clay County*
Named for Lt. Gen. Albert H. Blanding, a Floridian who had been chief of the National Guard Bureau. Camp Blanding was a World War II induction center where tens of thousands of young men were accepted or rejected for military service. Of some 72,000 acres of sun-baked flatland, with scrub oak, palmetto and pine, Camp Blanding has become a skeleton of rows of crumbling foundations where barracks and warehouses once stood. New quarters for summer encampments of the National guard have replaced the World War II barraks. A few warehouses survive. Gen. Blanding died in 1970.

World War II troops at attention on Camp Blanding's Company Street.

CAMP FOSTER • *Duval County*
See Camp Johnston.

CAMP JOHNSTON • *Duval County*
A military reservation on the St. Johns River, southwest of Jacksonville. In September 1917, during World War I, the government took over the camp-ground at Black Point, naming it Camp Joseph E. Johnston, in honor of the Confederate general. The name later was changed to Camp J. C. R. Foster during use for National Guard summer training. Still later this became the site of the Jacksonville Naval Air Station.

CANAAN • *Seminole County*
A dot on the State Department of Agriculture's big sectional map of Florida. Its name likely was derived from the Bible's promised land, flowing with milk and honey.

CANAL POINT • *Palm Beach County*
Situated at the point where the Palm Beach Canal enters Lake Okeechobee, this town derives its name from that fact.

CANAVERAL • *Brevard County*
A community settled in 1856.

CANDLER • *Marion County*
Laid out in the pine woods in the latter part of 1883. Candler is a family name.

CANTONMENT • *Escambia County*
The cantonment, or site of encampment, for Gen. Andrew Jackson's troops in 1814 while they were conducting a punitive expedition against the Spanish in Florida, and again in 1821 while the United States was awaiting transfer of Florida from Spain. Later this was Cantonment Clinch, for Gen. Duncan L. Clinch, who was ordered in March 1836 to enforce President Andrew Jackson's proclamation that the Seminoles must leave Florida. It was Gen. Clinch who represented the United States at the confrontation when a fiery young warrior named Osceola, after eight chiefs had signed an agreement to leave, stabbed a dagger through the paper and said, at least in effect, "This is the way I sign!"

CAPE CANAVERAL • *Brevard County*
A Spanish word meaning "a place of roots or cane." The Spaniards named the cape Canaveral because there was cane or reeds growing here. Ponce de León called the point The Cape of Currents, but the name Canaveral appeared on the earliest Spanish maps of Florida. This community, established in 1961, preserves the name originally given also to the missile facility and the geographical area but changed to Cape Kennedy after the 1963 assassination of President John F. Kennedy. The name was restored to the geographical area in 1973. *See also* Cape Kennedy.

CAPE CORAL • *Lee County*
Advertises itself as the "new city," and is indeed that. Not listed in the 1960 federal census, Cape Coral had grown to 77,082 by 1990. On the

Caloosahatchee River, four miles from the Gulf of Mexico, Cape Coral suggests by its name cool, casual, waterfront living—which was what its developers intended.

CAPE FLORIDA • *Dade County*
John Cabot is said to have named this, the southern tip of Key Biscayne, "The Cape of the End of April" in 1498. *See also* Biscayne Bay. Soon after the United States acquired Florida from Spain, planning began for a lighthouse on the cape. The tower was completed in 1825 and is one of the oldest structures remaining in south Florida. Indians attacked the lighthouse in July 1836, driving the keeper and a black helper to the metal platform surrounding the light. The helper was killed. Faced with the dilemma of being roasted by a fire the Indians had started inside the tower or of being killed by other means, Keeper John W. B. Thompson dropped some gunpowder into the fire. The explosion extinguished the flames and left Thompson still clinging to the platform, from which he was rescued the next day by the crew of a passing ship. A temporary Army post, Fort Bankhead, was established on the cape in 1838 by Indian fighters commanded by Col. William S. Harney. The lighthouse was raised to its present height of 95 feet in 1855. The light was wrecked and darkened during the Civil War, restored in 1867, and extinguished finally in 1878 when the Fowey Rock light took its place as a guardian of t h e coast.

Cape Florida light, 1925.

CAPE KENNEDY • *Brevard County*
Became the name of Cape Canaveral by order of President Lyndon B. Johnson on November 29, 1963, following the assassination of President John F. Kennedy. At the same time, Station No. 1 of the Atlantic Missile Range was renamed the John F. Kennedy Space Center by President Johnson. Because Cape Canaveral had been recognized as the oldest continuously used place name on the American Atlantic Coast, efforts were made to have the federal government restore the ancient name to the land mass, while retaining Cape Kennedy for the Space Center. When these efforts remained unsuccessful, the 1973 Florida Legislature enacted a law decreeing that "all public

maps and documents in Florida designate the geographical area as Cape Canaveral." Shortly afterwards, the U.S. Department of Interior, upon the recommendation of an inter-agency Committee on Domestic Geographic Names, acquiesced in the state's action, restoring the ancient name to the geographical area. *See also* Cape Canaveral.

CAPE ROMANS (OR ROMANO) • *Collier County*
Likely derived its name from Bernard Romans, the navigator, surveyor, and naturalist who was commissioned in 1769 by the Earl of Hillsborough to map the coasts of British Florida. At some point, the name was given a Spanish ending.

CAPE SABLE • *Monroe County*
Situated on a cape jutting into the Gulf of Mexico. *Sable* is Spanish for "saber," and the cape's shape may have suggested the heavy, single-edged, curved cavalry sword. The cape appears on a Spanish map as *Punta del Aguada* or *Punta de Muspa*.

CAPE SAN BLAS • *Gulf County*
A point on the Gulf of Mexico. The cape forms a short division between the gulf and Bay San Blas. This was formerly called Cape San Plaise. Blas seems to be a corruption of Plaise. The Spaniards probably sighted this land on February 3, the day the Roman Catholic church commemorates this saint.

THE CAPITOL • *Leon County*
Atop a hill in the capital city of Tallahassee are the two buildings which have housed the heart of state government since 1845. After the present Capitol was occupied in 1978, the 1845 structure with its 1902 additions has been referred to as the "historic" Capitol, except for a period when it was suggested that this meant all Florida's historic events happened in the past. After years of controversy, the old and the new Capitols face each other in what most now agree is a happy pairing.

CAPITOLA • *Leon County*
Named by reason of its nearness to the state's Capitol.

CAPONE ISLAND • *Broward County*
In the Intracoastal Waterway off Deerfield Beach and named for Al Capone, who bought it supposedly intending to build a home here. Meantime, Capone had a residence on Miami's Palm Island in the early 1930s. From this luxury estate he went away to another island (Alcatraz) in the middle of San Francisco Bay.

CAPTIVA • *Lee County*
An island and a community. The community has had a post office since 1902. Captiva is said by legend to be the island where the pirate Gasparilla handed over to his crew the eleven beautiful Mexican girls who, in 1801, were traveling to Spain for education when their ship was captured. A skeptic, however, has pointed out the island bore its name before Gaspar roved the seas. In *The Sea Shell Islands*, Elinore M. Dormer says "with no proof whatsoever we believe that the story of Capitva is the story of Juan Ortíz." Ortíz was captured by Indians in 1528 when he and three others left their ship to

look for Pánfilo de Narváez. Only Ortíz survived, and he remained a prisoner for 11 years. His rescue by the chief's wife and daughters preceded the famous Pocahontas story.

CARLOS • *Lee County*
Formed by the Spanish from *Calusa*, the name of the Indians living at the time of exploration in what is now the vicinity of Charlotte Harbor. *See also* Charlotte.

CAROL CITY • *Dade County*
The developer, Julius Gaines, had originally planned to call it Coral City and draw to itself "some of the magic of Coral Gables." All it drew, he said wryly, was a lawsuit from Coral Gables. Signs were ready to go, so Gaines merely switched the "a" and "o" and made it Carol City. The city capitalized on its name—a caroling party on the banks of the waterways was a Christmas custom.

CARRABELLE • *Franklin County*
A town was established here, near Dog Island Harbor, in 1877 by O.M. Kelly, who served as postmaster. Miss Carrie Hall reigned as the belle of the town, and it was named Rio Carrabelle in her honor. The Rio was later dropped. The name appears in an 1886 gazetteer as Carrabella.

CARYVILLE • *Washington County*
First settled in 1845 and later given the name Half Moon Bluff. In 1884, upon the advent of the Pensacola and Apalachicola Railroad, it was renamed Caryville in honor of a Pensacola businessman, R. M. Cary.

CASSADAGA • *Volusia County*
Also called Camp Cassadaga and founded by a group of spiritualists in 1893. Probably transplanted from Cassadaga, N.Y., whose Iroquois Indian meaning is given as "under rocks."

CASSELBERRY • *Seminole County*
Formerly known as Fern Park, and still thus referred to by many of its residents, this town was renamed during the 1940s by Hibbard Casselberry, a local horticulturist who had undertaken the development of the area. The earlier name came from the numerous extensive ferneries here.

CASSIA • *Lake County*
Established in 1850. Probably named for the Chinese cinnamon or cassia bark tree, which resembles the camphor tree, prevalent in Florida.

CASTILLO DE SAN MARCOS • *St. Johns County*
The sacking of St. Augustine by the English in 1586 and in 1668 caused Spain to build a defensive stone fort, the Castillo de San Marcos. Construction began in 1672 and continued with interruptions until 1763. The English twice besieged the Castillo, in 1702 and 1740. As a result of the French and Indian War, Spain ceded Florida to Great Britain for British-occupied Havana. The British garrisoned and held the Castillo during the American Revolution. Florida was returned to Spain in 1783 at the conclusion of the war, and then ceded to the United States in 1821. The Castillo was known to the Americans

Aerial view of the Castillo de San Marcos in the 1950s.

as Fort Marion, in honor of Gen. Francis Marion, the Revolutionary patriot of South Carolina popularly called the Swamp Fox. Fort Marion housed western Indians as prisoners in the 1870s. Confederate forces occupied the fort briefly during the Civil War. It was used during the Spanish–American War as a military prison. Fort Marion was declared a national monument in 1924 and the ancient name was restored afterwards. The Castillo was named for Saint Mark, a disciple of Christ.

CATAWBA • *Santa Rosa County*
Established about 1903 and said to have been named for the catawba grapes cultivated in this section of the county.

CAXAMBAS • *Collier County*
Appears as *Caximbas* on the Finley map of 1831 and as Caximba on the Melish map of 1816. It has been renamed Collier City. The meaning is obscure. The Portuguese word *caximba* means "pipe." There exists a Spanish word spelled similarly and meaning "a shallow well surrounded by rocks."

CAYO COSTA • *Lee County*
On the island of the same name off Florida's west coast. The name means "Coast Key" or "island near the coast." This island narrows toward the southern part, resembling a rib. *Costa* in Latin means "rib" or "side."

CEDAR GROVE • *Bay County*
In 1900, Jefferson Davis bought a homestead containing a number of large cedar trees. A settlement grew up and when it was incorporated 50 years later, the trees were still a feature of the place. The residents voted to name it Cedar Grove.

CEDAR KEY • *Levy County*
Although the Gulf island on which this town is located is called North Key, the name refers to the abundant growth of cedar trees which formerly covered all of the group of islands here. The town was established during the Civil War. Three pencil plants, formerly located here, were closed down when the cedar was depleted.

Railroad depot and wharf at Cedar Key.

CENTER HILL • *Sumter County*
Established in 1883 by Thomas W. Spicer, who became postmaster and gave the town its name. He liked to think of the hill on which it is located as the center of things.

CENTURY • *Escambia County*
The first settlement here was called Teaspoon. It was renamed when construction of the lumber mill began in the first month of the 20th century.

CHAIRS • *Leon County*
Near here stood the Spanish mission of San Pedro de Patali. The town developed beside the tracks of the Florida Railway and Navigation Company, and took its name from the Chaires family, prominent in early American development of Florida.

CHAMPAIGN • *Madison County*
Established during the early 1830s. Here lived some of the most prominent families of Madison County. From the French for "battlefield" or "level, open country."

CHARLIE APOPKA CREEK • *Hardee County*
Simpson (1956) says this signifies "trout (or bass) eating place," Charlie being a corruption of *chalo*, "trout or bass," and *apopka*, "place for eating."

CHARLOTTE COUNTY •
The fifty-seventh county, established April 23, 1921. The name is taken from that of Charlotte Harbor. Some authorities say Charlotte is a corruption of Carlos, in turn a corruption of Calusa, the Indian tribe. However, it is interesting to note that Charlotte Sophia was the queen of England when George III was king.

CHARLOTTE BEACH • *Charlotte County*
Takes its name from the harbor.

CHARLOTTE HARBOR • *Charlotte County*
Formerly Charlotte Bay. The name appears on Le Moyne's map of 1565 and is applied to the southern part of the Florida peninsula.

CHARM • *Seminole County*
Established in 1880. According to the sectional map of 1935, this place was formerly called Lake Charm. The fact that it is situated amid a group of charming lakes explains the name.

CHASSAHOWITZKA • *Citrus and Hernando counties*
The name of a river, bay, and point in Citrus County and a swamp in Hernando County. Simpson (1956) says the name was compounded from the Creek *chasi*, "pumpkin," and Creek *houwitchka*, "to open," with its meaning "pumpkin opening (place)." The name sometimes is humorously pronounced: "case o' whiskey."

CHATTAHOOCHEE • *Gadsden County*
A community was first established here about 1828, and took its name from the Chattahoochee River. The word is Seminole Creek and means "marked rock," deriving from the peculiarly colored and patterned stones found in the bed of the river. For part of its history, this town was known as River Junction because the Flint and Chattahoochee rivers join nearby to form the Apalachicola River. In 1681, the Spanish located their mission of Santa Cruz de Sabacola here.

CHERRY LAKE • *Madison County*
Established by Lucius Church in 1827 and named by him. A flourishing Indian village known as Ochoawilla was situated on a hill near the lake in 1827. The Indian word seems to be derived from two words meaning "slimy water." Cherry Lake was given the name because of the large number of wild cherry trees near the water.

CHETOLAH • *St. Lucie County*
Thought to be derived from the Indian word *chitola*, "rattlesnake."

CHICKASAW HATCHEE • *Orange County*
An obsolete name for Taylor Creek, a tributary of the St. Johns River, which it enters from the west, just below Lake Poinsett. Simpson (1956) reports that in the *Pena Journal* (1949:18) the old fields in the Apalachee country were spoken of as follows:

> *"These Chicazas abound in cattle, especially buffalo. The Chicazas (are) rich in fruit trees, such as figs, peaches, pomegranites, quinces, medlars, chestnuts, and acorns."*

There can be little doubt that *chicaza* (Chickasaw) refers to an old field or clearing, or place of settlement. In the Choctaw dialect, *chikki* means "old," and *asha*, "to sit or reside." One of the important places in the Chickasaw territory was known as the Chickasaw Old Fields and the tribal name itself may have originated there. The wild plum grows commonly in old fields and is called the Chickasaw Plum. The old name for Taylor Creek, Chickasaw Hatchee, probably means "old field stream," or stream where there are old clearings or settlements.

CHICORA • *Polk County*
Perhaps borrowed from the name once given to the Atlantic coast of South Carolina. There was a post office here from 1888 to 1920.

CHIEFLAND • *Levy County*
When hostilities in the Seminole War ceased in 1842, a Creek chief chose this site for his farm home and went extensively into the raising of corn, wheat, potatoes, etc. A number of other Indians did small farming nearby and assisted in the operation of the chief's farm.

CHILLOCHATCHEE OR HORSE CREEK • *Hardee and DeSoto counties*
Flowing southward through Hardee and DeSoto counties, this waterway derived its name from the Seminole Creek *chulako*, "horse," and *hachi*, "Creek."

CHIPLEY • *Washington County*
Originally known as Orange, renamed in honor of Col. William D. Chipley, a railroad official and state senator.

"Mr. Railroad of west Florida," William D. Chipley.

CHIPOLA • *Jackson, Calhoun, Gulf counties*
A river flowing through Jackson, Calhoun, and Gulf counties to discharge into the Apalachicola River. From the Chatot dialect, this word is said by Simpson (1956) to correspond to the Choctaw *champuli*, "sweet." The name also has been given to two communities in Calhoun County.

CHITE-HATCHEE • *Monroe County*
A stream shown on Ives map of 1856. Seminole-Creek *chitto*, "snake" and *hachi*, "river or creek"—snake creek. Now know as Rodger's River.

CHITTO HATCHEE • *Osceola County*
See also Chite-Hatchee. Judging from the Bruff map of 1846, this stream may have been the waterway known now as Ten-Mile Creek.

CHOCTAWHATCHEE • *Okaloosa and Walton counties*
A river, bay, and forest of west Florida. The name means "river of the Choctaws."

CHOKOLOSKEE • *Collier County*
Situated on one of the Ten Thousand Islands. Established in the 1880s by C. S. Smallwood and his father as an Indian trading post, but the place also appears as Chokoliska on an 1856 map. This name is formed from two Indian words, Seminole-Creek *chuka*, "house," and *liski*, "old." Through the energies of C. G. McKinney, the "Sage of Chokoloskee," a post office was established on November 27, 1891. However, Tebeau (1966) reports that the new post office bore the name Comfort, but it was changed on June 30, 1892, to Chokoloskee.

CHOSEN • *Palm Beach County*
Will (1964) reports that Chosen was promoted by J. R. Leatherman, a Dunkard preacher from Virginia. Leatherman's community got a school in 1921 but wanted a post office, and for that a name was necessary. "Leatherman's bailiwick decided on the name of Chosen, a good Bible name, because theirs was the Chosen Place. . . ."

CHRISTMAS • *Orange County*
Named in 1837, when a detachment of the U.S. Army, engaged in the war against the Seminoles, established a fort about halfway down the east coast of Florida on Christmas Day. The officers and men probably had little thought that their settlement would become the center of busy and famous annual activity connected with the greatest holiday which Christians celebrate.

Today the town of Christmas purveys each year a volume of Yuletide spirit disproportionate to its size. People from all parts of the United States send their holiday cards and letters to be posted from here with the official postmark "Christmas, Florida." Mrs. Juanita Tucker, commissioned postmistress in 1932, designed and added an extra imprint of her own—a Christmas tree and the words "Glory to God in the Highest, Christmas, Orange County, Florida" and the year.

The post office at Christmas about 1950.

The fame started in 1937, when the town of Christmas celebrated its 100th anniversary and receiv-ed considerable publicity. Since then, the early part of November each year brings the beginning of a steady flow of mail that swells and doesn't stop until the new year. In 1992, 150,000 pieces of mail from all over the world were postmarked.

Christmas received its name in 1837, shortly after the beginning of the seven-year Seminole War. A report of the gathering of a large number of braves in the upper St. Johns Valley caused Brig. Gen. Abraham Eustis to set out from Fort Mellon (Sanford) on December 17, 1837, with more than 1,000 men. The column took seven days to travel 25 miles, arriving at a point opposite Lake Cone on the St. Johns on December 25. Gen. Eustis (a Florida city recalls his name) ordered a site prepared for a fort which took the name Fort Christmas. Writing in *The Miami Herald*, Nixon Smiley reported "Fort Christmas was built eighty feet square, of pine pickets with two substantial block houses twenty feet square."

No battle ever occurred there, and Fort Christmas disappeared long ago, the log-constructed pickets and block houses becoming victims of decay or forest fire. No one knows now exactly where the fort stood, but as recently as 1950, the old military road between Christmas and Chuluota—the road cre-ated by the troop movement in 1835—was still in use.

The Christmas post office was established in 1892. The name Christmas—rather than Fort Christmas—always has been used.

CHUCCOCHARTS HAMMOCKS • *Hernando County*
An area 13 miles long and eight miles broad. From the Seminole-Creek word *chucko*, "house," and *chati*, "red." The name of the hammock was taken from that of the Indian town, in which the houses were daubed with red clay.

CHULUOTA • *Seminole County*
Appears to combine the Creek *chule*, "pine," and *ote*, "island," for this was an open area of pine surrounded by hardwoods. Another version says the name is Seminole for "fox den."

Just how the town received its musical Indian name has been forgotten, but Nixon Smiley reported in *The Miami Herald* that Robert A. Mills, who developed a community on nearby Lake Mills in the 1880s, is said to have named the place. But Mrs. Josie Jacobs Prevatt, who was born at Chuluota in 1883, told Smiley in 1968 that the area may have been known by the name when her grandparents arrived from North Carolina in 1866.

Residents smile when they tell still another story about the name's origin —a very corny one: A Seminole brave, courting a maiden named Luota, brought her some sassafras roots. "What am I to do with these?" asked Luota. "Chew, Luota," replied the brave.

Chuluota was one of the stations on Henry M. Flagler's abandoned railway division that swung away from Florida's east coast at New Smyrna and ran past Geneva, Bithlo, Holopaw, and Yeehaw to wind up at Okeechobee.

CHUMUCKLA • *Santa Rosa County*
Formerly called Chumuckla Springs. The year of origin is as confused as the meaning of the name. The Federal Writers Project (1939) said Chumuckla was settled about 1813 by the McDavid family, but the *Florida State Gazetteer* gives 1883 as the beginning date. Perhaps there were two starts as an organized community. Read (1934) is troubled about the derivation of the name, saying the Creek *chumuklita*, which signifies "to bow the head to the ground," closely resembles *chumuckla* in form, but the reason why a place-name of this peculiar meaning should have been selected is not apparent. The first syllable of *chumuckla*—to suggest another interpretation—may possibly be connected with *hitchiti ichi*, "deer," and the last two syllables with *imokli*, "its den,"—hence, "deer den" or "deer retreat."

CINCO BAYOU • *Okaloosa County*
When the Cocke family's homestead was subdivided, the property was given the name Cinco Bayou because it bordered Five Mile Bayou. In turn, Five Mile gave way to the more stylish Spanish name, so the waterway now also is called Cinco Bayou.

CITRA • *Marion County*
Named in 1881 by a group of men, among them Messrs. Wartmann, Harris, White, Hoyt, and the Rev. P. P. Bishop. As citrus production was the principal industry, Rev. Bishop suggested the name Citra, which was unanimously accepted.

CITRONELLE • *Citrus County*
Named about 1855, possibly for the prolific growth of citrons, the lemonlike fruit of a citrus tree whose preserved rind is often used in fruitcake (but also the small, hard-fleshed watermelon used especially in pickles and preserves and similarly found in central Florida).

CITRUS COUNTY •
The forty-fourth county, established June 2, 1887. The name stands as tribute to Florida's main agricultural product.

CITY POINT • *Brevard County*
Named in 1868 by Mr. J. Z. Dixon.

CLARA • *Taylor County*
A woman's name which signifies "clear, illustrious." It was conferred by turpentine people who worked here and by tradition refers to the Steinhatchee River near which the town is situated. But likely the wife of a company boss was the real source.

CLARCONA • *Orange County*
The origin of its name remains obscure. The long-settled Clarcona became a press service dateline in 1972 when Bill Herman bought the building that housed the post office. Wanting to call attention to the area's horse-breeding industry, Herman put up a sign picturing a rider on horseback with the words "Pony Express Station, Clarcona, Florida." A postal official said the sign didn't conform to post office regulations and asked Herman to take it down.

CLARKSVILLE • *Calhoun County*
The name honors the Clark family, prominent in the area. There has been a community here since the 1890s, with the present name since 1905.

CLARKWILD • *Hillsborough County*
Named for two pioneers, Messrs. Clark and Wilder.

CLAY COUNTY
The thirty-seventh county, established December 31, 1858. Named for Kentucky's Henry Clay, secretary of state under John Quincy Adams, and author of the saying, "I'd rather be right than be President."

CLAY SPRINGS • *Orange County*
Now known as Wekiwa Springs, its water flows into the Wekiwa River.

CLEARWATER • *Pinellas County*
Pánfilo de Narváez landed here on what is now the Pinellas Peninsula in 1528. Early in the nineteenth century some fishermen attempted citrus culture here, but were unsuccessful because of trouble with the Seminoles. After the establishment of Fort Harrison near here in 1841, a group of settlers under the leadership of James Stevens took up homes and farms under the Armed Occupation Act. The town was first called Clear Water Harbor, because of a spring of sulphated water which bubbles up in the Gulf near the shore, making the water usually clear and sparkling. Later the harbor part of the name was dropped and the other two words merged into one. The city is the county seat of Pinellas County.

CLERMONT • *Lake County*
Established about 1884 by the Clermont Improvement Company, whose manager, A. F. Wrotniski, had been born in Clermont, France. Today, in addition to the French name with its ancient associations, Clermont uses the designation "The Gem of the Hills," since it is situated amid 17 lakes and a group of rugged green-gold hills, at an altitude of 105 feet above sea level.

CLEVELAND • *Charlotte County*
Named in 1886 for Grover Cleveland, who had been inaugurated as president for the first time in the previous year. Dr. A. T. Holleymon, of Georgia, was responsible for the name. He had brought and developed extensive property on the Peace River.

CLEWISTON • *Hendry County*
In 1922, when the Atlantic Coast Line railroad was extended from Moore Haven to Sand Point, a community at the site of Clewiston was named in honor of A. C. Clewis, a Tampa banker who had provided the capital for the extension of the railroad. The town was platted and developed in 1925, and incorporated in 1932.

CLIO • *Liberty County*
The Greek muse of history. It has been used as the name of a number of American cities and the belief is that such use reflects more an appreciation of the shortness of the name than of the goddess. Florida's Clio had a post office from 1911 until 1913.

CLOUD LAKE • *Palm Beach County*
One of the famous war chiefs of the Seminoles during the Second Seminole War of the 1840s was Yaholoochee or "Cloud." In the 1940s, when Kenyon Riddle developed a subdivision here, he excavated about five acres and named the resultant lake Cloud Lake after the warrior. Several years later, the people of the platted area decided to incorporate and the name was used for the new town.

CLYDES • *Seminole County*
The Lord and Tanner families established Clydes in 1867 and named the place for their former home in Great Britain.

COACHMAN • *Pinellas County*
Named for S. C. Coachman.

COATSVILLE • *Holmes County*
Established by Marvin Coats, who had a gristmill and a cotton gin here in the 1890s.

COCKROACH CREEK • *Hillsborough County*
See Lakes.

COCOA • *Brevard County*
There are two widely varying accounts of how this unique name came to be attached to this community. One says that it came from the coco-plum (*Chrysobalanus icaco L.*) which grows along the Florida east coast and is particularly profuse in this area. The other explanation says that while a group of citizens was seeking a name for the town, an old African-American woman, standing near a landing at the foot of Willard Street, received inspiration from the label on a box of Baker's Cocoa. Her suggestion was adopted. Either route would have involved a little misspelling ("cocoa" is a corruption

An 1885 waterfront view of Cocoa.

of "cacao") but in any event Cocoa-ites claim there is no other town in the world with the same name. It was founded by fishermen very early in Florida's history, and in 1871, a post office was established at Magnolia Point, some two miles north of here, but the town of Cocoa was not incorporated until 1895. Cocoa Beach is on the beach peninsula across the Indian and Banana rivers from Cocoa.

COCONUT CREEK • *Broward County*
Incorporated in 1967, Coconut Creek derived its name from the density of coconut palms and the presence of a number of canals and small lakes. Originally named Edgefield.

COCONUT GROVE • *Dade County*
Once known as Jack's Bight, for John Thomas (Jolly Jack) Peacock, the Englishman who in 1863 homesteaded 160 acres by the side of Biscayne Bay. Jack's Bight (bight: the land beside a bend in a shore) came to be known more formally as Cocoanut Grove because of the grove of coconut trees here. When the area was incorporated in 1922, the "a" was dropped, largely through the energies of Kirk Munroe, a local resident and nationally-known writer of juvenile and other fiction who argued the coconut palm had nothing to do with cocoa, the roasted, husked, and ground seeds of the cacao. Coconut Grove was swallowed up by neighboring Miami in 1925, but still protests the annexation in periodic, unsuccessful secession movements.

CODY • *Jefferson County*
Believed named for a family, Cody had its own post office from 1912 to 1937.

CODYVILLE • *Flagler County*
Established about 1901 by the Cody's Turpentine and Farm Land Company.

COLDWATER • *Santa Rosa County*
On the Coldwater River. The town took its name from the river in 1912.

COLEE • *St. Johns and Broward counties*
Named for a St. Augustine family.

COLEMAN • *Sumter County*
Settled in 1882 and named for an early settler, B. F. Coleman, who was a physician, orange grove and farm owner, and the first postmaster.

COLLIER COUNTY
The sixty-second county, established May 8, 1923. Named for Barron G. Collier, who was one of the leading developers of the southern part of the state and had extensive land holdings in this area. Born in Memphis, Tenn., March 23, 1873, he graduated from Oglethorpe University. He entered the advertising business in 1890 and became one of the first great advertising tycoons, particularly in "car cards" on New York street cars, subways, and elevated trains.

COLLIER CITY • *Collier County*
By an interesting coincidence, this community had the same name as its county but derived the name from another source. William R. Spear, editor of *The Fort Myers News-Press*, explained: "The first settler at Marco Island was

W. T. Collier from Tennessee, no relation of Barron (Collier), who settled there in 1870 after an earlier stay at Fort Myers. He had eight children, the most prominent of whom was Captain William D. Collier. In 1927, when a New York syndicate promoted a big boomtime development there, they got the Legislature to incorporate all Marco Island as a city and named it Collier City. Whether it was named for W. T. or William D. is uncertain. There is no such place today as Collier City. Captain William D. Collier became post-master of Marco in 1888. In 1908 he invented a clam-dredging machine which gave rise to the big Doxsee clam industry here."

COLOHATCHEE • *Broward County*
Read (1934) thinks the name is a combination of Seminole Creek words, *kala,* "white oak," and *hatchee,* "river." Another view says colo is a combination of part of the name of William Collier, an early settler, with *hatchee.*

COLUMBIA COUNTY •
The sixteenth county, established February 4, 1832. This county took the poetical name of the United States, which had been formed from that of the discoverer of America.

COMBEE SETTLEMENT • *Polk County*
Named for the Combee family.

COMFORT • *Collier County*
See Chokoloskee.

COMPASS LAKE • *Jackson County*
Established in 1885. Named for the lake, which is round like a compass.

CONANT • *Lake County*
The post office was established here in 1884. The town was named in tribute to Maj. Sherman Conant, one of the principals of the Florida Southern Railway. Kennedy (1929) relates that "Conant would have been a good city of today with its promising start, but its promoters went in for snobbery and 'cut' all who did their own work or who sent their children to public school instead of a private school that was opened in Conant." Kennedy concluded: "It is, within any recollection, the only town that made this practice of snob-bery, for the usual spirit of the communities in Lake County was comrade-ship, helpfulness, and hospitality. All that marks [in 1929] the site of the once flourishing town of Conant is the railroad sign at the siding."

CONASAUGA • *Manatee County*
A river in Georgia and a village in Polk County, Tenn. It occurs in the narra-tive of the *Gentleman of Elvas.*

CONCH KEY • *Monroe County*
Native residents of the Florida Keys are called Conchs. Generally, they have Bahaman ancestry. This is the name also of the shellfish whose meat is the base for a delicacy, conch salad.

CONWAY • *Orange County*
England furnished the settlers for a number of British colonies in central

Florida during the 1880s, and Conway, beside a lake of the same name, was typical of these. Settlers were attracted both by the mild climate and by sport. At the Conway home of Dudley G. Cary-Elwes, a retired British army officer, many young people gathered every Wednesday in the 1880s to play tennis. Deer, quail, and pigeon were abundant in the woods just outside the town. The Episcopal churches had more than the usual Church of England flavor. *See also* Narcoossee.

COOK • *Bay County*
Settled in 1898 and named for an early resident.

COOPER CITY • *Broward County*
Morris Cooper, founder, gave his name to this community in the 1950s.

COPELAND • *Collier County*
Named for D. Graham Copeland, general manager for the Collier properties and member of the Florida House of Representatives in 1949.

CORAL COVE • *Sarasota County*
A neighborhood named for the yellow-red coral.

CORAL GABLES • *Dade County*
Seat of the University of Miami, it took its name from the home built there earlier by the Rev. Solomon Merrick, whose son, George E. Merrick, subdivided the area during Florida's great land boom of the 1920s. The son perpetuated in the name of the community the coral rock walls and many gables of his father's house.

CORAL REEF STATE PARK, JOHN PENNEKAMP •
Monroe County
Here are the nation's only living reef formations of coral, the underwater anthozoan animal which has given its name to a number of Florida communities: Coral Gables, Coral Springs, Coral Cove and even, by misadventure, Carol City. Within John Pennekamp Coral Reef State Park are 40 of the 52 species of coral found in the Atlantic reef system. As for John Pennekamp, he was the Miami editor who led the successful campaign to preserve the coral reefs against commercial shell collectors, tropical fish hunters, skin divers, and most recently, pollution.

CORAL SPRINGS • *Broward County*
An officer of Coral Ridge Properties, developers of the 21-square-mile community west of Pompano Beach, gave this explanation in 1972 for the choice of name: "This area has been known since Indian times for the purity of the natural spring water. In order to give it our own continuity, we merely added the 'coral' to 'springs.' Also, underlying the land is a solid formation of coral rock, which had, however, nothing to do with the name."

COREYTOWN • *Pinellas County*
The once incorporated and later "decorporated" community of Coreytown was named for the Corey Causeway to St. Petersburg Beach. The town is located at the eastern end of the causeway, which was named for one of the Pinellas County commissioners in office at the time it was built.

CORK • *Hillsborough County*
For a time the name of the community now known as Plant City. It came about after a mail route was opened on April 14, 1851, from Tampa to Ichepuckesassa to Jernigan (Orlando) to Mellonville (Sanford). H. E. Ostera contracted to make the 108-mile once-weekly round trip for $635 a year. E. H. Gore (1949) picks up the story: "Ichepuckesassa was an Indian name meaning 'tobacco blossoms' or 'fields.' An Irishman was made its postmaster but he had so much trouble trying to spell or pronounce the name that he had it changed to Cork after his hometown in Ireland." It was changed again, in 1885, to Plant City in honor of the railroad developer, Henry B. Plant.

CORKSCREW (Swamp, Village, Sanctuary) • *Collier County*
The late Dr. Robert O. Vernon, former director of the Division of Interior Resources, State Department of Natural Resources, said the name of the swamp likely was derived from its shape. The outline of the swamp resembles a corkscrew with a handle across the top, then dwindling to a point. The sanctuary is under the protection of the National Audubon Society. At its heart is an untouched stand of bald cypress trees, their roots underwater and their branches reaching 100 feet or more into the sky. Beneath these towering giants is a lush tangle of vines, Spanish moss and aquatic plants so impenetrable that until a few years ago most people were content to leave it to the alligators. Then, in the mid-1950s, the pressures for land in south Florida became so intense that even this inaccessible swamp was threatened with drainage and development. Conservationists stepped in to preserve this unforgettable remnant of the original Florida wilderness as a wildlife sanctuary. Today, visitors can stroll among the cypresses on a boardwalk. Corkscrew is the largest remaining nesting place for the wood ibis, the only North American member of the stork family. Near the sanctuary is the village of Corkscrew.

CORONADO BEACH • *Volusia County*
F. C. Austin homesteaded a portion of the beach known by this name about 1885.

CORONET • *Hillsborough County*
The residential community of the Coronet Phosphate Company, which began mining operations here in 1909. Coronet was known as The Spotless Town because of its general cleanliness.

CORTEZ • *Manatee County*
Named in 1888 for Hernando Cortés, Spanish explorer.

COSME • *Hillsborough County*
The railroad station was established in 1914. This name seems to have been taken from the Greek word *cosmos*, meaning "harmony, order, the world."

COTTAGE HILL • *Escambia County*
So named in the 1890s because cottages were built on the hill.

COTTONDALE • *Jackson County*
Established by railway hands in 1882 and named for the surrounding cotton farms.

COTTONWOOD PLANTATION • *Citrus County*
On the Homosassa River stand the ruins of the antebellum sugar plantation of Sen. David Levy Yulee, pioneer Florida railroad builder. Yulee was president of the Florida Railroad Company, which was completed in 1861 and linked the Atlantic with the Gulf of Mexico between Fernandina and Cedar Key. Cottonwood was raided and pillaged in 1863 and again in 1864 by federal forces based at Cedar Key. As a result, the plantation never recovered its productivity.

COURT MARTIAL LAKE • *Bay County*
Named because a court martial was held here by Gen. Andrew Jackson, who tried two deserters from the army. The alternate water route of the Old Spanish Trail passed near this pond, called Southernmost Great Pond on the Purcell map of 1778.

COURTENAY • *Brevard County*
A homesteader of that name settled here about 1870.

A Courtenay ostrich farm in the 1890s.

COURTNEY CAMPBELL CAUSEWAY • *Hillsborough and Pinellas counties*
Crossing Old Tampa Bay to link Hillsborough and Pinellas counties, it was named for Courtney W. Campbell of Clearwater, who served on the State Road Board 1945-49 and as a member of Congress 1952-53. The causeway has a bridge 3,202 feet long with a vertical clearance of 22 feet.

COW CREEK • *Volusia County*
An early cattleman was responsible for this name.

COW FORD • *Duval County*
A marker on Bay Street, near the courthouse in Jacksonville, concisely tells the story of Cow Ford: "This narrow part of the St. Johns River, near a clear, freshwater spring, was a crossing point for Indians and early travelers. The

Indian name *Wacca Pilatka*, meaning 'Cow's Crossing,' was shortened by the English to Cow Ford, and Jacksonville was known by this name for many years. This crossing was used by the English when they made an old Timucuan Indian trail into King's Road." *See also* Jacksonville.

CRACKER SWAMP • *Duval County*
After the Battle of Olustee on February 20, 1864, Confederate troops found an abandoned federal railway box car, between Baldwin and Ten-mile Station (now Whitehouse), containing some 400 boxes of hard biscuits or crackers. At that point, the railroad crossed a branch of McGirts Creek and for this reason the place since has been known as Cracker Swamp.

CRACKERTOWN • *Levy County*
A riposte to nearby Yankeetown. There once was also a Crackertown in Duval County. Floridians are known as "crackers," but Allen Morris and Ann Waldron, in their book *Your Florida Government,* suggest the nickname should be used with care. Its acceptance by Floridians depends upon the person and, in some measure, upon the section of the state. A historian illustrated this shading by saying that if, while out of the state, someone hailed her as a cracker she would respond affirmatively. If, however, someone in Florida described her as a cracker, she would want to think it over. A number of origins are suggested. Francis R. Goulding, in *Marooner's Island* (1869), thought the name was derived from Scottish settlers in whose dialect a "cracker" was a person who talked boastingly. John Lambert, in *Travels Through Lower Canada, and the United States of North America* (1810), wrote: "The wagoners are familiarly called crackers (from the smacking of their whip, I suppose)." Emily P. Burke, in *Reminiscences of Georgia* (1850), said crackers were called that "from the circumstance that they formerly pounded all their corn, which is their principal article of diet." Two modern historians, A. J. and Kathryn Abbey Hanna, wrote in 1948: "The name 'cracker' frequently applied to countrymen of Georgia and Florida is supposed to have originated as a cattle term." Florida cowboys popped whips of braided buckskin, 12 to 18 feet long. The "crack" sounded like a rifle shot and at times could be heard for several miles. The writer of the newspaper column "Cracker Politics" suggested it might be prudent to accompany the nickname with a smile.

CRAIG • *Monroe County*
Gained two national distinctions in the 1930s while hardly more than a building or two to serve motorists and fishermen. Craig, named for its merchant, appeared in Ripley's "Believe It or Not" as a "town built on a highway, instead of a highway built through a town." Craig also is the place where the lowest sea-level barometric pressure in the Western Hemisphere was ever recorded—26.35 inches on Labor Day, September 2, 1935 (until Hurricane Gilbert in 1988). This 1935 hurricane, accompanied by tidal waves, smashed a relatively small area of the Middle Keys, killing some 400 persons, including 200 veterans of World War I engaged in a federal work relief highway project. The storm also put the Florida East Coast Railway's Overseas Extension forever out of use.

CRANDALL • *Nassau County*
Once called Township, then Fort Henry, Crandall gained its name from a family who lived here in 1884.

CRAWFORD • *Nassau County*
Established in 1883 by W. R. Crawford.

CRAWFORDVILLE • *Wakulla County*
This seat of Wakulla County derived its name from the Crawford family, two of whose members, Dr. John L. and his son, H. Clay, served as secretary of state for 48 years, from 1881 until 1929.

CRAWL KEYS • *Monroe County*
These keys along the Overseas Highway gained their name by the use of "crawls," or pens extending from the land into shallow water, in which turtles were kept until shipped to market. The green hawksbill turtle and loggerhead turtle were sought in the Keys for soup and other dishes. The hawksbill also was valued for its shell. The trunk turtle grew to great size but seldom was used for food. The naturalist John James Audubon, while cruising the Keys in 1832, watched seiners as they stretched nets across the mouths of streams to trap turtles then prolific there. He bought turtles to feed herons which he was taking back to friends in Charleston. Most sea turtles are now endangered.

CREIGHTON • *Volusia County*
Named for E. R. Creighton. In 1911, a mill bearing this name operated here.

CRESCENT CITY • *Putnam County*
Named by Mrs. Charles R. Griffin of New York City, who came to this location with her husband soon after the close of the Civil War. There were two lakes in the vicinity, one of them—Crescent Lake—shaped like a moon in crescent, and the other—Lake Stella—positioned like a star nearby. The town took its name from Crescent Lake, which was known as Dunn's Lake during the Civil War and before. Dunn's Creek, which flows out of the lake, is still called Dunn's Creek; in this creek the famous sailing yacht *America* was scuttled by the Confederates and raised by the Unionists.

CRESTVIEW • *Okaloosa County*
Situated on the top of a high hill, the highest point on the old Pensacola and Apalachicola Railroad, Crestview took its name from that fact. It is 223 feet above sea level.

CROOKED ISLAND • *Bay County*
Off the coast in the Gulf of Mexico, the island has an irregular outline.

CROSS CITY • *Dixie County*
Two public roads, one from Perry to old Archer, the other from Branford to Horseshoe, crossed at this point. W. H. Matthis, who conferred the name, seemingly wanted it clear that a Cross City was something more than a mere crossroad.

C R O S S   C R E E K • *Alachua County*
See Island Grove.

C R O W N   P O I N T • *Orange County*
Named for the local terrain, which forms a point or peninsula into Lake Apopka.

C R O W S   B L U F F • *Lake County*
E. H. Crow was among those who settled here on the St. Johns River in the 1850s. The community then was called Ledworth Camp, after a timbering operation for the U. S. Navy. Crow changed this to Osceola but confusion resulted, with freight shipments for Ocala arriving here and those for Osceola turning up in Ocala. The name again was changed, in 1858 to Hawkinsville, and finally in 1888 to Crows Bluff. It was the site of an early free bridge across the St. Johns to link Lake and Volusia counties.

C R Y S T A L   R I V E R • *Citrus County*
On the Taylor War Map of 1839 a stream designated as Weewa-hiiaca appeared. In Seminole-Creek the word *wiwa* means "water," while *haiyayaki* means "clear or shining." The English name Crystal River was given as a translation of this, and by the time the Davis Map of 1856 was published, the Indian name had disappeared. The town takes its name from the river.

C U D J O E   K E Y • *Monroe County*
Stevenson (1970) relates a story worth retelling about how this key may have gotten its name. Aggravated by the bustle of Key West in the 1880s, writes Stevenson, a member of a family there left for the isolation of this key. "He selected a pleasant spot and his family used to visit him frequently, upon Cousin Joe's key." Whether Cudjoe took its name from Cousin Joe or from the fragrant little tree there known as joewood, or cudjoewood, no one knows.

C U S C O W I L L A • *Alachua County*
The Indian village of Cuscowilla once was near the present town of Micanopy. It was there that the Pennsylvania Quaker naturalist William Bartram visited the Seminole chief, Cowkeeper, in May 1774. William Bartram first visited Florida in the company of his father John, the renowned botanist, and returned alone a decade later. William Bartram wrote his famous *Travels*, which Samuel Taylor Coleridge described as the last book "written in the spirit of the old travellers."

C U S H I N G ' S   P O I N T • *Collier County*
At this place in 1895-97, Frank H. Cushing, of the Bureau of American Ethnology, discovered artifacts so different from any found elsewhere in Florida shell heaps that he regarded them as belonging to an aboriginal culture previously unrecorded.

C U T L E R   R I D G E • *Dade County*
Dr. C. F. Cutler of Chelsea, Mass., came here in 1884, started a settlement, and built a coontie (or komptie) mill to grind an arrowroot starch which was used for bread. The Seminoles first ground coontie. This area was known before his coming as Big Hunting Ground.

CYPRESS • *Jackson County*
Named for the large number of cypress ponds to be found in this vicinity, Cypress was established in 1873.

CYPRESS GARDENS • *Polk County*
The late promotional genius Richard Downing Pope converted what in the 1930s was a swamp bordering Lake Eloise into an internationally known center for water ski shows and "gardens of the world." An unincorporated community by the same name has grown up about Cypress Gardens largely to serve the thousands of tourists attracted here.

Aquamaids posed around the Florida-shaped swimming pool at Cypress Gardens soon after it was dedicated by champion swimmer/movie star Esther Williams and Governor Dan McCarthy

DADE COUNTY •

The nineteenth county, established February 4, 1836. When the news reached Tallahassee of the Dade massacre (*See* Dade City), the Legislative Council inserted Dade's name in a pending bill to create a new county. This county is today the most populous in Florida, the site of Greater Miami.

A curiosity among Florida maps is one from 1838 which shows Dade County between Alachua and Hillsborough counties. Apparently, a Northern cartographer assumed that the lawmakers would recognize the area of the massacre in creating a new county.

DADE CITY • *Pasco County*

Named for Maj. Francis Langhorne Dade, U. S. Army. The commanding officer of a detachment of about 110 which was on its way from Fort Brook (Tampa) to relieve Fort King (Ocala), Dade and all but three of his men were ambushed and slaughtered by Seminoles near the present Bushnell on December 28, 1835. The date marks the opening of the Second Seminole War, as tragic an event and as tragic a war as the pages of history have to show. *See also* Dade County.

The Second Seminole War also gave names to many of Florida's "fort" cities. The Seminoles fought guerrilla-style, characterized by former *Miami Herald* reporter Jeanne Bellamy as "hit and hide." Most encounters involved only a handful of men on each side. The last big battle occurred on the eastern shore of Lake Okeechobee on Christmas Day, 1837, and perhaps would be forgotten today but for the presence as commander of the U. S troops of Gen. Zachary Taylor, afterwards president of the United States.

DAHOMA • *Nassau County*

This name was carried on postal markings for 20 years at the turn of the century.

DANIA • *Broward County*

Danes gave this town its present name, after the name of their own people. The community was founded by the Florida East Coast Railroad's Model Land company, whose officials named it Modello. But later a group called the Danish Brotherhood came from Wisconsin, under the leadership of A. C. Frost, and provided the new name. The town was incorporated in 1927. It is the center of the county's tomato-growing district, and the seat of the Seminole Indian Agency. Incidentally, the thrifty railway men again used the name Modello for another community in south Dade County.

DAVENPORT • *Polk County*

Some say this town, founded about 1883, was named after a colonel; others say it was named after a conductor. The military officer was Col. William Davenport, who commanded a military camp located about 12 miles northwest of the present site, during the Second Seminole War. The gentleman honored according to the other version was a conductor named Davenport on the old South Florida Railroad.

DAVIE • *Broward County*
Formerly called Zona, this community took its present name from a developer, R. P. Davie, who bought 25,000 acres of black muck by the South New River Canal north of Miami and advertised the quality of Everglades land in the West. Davie bought at $2 an acre and sold at $30.

DAVIS ISLANDS • *Hillsborough County*
Once there were two mud flats known as Big Grassy and Little Grassy off Tampa's Bayshore Boulevard at the mouth of the Hillsborough River. David P. Davis, remembering the emergence of Miami Beach from the mangrove swamp and sand, sold local people and others on a development at Tampa's doorstep. Down payments on lots, mostly still underwater, totaled $3 million at the opening sale. Davis enlarged and gave substance to the Grassys in what was the Florida west coast's most spectacular real estate enterprise of the 1920s. With construction underway of apartments, residences, and other buildings of Mediterranean architecture at Davis Islands, the restless promoter commenced a similar project known as Davis Shores at St. Augustine. Collapse of the land boom delayed fulfillment of the Davis plans but, as with so many other subdivisions of the 1920s, the dreams ultimately came true, in this case after World War II. Davis never saw the finished dream. He had slipped into a storm-tossed Atlantic from the liner *Majestic* in October 1926. No one ever was to know whether his drowning was by accident or by his own wish.

DAY • *Lafayette County*
Named for a family, this community dates at least from 1892, when the post office was established.

DAYTONA BEACH • *Volusia County*
Mathias Day, of Mansfield, Ohio, is the man whose name lives on in the rather unusual name of this world-famous seaside town. He was its founder, in 1870. Two years later, a committee consisting of himself, Mrs. William Jackson and Mrs. Riley Peck was commissioned by the settlers to select a name from among three suggested versions: Daytown, Daytonia, and Daytona. The city now encompasses a business and residential section on the mainland west of the Halifax River, as well as a residential and resort section on the beach and peninsula between the river and the ocean; but until they were consolidated in 1926, these were three separate municipalities called Daytona, Daytona Beach, and Seabreeze. The broad, hard beach has been the scene of many automobile races and speed trials, including those of Sir Malcolm Campbell. Campbell was honored with knighthood after setting a world auto speed record at Daytona in 1931.

DEADENING, THE • *Polk County*
Fort Meade was settled in a tract, about 20 miles square on the west side of Peace Creek, known as The Deadening. Heatherington (1928) says the tract was called The Deadening from the fact that "years before, all the large timber in that area had died. Indians say that there was a very heavy hail at one time, and the stones were so large and fell with such force, that they bruised the trees, and worms got into the bruised places and killed the trees."

DEAD LAKE • *Gulf County*
With a surface area of 3,655 acres draining an area of 1,206 square miles, it presents to first viewers an eerie appearance, with many dead trees standing in the water as though the forest had drowned; hence, the name. Streams run both in and out of Dead Lake.

DEADMANS BAY • *Dixie County*
In the Gulf of Mexico off the coast of Dixie County. The name appears on eighteenth-century English maps, likely because of the loss of a sailor in the area.

DEAD RIVER • *Lake County*
A waterway dug in 1878 to connect Lake Harris and Lake Eustis, and so named because of the slowness of its current. There also are Dead rivers in Osceola, Santa Rosa, Wakulla, and Sumter counties.

DEBARY • *Volusia County*
Named for Baron Frederick DeBary, German-born of Belgian ancestry, who came to the United States in 1840 as agent for Mumm's champagne. The baron came here in 1868 and built the handsome residence known now as DeBary Hall. His Florida estate of some hundreds of acres, with its hunting and fishing, attracted many notables of the era, including presidents Grant and Cleveland. Their visits were facilitated by the baron's ownership of steamboats plying the nearby St. Johns River. In the 1960s, DeBary gained occasional national attention as the winter home of U.S. Sen. Everett K. Dirksen of Illinois, colorful minority leader.

Look carefully and you will see a pig in the surf in this 1904 photo of Daytona Beach.

DEEP CREEK • *St. Johns County*
So called because an adjacent stream was deep enough to be navigable.

DEERFIELD BEACH • *Broward County*
Originally called Hillsborough, this town adopted the name Deerfield about 1907, when deer were plentiful in the hammocks west of the town and beach.

DEER, RIVER OF THE
The River of the Deer mentioned in diaries of Hernando De Soto's expedition has been identified as the Suwannee by the U.S. Commission that studied De Soto's route. The river was so named "because there the messengers from Ocachile brought thither some deer, of which there are many fine ones in that land." The expedition bridged the Suwannee on September 24-25, 1539.

DEFUNIAK SPRINGS • *Walton County*
Col. Fred DeFuniak of Louisville, Ky., an official of the Louisville and Nashville Railroad, gave his name to this town. It was at first called Lake DeFuniak. DeFuniak Springs is the county seat of Walton County. Around the lake, which is a mile in circumference and was known in early days as Open Pond, developed not only the business district but also a Chautauqua building which attracted widely known speakers and large audiences. When established in 1885, the institution was called the "Chautauqua that began under a tree" because its organizers met under a large oak to plan for the building beside the spring-fed lake. Chautauquas were assemblies in a nationwide system of lectures, concerts and dramatic performances that flourished in the late nineteenth and early twentieth centuries. The assemblies originated at Lake Chautauqua, N.Y.

DELAND • *Volusia County*
Henry A. DeLand, a New York baking-powder manufacturer, came to Florida on a visit in 1876 and purchased a homestead at the site of this town. A group of the people in the vicinity, visiting at a home where DeLand was being entertained, resolved to obtain a post office and name it after him. John B. Stetson, the world-famous Philadelphia hat manufacturer, also had a part in the founding of the town. In 1883, DeLand established an academy here and gave it his own name. Stetson thereafter became a great financial benefactor of the institution, and when it was finally incorporated as a university it was DeLand himself who suggested that its name be changed to honor Stetson. Because of the university, the city calls itself "The Athens of Florida." It is also the county seat of Volusia County. Branching oaks planted long ago beautify its streets. These trees have caused some aviators to call DeLand "the city of the forest." The Spanish mission of Antonico stood near here.

DELEON SPRINGS • *Polk County*
Named for Ponce de León, the Spaniard who discovered Florida in 1513. (*See also* Florida.)

DELEON SPRINGS • *Volusia County*
Once known as Garden Springs and earlier as Spring Garden, a plantation here was visited in 1831 by the naturalist John James Audubon. There were two springs but one ceased to flow. Named in 1885 for Ponce de León. Gold (1927) states this place was named De Sota (sic) in 1882, but the Post Office Department refused to recognize the name because of a De Soto elsewhere, so Ponce de León was honored. Near here stood the Spanish mission of San Salvador de Maiaca.

DELESPINE • *Broward County*
Situated on the west bank of Indian River. This site is a part of the Spanish land grant of 42,000 acres to Joseph Delespine, for whom it was named.

DELL • *Lafayette County*
This community on the Suwannee River managed to support a post office for a year and a half in the early 1900s.

DELLWOOD • *Jackson County*
Settled in 1840 or earlier. The beauty of the wooded land on a ridge overlooking lakes and streams prompted the name.

DELRAY BEACH • *Palm Beach County*
May be simply a corruption of the Spanish words *del rey*, meaning "of the king." It was originally named Linton, after Congressman Linton of Michigan, who platted the town about 1892. In 1895, the town was reorganized as Delray. One story has it that the settlers named the town for a neighborhood in Detroit called Delray. The Beach was added in the 1930s when the area along the beach was consolidated with the city on the mainland.

DELTA • *Escambia County*
Situated at the mouth of the Escambia River. In 1830, this was called Ferry Pass for the narrow pass leading to the ferry across the Escambia River. At one time it was also named Beelerville and finally Delta, for the common usage of the word as an alluvial deposit at the mouth of the river.

DELTONA • *Volusia County*
Started virtually from scratch in the 1960s, it is approximately midway between DeLand (Del-) and Daytona Beach (-tona).

DEMORY HILL • *Dixie County*
First named Demory Hill in 1930, the community has been known since 1948 as Suwannee.

DENNETT • *Madison County*
On the South Georgia and West Coast Railroad. Established in 1904 and named for Dennett H. Mays, a prominent citizen and planter who owned the surrounding property.

DE SOTO COUNTY •

The forty-second county, established May 19, 1887. This is one of two counties in Florida bearing parts of the name of the same person—the Spanish explorer Hernando De Soto—with Hernando being the other.

DE SOTO CITY • *Highlands County*

Named for Hernando De Soto, the Spanish conquistador. It was founded in 1916.

DESTIN • *Okaloosa County*

Proud of its New England atmosphere, an inheritance from Captain Leonard Destin of New London, Conn., who used this area as a base in pioneering the snapper fishing industry more than a century ago.

DETROIT • *Dade County*

Now known as Florida City, Detroit was established in 1910 by the Tatum Brothers—B.B., J.R., Smiley, and J.H.—land developers in Dade County who preceded the great boom of the 1920s.

DEVILFISH KEY • *Lee County*

President Theodore Roosevelt was one of the many presidents of the United States who found relaxation in Florida. Fishing off Captiva Island in the early 1900s, President Roosevelt hooked a giant devilfish, or manta, which he landed after an all-day battle. The creature, measuring 30 feet across and weighing more than two tons, was beached on a small island in Blind Pass. The island was thereafter known as Devilfish Key. Nearby Roosevelt Beach also commemorates the president's visit.

DEVIL'S GARDEN • *Hendry County*

Capt. Francis Asbury Hendry is believed to have given the name to the area and also to an Indian who was his friend. The Indian, known as Devil's Garden Tom, guided Capt. Hendry from Immokalee through an area which Hendry had found virtually impenetrable until Devil's Garden Tom showed him how easy it was to traverse on horseback. The name, The Devil's Garden, appears on the state's road map today.

DEVIL'S MILL HOPPER • *Alachua County*

Two miles northwest of Gainesville, this sink was caused by the collapse of the surface by the eroding action of an underground waterway on the limestone. The sink is a funnel-shaped depression with a surface area of five acres, sloping to a depth of approximately 100 feet. Former state geologist Robert O. Vernon said seepage from underground water fills a pool and drains through an underground outlet. Violets, ferns, dogwood, and magnolia grow in profusion. The rim of the sink is surrounded by dense stands of hardwood. The name appears to stem from the international custom of using devil to indicate something unusually bad in terrain or formation.

DEVIL'S PUNCH BOWL • *Hernando County*

A dry sink an acre in extent and from 60 to 80 feet deep. About three and a half miles west of Brooksville, this sink resembles a mammoth punch bowl, with steep sides.

DEWEY • *Hillsborough County*
Named by railroad officials to honor the Spanish-American War hero of Manila Bay, Adm. George Dewey.

DICKERT • *Suwannee County*
A railroad siding at the farm of Judge C. P. Dickert.

DICKSON BAY • *Wakulla County*
An inlet of Apalachee Bay.

DIEGO PLAINS • *St. Johns County*
Since the early 1700s, the cattle ranch of Don Diego de Espinosa bore the name San Diego. It was located in the natural grasslands along the North and San Pablo rivers about 20 miles north of St. Augustine. Espinosa fortified the ranch house by erecting around it a palisade of cedar posts 15 feet high. As Fort San Diego, it fell in 1740 to Gen. James Oglethorpe of Georgia, who made it his headquarters in an unsuccessful attempt to capture St. Augustine. Even today the grasslands are known as Diego Plains, but the small settlement, once called Diego, became Palm Valley in 1907.

DINNER ISLAND • *Flagler County*
Was this a place where folks gathered for Sunday picnics or was there once a restaurant here that attracted them? Dinner Island survived as a postmark for 12 years in the early 1900s.

DINSMORE • *Duval County*
This former dairying community near Jacksonville was previously known as Pickett. It was founded in 1854 by James E. Pickett

DISCORDS, RIVER OF •
The report of the U.S. De Soto Expedition Commission states the expedition built a bridge on August 16, 1539, across the River of Discords, so named "because of some disturbance in the army, the nature of which the chroniclers chose to conceal." The River of Discords was identified by the Commission as the Santa Fe, and the De Soto crossing likely was between the mouths of New River and Olustee Creek.

DISSTON CITY • *Pinellas County*
Hamilton Disston saved Florida from bankruptcy by purchasing 6,250 square miles of land from Orlando to south of Lake Okeechobee, for one million dollars. Two lakes, in Flagler and Pinellas counties, bear his name. Disston City now is Gulfport. Disston City was not a part of Hamilton Disston's huge Florida undertaking, but appears to have been an effort in 1884 by other, small-scale developers to interest him. The first bid for his attention was frustrated because there already was a town called Diston in Pasco County, so the town was called Bonafacio. By the time

Disston

the name Disston became available (through Diston changing its name to Drexel), Hamilton Disston was busy dredging canals in south-central Florida. Straub (1929) suggests that a new generation of developers sought to woo former military men by changing the town's name to Veteran City in 1905. Gulfport emerged in 1910 and that name clicked.

DIXIE COUNTY •
The fifty-ninth county, established April 25, 1921. Named for the lyric name of the South.

DIXIE • *Hernando County*
This community, for ten years at the turn of the century, bore the name of the synonym for the South.

DOCTOR PHILLIPS • *Orange County*
A town named for the Dr. Phillips who once may have been the largest grower of citrus fruit in Florida.

DOG ISLAND • *Franklin County*
At the entrance to St. Georges Sound in the Gulf of Mexico off Carrabelle, Dog Island appears on the earliest map, in 1690, as *Isles aux Chiens*. It is speculated variously that there were wild dogs on the island when the French explored or that the island to a shipboard observer resembled a crouched dog. Dog Island, of some 2,000 acres, is seven miles long. Once there was a federal government reservation here, including a lighthouse and quarantine station as a port of entry for the vessels serving Carrabelle, then an important port for the worldwide shipment of lumber. Dog Island today serves primarily as an escape for those desiring to exchange the mainland's problems for white sand dunes and surf.

DOGTOWN • *Gadsden County*
State Sen. Pat Thomas reports that Dogtown gained its name many years ago as a place where dogs were pitted to fight.

DOUBLESINK • *Levy County*
Established about 1870, the name recalls two natural sinks or spring-fed depressions here.

DOVER • *Hillsborough County*
Once Sydney, then Cork (the second Hillsborough community of that name), Dover is believed to have received its third name from settlers who came from Dover, the capital of Delaware.

DOWELL • *Hillsborough County*
Said to honor the name of a son-in-law of the Capt. Davis who founded the town of Wimauma in the same county.

DOWLING PARK • *Suwannee County*
Called Charles Ferry on J. L. Williams' map of 1837. Later owned by Thomas and Robert L. Dowling, it was a turpentine camp. Thomas Dowling, uncle of Robert L. Dowling, gave a large acreage to the Advent Church for an orphanage. Near here stood the Spanish mission of San Francisco de Chuayain. The Spanish explorer Pánfilo de Narváez may have crossed the Suwannee near here.

D R AY T O N   I S L A N D   •   *Putnam County*
Al Burt writes that the Indians were the first residents here and they quarreled over the fine hunting offered on the island. Finally, a subchief named Edelano won control and the island took his name. The French artist Jacques LeMoyne saw the island in 1565 and called it "the most delightful of all islands in the new world." During the English occupation, 1763-1783, this Lake George island was renamed for Chief Justice William Drayton.

D RY   C R E E K   •   *Jackson County*
So named because most of its five branches go dry during the seasons of little rain.

D RY   T O R T U G A S   •   *Monroe County*
On the exploratory voyage of Juan Ponce de León along the Florida coast in 1513, a landing was made on some rocky islets which he called *Las Tortugas* because the crew took 160 tortoises (turtles) here. On the return to Puerto Rico after coasting to the Tampa Bay area, the fleet of three ships again paused at Las Tortugas. As Bickel (1942) said, "Here they restored their larder with turtles, manatee—which they called seal — pelicans and terns. Not dainty fare, but filling. The Spaniard of the early sixteenth century in the Indies enjoyed strange food and grew fat on it." Now, the great ruins of Fort Jefferson stand on an island of the Dry Tortugas: a fortress never to fire its cannon in anger but to earn infamy as the prison of Dr. Samuel A. Mudd, an innocent victim of John Wilkes Booth, President Lincoln's assassin.

Inside Fort Jefferson in the Dry Tortugas, 1897.

DUDLEY • *Jackson County*
Named for a pioneer family, Dudley existed as a post office from 1902 until 1906.

DUETTE • *Manatee County*
There are two versions of the origin of this name, but the one commonly accepted is this: Prior to 1930, the community had a church, the Dry Prairie Baptist, but no other name. The need for a name arose with school consolidation, and at a community meeting Mrs. Susie Wilkins, who had donated money for the new school, suggested "Duette." There was no disagreement. Another version is that the name was that of an early Canadian settler.

DUMMITT CREEK • *Brevard County*
On Merritt Island. Named for Douglas D. Dummitt, who planted orange trees in this area between 1830 and 1835.

DUNDEE • *Polk County*
The name was taken from that of the famous town in Scotland. When the railroad was built from Haines City to Sebring, Dundee was the first new town to be platted along the line, and the first depot was erected here. Development of the town was begun about 1911 by William W. Shepard, who organized the Florida Highlands Company.

DUNEDIN • *Pinellas County*
This is the old Gaelic name for Edinburgh, Scotland, so this Florida town is named for a more important Old World city than you might think. It vies with Clearwater for the distinction of being the oldest town on the Florida west coast between Cedar Key and Key West, with the exception of Tampa. It was established in the late 1860s, and at first was called Jonesboro, after the general store proprietor George L. Jones. The name change occurred in 1878 when J. O. Douglass and James Somerville, two Scotsmen, arrived on the scene. "Dun" is a form of "town" and "edin" derives from an Irish saint, Edana, for whom many Scottish churches were named.

The Dunedin waterfront about 1909.

DUNNELLON • *Marion County*
This town near Rainbow Springs is named for an early railroad promoter, J. F. Dunn. This point is probably where the Spanish explorer Pánfilo de Narváez crossed the Withlacoochee River. Albertus Vogt discovered hard rock phosphate here in 1889 and caused Dunnellon to become a boom town. The Tiger Rag, Early Bird, and Eagle mines were among the most valuable.

DUPONT • *Flagler County*
Established about 1835 by Abraham DuPont.

DURANT • *Hillsborough County*
Named in the 1900s for a resident who owned a farm here.

DURBIN • *St. Johns County*
Formerly known as the Heights of Dublin. A family named Durbin settled this district.

DUVAL COUNTY •
The fourth county, established August 12, 1822. Named for William Pope DuVal, first territorial governor of Florida. DuVal was born at Mount Comfort, near Richmond, Va., in 1784, the son of William and Ann (Pope) DuVal. DuVal was of French Huguenot forebears. His father was associated, as a lawyer, with Patrick Henry in British debt cases and, as a major of riflemen, captured a British vessel becalmed in the James River during the revolution. Young DuVal left home at the age of 14 for the Kentucky frontier, settling in Bardstown to study law. He was admitted to the bar at 19. He served as a captain in the mounted rangers in 1812, and as Kentucky representative in the 13th Congress (1813-1815). He came to Florida as a territorial judge, having been appointed by President Monroe upon the recommendation of DuVal's friend, John C. Calhoun, then secretary of war. He served about a month at St. Augustine. He was appointed governor of Florida Territory in 1822 by President Monroe; he was reappointed by presidents Adams and Jackson. His administration was notable for the confidence which he enjoyed with the Indians. The capital was established at Tallahassee during his tenure. He was a friend of Washington Irving, who wrote of him in "The Early Experiences of Ralph Ringwood," an essay in his *Knickerbocker Sketch Book*. James K. Pauling also wrote of him in an essay as "Nimrod Wildlife." Duval County perpetuates his name. DuVal uniformly signed himself as "DuVal," though the name usually appears in print as "Duval." DuVal moved to Texas in 1848. He died on March 18, 1854, in Washington, D. C.

EAGLE LAKE • *Polk County*
A town that takes its name from the body of water on which it is located.

EARLETON • *Alachua County*
Once known as Rosetta, the community's name was changed in 1887 to honor George Bliss Earle, a horticulturist.

EARLY • *Gulf County*
Local legend says the name of this naval stores community was suggested by some postal official; why, no one now remembers.

EARLY BIRD • *Marion County*
An intriguing name, with three starts at being a post office between 1891 and 1914, but no known record of who selected the name or why. It was a station on the Cummer Lumber Company's railroad from Early Bird to Archer, in neighboring Levy County.

EARNESTVILLE • *Escambia County*
Named for W. T. Earnest, a mill owner, and later called Bay Springs.

EASTLAKE • *Marion County*
Established in 1866 on the east side of Lake Weir; hence, the name.

EASTPOINT • *Franklin County*
Apparently named for the community's location on the east point of a peninsula where the big Apalachicola River empties into Apalachicola Bay. East Point (spelled then as two words) was the site of an experiment in cooperative living at the turn of the century. A promotional guide to Franklin County, published in 1901, had a page describing how "the Co-operative Association of America has secured a thousand acres of land with sea front and is establishing a co-operative colony there."

The Rev. Harry C. Vrooman, manager for Florida, said the "Association means to organize industry in departments—like a huge department store, only on the co-operative plan—so that all the profits of industry go to the workers. Each member must deposit $300 before he is guaranteed employment. This $300 may be paid in installments. Retiring members are guaranteed their money."

Members had a choice of employment at Lewiston, Maine, or East Point. Persons not wishing to participate in cooperative living could become

David H. Brown boiled and bottled Bay Croft Brand pure cane syrup at Eastpoint in the early 1900s.

associate members at $2 a year and "enjoy all the commercial and social advantages." Associate members could "buy good land for farm, garden or fruit, fronting the sea if desired, near good fishing and oystering."

Eastpoint today remains a center for fishing and oystering.

EATON PARK • *Polk County*
Once known as Pauway, Eaton Park near Lakeland was another of Polk County's phosphate centers. Eaton may have been derived from State Sen. O. M. Eaton, who represented Polk in the 1920s about the time the name was changed.

EATONVILLE • *Orange County*
Incorporated August 18, 1888, as a black community; some say the first in the country. *The Eatonville Speaker* capsuled the purpose of the town in this advertisement on January 22, 1889: "Colored people of the United States— Solve the great race problem by securing a home in Eatonville, Florida, a Negro city governed by Negroes." This description remains true in the 1990s. The community of 2,170 inhabitants is virtually all African-American. Yet the town takes its name from a white man, Capt. Joshua (or Josiah) C. Eaton of Maine, a retired Navy paymaster who settled with other Union veterans at nearby Maitland after the Civil War. Blacks joined with whites in an election at Maitland, and a black, J. E. (Tony) Clarke, became mayor. Clarke had the dream of an all-black town and enlisted the aid of Eaton and two other white Union veterans. They bought a 500-acre tract a mile west of Maitland for the site of Eatonville. Among those lured to Eatonville was John Hurston, a master carpenter and Baptist preacher who became the father of Zora Neale Hurston, who alone would give the town more distinction than many small towns ever receive. She wrote about Eatonville in her remarkable autobiography, *Dust Tracks on a Road*, and impressions of her life there may be found in her other books, including *Mules and Men*. The late novelist Theodore Pratt said Zora Neale Hurston was the "only first-class native-born Florida author."

EAU GALLIE • *Brevard County*
Authorities are agreed that the *eau* is French for "water," but they differ as to the *gallie*. Some say it is French for "bitter" (like gall); others that it is an Indian word for "rocky." The water referred to is that of the Indian River, which is salty. Where we use the words "salt" and "fresh," Europeans often use the equivalent of "bitter" and "sweet." In any event, the town was established soon after the Civil War by William H. Gleason, who is said to have named it. He had been commissioned by the federal government to ascertain whether Florida was suitable for Negro colonization; finding that the natural resources of the country required capital for their development, he reported adversely on this matter, but settled in Florida himself. The name is pronounced "Oh, galley" and not "Oh, golly!" Eau Gallie merged with Melbourne in 1969.

EBB • *Madison County*
The nickname of A. W. Edwards, postmaster when the office was opened in 1904.

EBRO • *Washington County*
Believed to have gained its name from Spain's Ebro River.

ECHAS-HOTEE RIVER • *Pasco and Pinellas counties*
Simpson (1956) suggests this small stream, which rises in Pasco County and flows into the Gulf of Mexico through the coast of Pinellas County, is derived from the Creek *echas*, "beaver," and *hute*, "house or den." Simpson says the Seminoles called the manatee *echaswa* "and the name may have originally related to this animal rather than to the beaver, although the evidence appears to indicate otherwise."

ECHO • *Levy County*
While *echo* was the Seminole word for "deer," of which there were many around this area, the Federal Writers Project was informed by a longtime resident that the place actually was named for a brand of whisky.

ECONFINA, ECONFENA
The first spelling is applied to a small river in Bay and Washington counties and a community in Bay County and the second to a small river in Taylor County. Simpson (1956) says each has the same meaning, Creek for natural bridge: *ekana*, "earth," and *feno*, "bridge or footlog."

ECONLOCKHATCHEE RIVER • *Orange and Seminole counties*
Rises in Orange County and flows through Seminole County to empty into the St. Johns River. The name has been translated as Mound River, from the Creek *ekana*, "earth," *laiki*, "site or mound," and *hatchee*, "creek."

EDDY • *Baker and Hendry counties*
Baker County's Eddy, dating from 1885, is said by local legend to be named for a settler, Washington Eddy. There is no information on Hendry County's Eddy, except that a post office by that name existed for two years from April, 1916.

EDEN • *St. Lucie County*
Thomas E. Richards started growing pineapples in 1880 on a high ridge facing the Indian River. The lushness of the scenery, the fertility of the soil, and the protection against winter cold caused Richards to regard the area as an Eden.

EDEN • *Walton County*
A lovely estate and mansion built with elaborate Victorian trimmings in 1895 by lumberman William Henry Wesley. Bought in 1963 by Lois Genevieve Maxon, the mansion was restored in antebellum style with a formal garden and given to the state by Mrs. Maxon in memory of her parents. The restoration fulfills a local legend which claims the original design was inspired by an antebellum plantation house in which the builder was given shelter on his way home from the Civil War.

EDGEWATER • *Volusia County*
Dr. John M. Hawks bought property here in 1865 and settled it about 1872, naming it Hawks' Park. The name was changed in 1924. It refers to the town's location at the edge of Mosquito Lagoon.

EDGEWATER GULF BEACH • *Bay County*
Incorporated as Edgewater Gulf Beach Apartments in 1953. It consisted almost entirely of the resort facility of that name.

EDGEWOOD • *Orange County*
Likely gained its name from a desire to stimulate the desirable image of a community at the edge of woods.

EGLIN AIR FORCE BASE • *Santa Rosa, Okaloosa, and Walton counties*
Named in honor of Lt. Col. Frederick I. Eglin, an Army Air Force aviator who was killed in the crash of his airplane near Anniston, Ala., on January 1, 1937. Eglin Field was a redesignation on August 4, 1937, of the Valparaiso Bombing and Gunnery Base, which had been activated on June 14, 1935, with a detachment of 15 enlisted men under the command of Capt. Arnold H. Rich, as a sub-post of Maxwell Field, Ala.

EGMONT KEY • *Mouth of Tampa Bay*
A mile-long stretch of palmettos and pines which once guarded the entrance to Tampa Bay, it derives its name from the Earl of Egmont, brother-in-law of the second Viscount Hillsborough, who received a large grant of Florida land during the English occupation (1763-1783). The first Spaniard to die in battle within the boundaries of the present United States was killed in 1513 either here or on one of the keys of Charlotte Harbor. He was a member of Juan Ponce de León's exploratory expedition cruising the coasts of Florida. Because of its strategic location, Egmont was fortified by the Spanish and the Americans. From a collection center here in 1858, Billy Bowlegs and 139 other Seminoles were taken aboard ship for transport to the West. During the Spanish-American War, a fortification called by an old name—Fort Dade— was built on Egmont.

A 1910 photo of Egmont Key light "taken after sunset."

EGYPT LAKE • *Hillsborough County*
Largely an apartment house complex bordering the 67-acre lake of the same name, it appeared for the first time in 1970 on the U. S. Census listing of places of more than 2,000 inhabitants.

EIGHT OAKS • *Orange County*
When settlers first came here in 1885, there were eight large oaks.

EL CAMINO REAL   (The Royal Road)
A Spanish name meaning "The royal road," which conjures an image of a thoroughfare that certainly did not exist in early Spanish Florida. Here, over-land travel was by trails or footpaths. Freight moved on the backs of Indians. Boyd (1951) cites examples which evidence the nature of travel. The use of pack mules instead of Indians still was under consideration in 1686, although the Spanish had been thrusting out from St. Augustine since 1565. Capt. Enrique Rivera obtained a contract for the transport by cart of missionary supplies and foodstuffs in 1688, but could not fulfill the contract. He was unable to proceed more than 20 leagues (approximately 40 miles) from St. Augustine because of impassable streams and swamps. By 1704, the path between St. Augustine and Apalachee evidently was suited to mounted trav-elers, for a dispatch rider covered the 200-mile journey from San Luis (Tallahassee) to St. Augustine in approximately three and a half days. Later, the Spanish built a number of graded roads. Most Spanish trails could be called *el camino real* since the king paid whatever cost was involved for devel-opment. A country road and city street in Tallahassee still known as the "Old Augustine Road" follow an early Spanish trail.

EL DESTINO • *Jefferson County*
A mile-long avenue of spreading live oaks was a memorable feature of this virtually self-sufficient antebellum plantation. The vast tract, of thousands of acres, was acquired from the federal government in 1828 by John Nuttall, a Virginia planter, and his sons, James and William. William Nuttall added to the family's fortune and labor resources in 1832 by marrying Mary Wallace Savage, a Savannah heiress. Cotton was the chief product, but corn, oats, sugar cane, potatoes, and rice also were raised. The plantation largely escaped the rigors of the Civil War and Reconstruction, during which the former slaves remained to work the fields as sharecroppers. The big house was destroyed by fire in 1925. The destiny of El Destino was to outlive its founders and their descendants. The Nuttall name survives in Nuttall Rise, where water emerges from the earth and flows into the Aucilla River.

ELDORADO • *Lake County*
The golden color of the heavy-laden citrus trees at harvest time suggested this name. The community had its own post office from 1886 until 1910.

ELECTRA • *Marion County*
Electra, in classic mythology, was the daughter of Agamemnon and Clytemnestra who incited her brother Orestes to kill Clytemnestra and her lover Aegisthus. But Electra also is a girl's given name. As to the origin of the name of the Florida community, between the Oklawaha River and the Ocala National Forest, take the version most pleasing to you.

EL JOBEAN • *Charlotte County*
Once known as Southland but in 1924, during the great land boom, the Spanish-sounding name El Jobean was substituted. In actuality, Joel Bean, a developer, twisted his name around to produce El Jobean.

ELKTON • *St. Johns County*
Local legend says B. Genovar bought property here simultaneously with being initiated into the Elks Lodge at St. Augustine. In commemoration, he named the site Elk Town, which usage corrupted to Elkton.

ELLAVILLE • *Madison County*
Little is left today to suggest that Ellaville once was a busy lumber port on the Suwannee River. Obviously named for a woman, Ellaville was the site of a large lumber mill owned by George F. Drew, governor of Florida from 1877 to1881.

ELLENTON • *Manatee County*
Here is the Gamble Mansion built in the 1840s, a duplicate of Waukeenah, the homestead near Tallahassee that Maj. Robert Gamble left after the crash of the Union Bank. It has thick walls, shuttered windows, and wide verandahs out of "tabby," a combination of marl, burnt shell lime, oyster shell, and sand. This mansion is said to have sheltered Judah P. Benjamin, secretary of state in the Confederacy, as he escaped to England by way of Florida and the Bahamas. But who was Ellen?

The Ellenton mansion is now the Judah P. Benjamin Confederate Memorial at Gamble Mansion Plantation Historic Site.

ELLIOTT KEY • *Dade County*
Years ago, when England owned Florida, the key was known as Ledbury. In 1769, a British sailing vessel, the *Ledbury*, foundered on the reef near the south end of the Key. Bernard Romans, who was surveying the area for the British, changed its Spanish name to Ledbury Key. Sometime later, the name was changed to Elliott Key.

ELLZEY • *Levy County*
The Rev. R. M. Ellzey, who settled here in 1876, is remembered in this name.

ELOISE • *Polk County*
Nearby is Lake Eloise, the site of the world-famous Cypress Gardens.

EL PORTAL • *Dade County*
Took its name from a subdivision developed during the boom of the 1920s at what was then the highway entrance to Miami from the north. The name in Spanish means "the gate."

EMATHLA • *Marion County*
Charley Emathla was one of the Seminoles who was agreeable to the U. S. Army's efforts to move the Indians from Florida. As a consequence, he was murdered by Indians led by Osceola. Simpson (1956) says Charley is a corruption of the Creek *tsala* or *chalo*, "trout," while *emathla* or *imala* signifies "leader." The settlement of Charley Emathla was in the vicinity of the Marion County community.

EMERALDA • *Lake County*
Kennedy (1929) reports that Emeralda, situated at the upper end of Lake Griffin, is an island only in time of high water. "Frances Hodgson Burnett's story *Esmeralda* was popular about the time when a post office was established (in 1890) on the island, so the place was named Esmeralda," says Kennedy. "As some of the older residents objected to this, the name was changed and it is now called Emeralda." The present name is thought to convey the thought of Ireland, the Emerald Isle.

EMPORIA • *Volusia County*
Established in 1881, the community gained its name from Emporium, Pa., the former home of many settlers in the area.

ENGLEWOOD • *Sarasota County*
Herbert, Howard, and Ira Nichols—three brothers from Englewood, Ill.—laid out and promoted this community. An exhibit about the new community at the Columbian Exposition in Chicago in 1893 attracted new residents.

ENSLEY • *Escambia County*
Once called Fig City because of its fig production. Established about 1912, it was renamed for Fred B. Ensley.

ENTERPRISE • *Volusia County*
Once the southern terminus of shipping on the St. Johns River. The community on Lake Monroe was founded in 1841 by Maj. Cornelius Taylor, cousin of Zachary Taylor. Enterprise first was known as Fountain Place, then Enterprize, with the present spelling emerging in 1937. Until 1888, Enterprise was the seat of Volusia County. In the mid-1900s, Daytona Beach tried to wrest from DeLand the honor of being the seat of Volusia County. This was ironic, for in 1888 Enterprize lost the seat to DeLand by a vote of 439 to 1,003 (seven other communities were in the running, with Daytona receiving three votes).

E R I D U • *Taylor County*
On your way from Tallahassee to Perry on U. S. 19 and 27, just after crossing into Taylor County, you'll come to a little place called Eridu. If you happen to be a classical scholar, you'll recognize the name as Latin for the River Po —or maybe we'd better say a derivative of that name, which in full was Eridanus. M. S. Rose, who retired to Vero Beach from Pittsburgh in 1969, wrote that Eridu was given its name in 1926 by J. E. Welloughby who, at that time, was chief engineer of the Atlantic Coast Line Railroad. "I was a young engineer on Mr. Welloughby's staff and believe that I probably produced the first map showing Eridu as a town," Mr. Rose said. In the building of tracks to join existing lines at Thomasville, Ga., and Dunnellon, Fla., two other names, apparently from ancient lore, were applied: Iddo and Secotan. Secotan has not been found, but Iddo is from *2 Chronicles 9:29*—"Now the rest of the acts of Solomon, first and last, are they not written in the book of Nathan the prophet, and in the prophecy of Ahijah the Shilomite, and in the visions of Iddo the seer against Jeroboam the son of Nebat?" In 1863, a great many Confederate deserters and draft evaders hid out in the wilds near here. Confederate cavalrymen were unsuccessful in their effort to round them up, but drove off their livestock, burned their houses and in some instances took their families into a concentration camp at Tallahassee until an outraged community forced their release.

E R I E • *Manatee County*
Appears to have been a transplant from the numerous Eries of the New York and Pennsylvania, where the name was derived from the Huron or Iroquois *yenresh*, "people of the panther."

E S C A M B I A   C O U N T Y   A N D   R I V E R •
Escambia shares with St. Johns the distinction of being one of the first two counties, each having been established July 21, 1821. The river divides Escambia and Santa Rosa counties. Simpson (1956) reports the river was shown on a 1693 map as the *Rio de Jovenazo,* apparently honoring the Duke of Jovenazo. It also was referred to at the same time as the Pensacola River. Simpson goes on to say that while the word might be derived from the Spanish *cambiar,* "to change or barter," "it more likely has an Indian origin, even though the derivation is unknown." Justification for this belief, he con-tinues, "is afforded by the existence in Apalachee during the mission period of an Indian village called San Cosmo y San Damian de Escambé (or Scambé). It is possible that the prefixed 'E' represents the Spanish pronunciation of the letter 'S' when before a consonant."

E S T E R O • *Lee County*
Spanish for estuary. It was here in 1892 that Dr. Cyrus Read Teed, founder of the Koreshan Unity, established his "college of life" as a cooperative com-munity in the spirit of Christ's teachings. Koreshans believe "we live inside the world." The Guiding Star Printing House at Estero published *The Cellular Cosmogony* and other books, magazines, and newspapers. The Koreshan

Nursery was world-famous for its subtropical plant life. In 1961, the last of the Koreshans gave their 305-acre homestead to the Florida Park Board. Some of their buildings and their tropical garden are now part of the Koreshan State Historic Site.

ESTO • *Holmes County*
The name of one of the earliest settlers in this community, before the railroad was built. But before "old man Esto"—as the federal writers characterized him —was honored, the place was known as Hutto.

ETONIA • *Putnam County*
Simpson (1956) concludes the name is a Muskogee word combination of *atan*, "from," and *aia*, "go, or go elsewhere." Eton Lake and Eton Creek, in the Big Oklawaha Scrub, may have been similarly corrupted from *atan-aia*.

EUCHEE, EUCHEEANNA • *Walton County*
The names of a community, valley, and creek. Once a tribe of Indians lived along the nearby Choctawhatchee River. They were known as the Euchee, Uchee, or Yuchi because once when asked by other Indians where they came from, they replied, *"yui-tci,"* meaning "at a distance." But the Euchee Valley is better known because Neil McLendon, a native of Scotland, brought his family and others in 1822 to this valley, some 25 miles long and 12 miles wide. The McLendon group dealt fairly with the Indians and the Euchee tribesmen helped the settlers repel raids by hostile Indians from Alabama. Shortly after the Civil War, women of Walton County organized a "Ladies' Memorial Association," with Jeannet I. McKinnon as president, to erect a marble monument honoring Walton County's Confederate dead. The monument first was erected in 1871 at Valley Church, then moved to Euchee Ann, the county seat, and then to DeFuniak Springs when it became the county seat. The white marble shaft, its apex a hand with index finger pointing skyward, is regarded as Florida's first Confederate monument.

EUREKA • *Marion County*
On the Oklawaha River at the edge of the Ocala National Forest, Eureka has been settled since 1873. From the Greek "I have found (it)," the name has been applied to many places where people have found what they sought: gold in California, spring water in Kansas, and perhaps happiness in Florida.

EUSTIS • *Lake County*
There is some question as to which member of the Eustis family gave his name to this town. The lake on which it is situated is called Lake Eustis, and is said to have been named for Brig. Gen. Abraham Eustis, who served in Florida during the Seminole War and was one of the officers who favored closing the war by allowing the Indians to remain within a small territory to be given them in the southern part of the state. The community itself was established in 1881 by James A. McDonald, a Scottish engineer, and was first called Highlands, then Pendryville, then Lake Eustis. Another authority says that the Eustis honored was Gen. Henry Lawrence Eustis, the son of Abraham, who was a Civil War soldier, engineer, and professor, first at West Point and then at Harvard.

E V E • *Levy County*
See Adam.

E V E R G L A D E S   C I T Y • *Collier County*
Takes its name from the great primeval "river of grass" on whose western edge it lies. An Indian trading post was established here at the mouth of the Barron River in 1873, and soon became the center of a farming community. Around 1880, farmers began calling it Everglades when they needed a trade name for their produce. A post office was established in 1892. W. S. Allen built the first home on the south bank of the Barron River, then known as Allen's River, and used the spot as a shipping point for his produce. The principal agricultural product today is tomatoes. The community first was known as Everglade. The "s" was added locally in 1923 and by the post office department in 1925.

The Everglades, "the big swamp of Florida," 1906.

E V E R G R E E N • *Nassau County*
The pleasant greenery of this area near the St. Marys River likely suggested the name.

E V I N S T O N • *Alachua County*
Evinston or Evanston? Here is a fascinating example of how an ancient argument lives in a place name. Joseph Judge, assistant editor of the *National Geographic,* wrote about Evinston in the magazine's issue of November 1973. Judge wrote that he had been driving a back road in Florida's countryside, past moss-covered hamlets of weathered houses with tin roofs sloping against a chill rain, when he came to a highway marker designating Evanston. Yet the

ancient post office and general store bore an old sign proclaiming "Evinston P.O." Inside, reported Judge, Mr. Fred Wood addressed the question. "There were two brothers," he said, "who came from England. My forebears. Their name was Evans, with an 'a.' During the war they took opposite sides." "The Civil War?" assumed Judge out loud. "Lord, no, man, the Revolution," corrected Wood. "The colonist got so mad at the loyalist that he changed his name to Evins, with an 'i.' No highway department knows much about history, or cares."

EXCELSIOR PARK • *Polk County*
From the Latin "higher," Excelsior Park was so named because of its location in the 1890s on a ridge near Bartow.

EZRY • *Sarasota County*
Supported a post office for nearly ten months in 1885; then neighboring Osprey took over its mail service. The origin of the name is a mystery.

FAHKAHATCHEE **(BAY, SWAMP, RIVER, ISLAND)** •
Collier County
From Creek *fakka*, "clay or mud," and *hatchee*, "creek." Nearby is a river known as the Fahkahhatchoochee, or "Little Fahkahatchee."

FAIRBANKS • *Alachua County*
Recalls Samuel Fairbanks, who was granted 500 acres here in 1823.

FAIRFIELD • *Marion County*
Another of the image names, albeit a prophetic one because of the fair fields of the horse country of Marion County.

FAIRMOUNT, FAIRMOUTH • *Citrus County*
The Federal Writers project of the 1930s reported the early settlers here to be mostly Pennsylvania Dutch, divided into two groups. One group brought into being Fairmount; the other, Fairmouth. The original post office was at Fairmouth. A dispute resulted in there being two post offices, Fairmount and Fairmouth, for some years until a reconciliation was effected, in all likelihood by postal authorities, and Fairmount survived.

FAIRVIEW • *Putnam County*
An image name, given by someone who found the view pleasing or hoped it would be to others.

FAIRYLAND • *Brevard County*
One of a string of old-time Florida settlements that exist within sound of the takeoffs of spacecraft from Cape Kennedy. On Merritt Island, Fairyland, Tropic, and Georgiana are among the communities on what now is known as the Scenic Drive but once was called the Tropical Trail. The late Nixon Smiley, author and columnist for *The Miami Herald,* said, "Driving about the byways and backways one still can find a few scenes of a bygone era." The Scenic Drive on Merritt Island is one of those scenes.

FALLING WATER HILL (Falling Waters State Park) •

Washington County

The elevation of some 322 feet affords a view of several miles in all directions. Below the summit, on the southeast slope, there is a spring of sufficient flow to create a waterfall from a ledge for an almost vertical drop of some 50 feet into a limestone sink. The limestone has weathered into attractive shades of green. Once there was a grist mill and a whisky still here. Indians and others mined the area for colorfully pigmented rocks they used to make paints and dyes.

Visitors admire the cascade three miles south of Chipley, for which Falling Waters State Park was named.

FALMOUTH • *Suwannee County*

Once known as Peacock, but a Col. Duval, an influential resident, had a pointer dog named Falmouth which he prized highly. Local legend says that when Falmouth was killed while hunting, the colonel gave the community his name. For whatever reason, the change of name occurred in 1906.

FANLEW • *Jefferson County*

A railway distribution center, serving the sawmills and turpentine stills once in this area, with supplies moving in and timber and naval stores moving out. Fanlew likely was named for an Atlantic Coast Line superintendent.

FANNING SPRINGS, FANNIN SPRINGS • *Gilchrist County*

On the south bank of the Suwannee River at U.S. 19 and 98, a cluster of tourist-oriented establishments was known variously as Fanning Springs and Fannin Springs. The high bank and the clear, cool water flowing from a spring attracted Col. Alexander C. W. Fanning and his Seminole War contingent just as it had attracted the Indians who used it as their campground. After the war, the place was called Sykesville after an early settler, but the old name was restored as first the springs and then a big wooden dance pavilion invited boaters, campers, picnickers, and fun-seekers. After World War II, better roads, better cars, and the boom in boating gave greater range to those who had patronized Fanning Springs. In 1965, residents sought to improve the image by incorporating so they could change the name of Fanning Springs to Suwannee River.

FARGO • *Polk County*
One of the five names by which the present town of Lake Alfred was known—Wahneta, Bartown Junction, and Chubb being the others—before the present name was adopted in 1913. A group from Fargo, N.D., bought a large tract of land here for development and gave the prospective community the name of their hometown. Fargo often was confused with Largo by mail handlers and thus the name gave way to Chubb.

FARMDALE • *Bay County*
Named by a Northern developer who sought to interest settlers by its pleasant combination of farm and dale.

FARMTON • *Volusia County*
Formerly known as Celery City, the name Farmton was given about 1904 by James A. Burns, who was interested in agricultural development. Now the map shows the Farmton Wildlife Management Area of the Florida Game and FreshWater Fish Commission.

FAT DEER KEY • *Monroe County*
Named for the small deer peculiar to the Florida Keys, a species saved from extinction by the energies of the Audubon Society and other conservationists. The Key Deer is a dwarf white-tailed deer that might weigh 50 pounds and stand two feet six inches tall.

FAYETTE • *The lost county*
Established in 1832 and extinguished in 1834, the only Florida county ever to pass completely out of existence. Presumably named for the Marquis de Lafayette, who died in the same year as the county, Fayette filled the "V" of the coverging Chipola and Apalachicola rivers, with Alabama's boundary as the crossbar. Fayette was reincorporated in Jackson County.

FELDA • *Hendry County*
Felix Taylor, a mailman, changed the name of Eddy to Felda, combining syllables of his first name and that of his wife, Ida.

FELLSMERE • *Indian River County*
The Miami Herald reports hundreds of farmers moved here in 1910 to sow their dreams in the muckland. Roads were platted, waterways planned: It was to be the marketing hub of the region. But then after only five years, nature purged the dreams in a huge flood. An abandoned, stuccoed fortress—the words "Fellsmere Estates Corporation" chiseled above its white columns—stood as a reminder of the dreams of Nelson Fells, an English millionaire.

FENHOLLOWAY • *Taylor County*
This river and community derive their name from the Creek *fena*, "foot log or bridge," and *halhauwe*, "high," with the meaning given as high bridge. When Gen. Andrew Jackson's army passed here in 1818, the topographic officer put down Slippery Log Creek on his map.

FENTRESS • *Santa Rosa County*
Formerly Red Rock, the name changed about 1912 to honor Calvin Fentress.

FERNANDINA BEACH • *Nassau County*
Everyone agrees about the great age of Fernandina; it claims to be the second oldest city in the United States, having been settled by Spaniards in 1567. Not everyone agrees, however, about the source of its name. Fernandina was the early name of Cuba, conferred upon it by Columbus in 1492 as a tribute to King Ferdinand of Spain, and it is presumed by some that the name was given to the Florida settlement for the same reason. But a large tract of land was granted to Don Domingo Fernandez in 1785, and other authorities say the town was named in his honor. Still others say the name comes from Fort San Fernando, built by Spain in 1686. It is the county seat of Nassau County, and is located on Amelia Island. It calls itself "The Ocean City." Beach is a recent addition to the city's name.

Fernandina's busy waterfront, April 16, 1902.

FERN PARK • *Seminole County*
Here various kinds of ferns are grown for use by florists nationwide.

FERRY OF SAN NICOLAS • *Duval County*
Here, on the south shore of the St. Johns River, the Spanish in 1740 erected Fort San Nicolas to guard the crossing. The British called the settlement Cow Ford, and we know it as a part of Jacksonville. On the north side, the British built a ferryman's house and a tavern—the first known buildings on the present site of downtown Jacksonville.

FIDDLE LAKE • *Lake County*
Kennedy (1929) says this lake near Eustis was named because of an accident. "One day K. D. Smith was bringing a miscellaneous load of goods, containing nails, groceries, and fiddles among other things, from the St. Johns River

to Fort Mason. As the day was hot, the haul a long and tiresome one, and the oxen very thirsty, they started on a run when they sighted a lake. The driver was so startled by their sudden stampede that he could not check them until they were almost completely submerged." The cargo, including the fiddles, was lost in the lake.

FIESTA KEY • *Monroe County*
The name since 1966 of the island formerly known as Greyhound Key.

FISHEATING CREEK • *Highlands and Glades counties*
This stream rises in Highlands County, flows southward into Glades County, then eastward into Lake Okeechobee. Once the name was *Thlothlopopka-Hatchee*, or Seminole for "the creek where fish are eaten." There was a community known as Fisheating Creek until someone decided this was not sufficiently dignified and changed the name to Tasmania.

FLAGLER COUNTY •
The fifty-third county, established April 28, 1917, and named for Henry Morrison Flagler, one of the two Henrys—the other being Henry B. Plant—who raced to open the east and west coasts of Florida by building railroads and hotels and operating steamships and land development companies. Flagler (1830-1913) lived two lives, the first as a Northern businessman and the associate of John D. Rockefeller in the Standard Oil Company, and the second as a promoter of Florida's east coast. *The Dictionary of American Biography* says Flagler, "brought up in poverty and trained in the stern Rockefeller school," was a grim, shrewd, rather ruthless man until he was 55. Thereafter, in Florida, he continued to work but with a new attitude toward humanity. "He thoroughly enjoyed his role of builder of a state, and seemed to feel a sense of personal responsibility for every settler on his railroads and for every one of his many employees," reports the *Dictionary*. "They, in turn, repaid him with admiration and loyalty." Flagler first visited Florida in 1883. Good businessman that he was, even on a holiday, he believed full advantage was not being taken of Florida's natural assets. He thought the state needed better transportation and hotel facilities, and he set about providing these for the east coast. His first project was building the Ponce de Leon Hotel in St. Augustine, formally opened January 10, 1888. He bought the rickety, narrow-gauge Jacksonville, St. Augustine & Halifax Railway on December 31, 1885. Thereafter, Flagler's Florida East Coast Railway paced the building of a chain of hotels down the coast until Key West was officially reached on January 22, 1912. Building the railroad brought Flagler more than a million and a half acres of state land, and he vigorously sought settlers, making concessions including free seed and reduced freight rates to encourage colonizing, which in turn would produce revenue for the railroad. Flagler died on May 20, 1913. Rail service to Key West was ended by hurricane damage in 1935, but a highway (U.S. 1) was extended to Key West over bridges and viaducts constructed for Flagler's railroad.

FLAGLER BEACH • *Flagler County*
Honors Henry M. Flagler, who did so much for the development of the east coast of Florida through his building of the Florida East Coast Railway. A settlement on the mainland side of the Intracoastal Waterway was earlier known as Ocean City, and was granted a post office under that name in 1915. But as more families built homes along the oceanfront, a post office was needed there. The name Ocean City Beach was first suggested, but the Post Office Department disapproved it because of its length and its similarity to others. Robert Tolan, real estate broker and promoter, who had been corresponding with the post office authorities, consulted George Moody, homesteader of the section, who said he would like it named Flagler Beach in honor of the late Henry Flagler, who had been a friend of his brother, I. I. Moody. Between Flagler Beach and Summer Haven stood the Spanish mission of San José.

FLAMINGO • *Everglades National Park*
Formerly the southernmost community on the mainland of the continental United States and now the southernmost headquarters for the Everglades National Park services and operations. Named in 1893 by the half dozen families living there. According to Tebeau (1963), "They felt it should be named for something characteristic of the place and easily hit upon the flamingo as the most distinctive of the many birds that frequented the area." Dr. Tebeau says flamingoes are not native to south Florida, which lies on the outer fringe of their natural range. "But they once came in relatively large numbers from Cuba, the Bahama Islands and possibly other nearby places where they nested. Several hundred were sighted in 1902, but rarely any after that time." Dr. Tebeau comments that later, when the presence of the long-legged birds in large numbers was largely forgotten, at least one writer surmised that Flamingo was so named "because the houses were 'long-legged,' being built in many cases on stilts to raise them above the hurricane flood waters that sometimes swept over the low-lying land."

FLIRT LAKE • *Glades County*
In the old steamboating days, river traffic moved along the Caloosahatchee from Fort Thompson to Lake Okeechobee through open country with shallow lakes and drowned prairies. These lakes included Lake Flirt, some five miles by two. The lake is believed to have taken its name from the Army supply boat *Flirt*. Will (1965) quotes a state engineer, Fred Flanders, as saying he found "a most bodacious collection of old fossil bones of dinosaurs and all them old timey critters, with mammoth's teeth as big as a cow man's hat" after the lake dried up. He said Flanders opined this must have been a bog during prehistoric times. Flanders gave the specimens he found to the National Park Service, but Will said no one should be surprised to see a "whopping big bone or vertebra hanging in some Cracker's porch thereabouts."

FLOMATON •
See South Flomaton.

FLOMICH • *Volusia County*
F. W. Skirlo, in establishing this sawmill community in 1918, combined the names of his home and adopted states, Florida and Michigan.

FLORA • *Hillsborough County*
A railroad official is said to have liked this name because of its brevity, sound, and floral imagery.

FLORAL CITY • *Citrus County*
A search for orchids and other rare flowers led a Vermonter to what in the 1870s was known as Cove Bend. His enthusiasm brought a change of the name to Floral Cove and subsequently Floral City.

FLORAL ISLAND • *Citrus County*
A development syndicate headed by Tom Ferris of Chicago in 1925 bought an island then known as Duval Island (after a homesteader, Jean Paul Fermy Duval), and changed its name for promotional reasons to Floral Island.

FLORIDA •
The first place name the Europeans brought to this continent. On Easter Sunday, 1513, Juan Ponce de León and those with him in three ships saw a small, unknown island. They sailed northwest for three days and then west-northwest for two days more. Again they saw land, but the coast was so long that they knew this was not an island like the one glimpsed five days before.

The lawyers who served the king of Spain thought possession could be cinched by naming places discovered by the explorers; thus, Ponce de León was faced with the problem of what to call this land on which he yet had not set foot.

Writing a hundred years later, court historian Antonio de Herrera told how Ponce de León solved the problem:

"Believing that land to be an island, they nam'd it *Florida*, because it appeared very delightful, having many pleasant groves, and it was all level; as also because they discovered it at Easter, which as has been said, the Spaniards called *Pasqua de Flores*, or *Florida*."

The Spanish pronounced it Flor-EE-da. The English, coming later, kept the name but changed the pronounciation to suit their tongues, so Flor-EE-da became FLOR-i-da.

FLORIDA CITY • *Dade County*
The southernmost mainland town in the United States. It was developed in 1905 by Miami realtors, and was incorporated in 1913. A group of settlers from Detroit, Mich., agreed to name the place after their home city, but the Post Office Department said this would be confusing. The name Florida City was then adopted by a vote of the residents.

FLORIDA KEYS •
Juan Ponce de León, on his exploratory voyage around the coasts of Florida in 1513, called the islands arcing southeast from the Florida mainland *Los Martires*, or The Martyrs, because they resembled men in agony. The islands now are known as keys, after an English modification of the Spanish *cayo*, or "small island." The keys are mainly in Monroe County, with others in adjoining Dade County, but key may be found as a part of the name of islands along the Florida coasts.

Souvenirs of a 1900 trip to Florida.

FLORIDATOWN • *Santa Rosa County*
One of the oldest place names in the state. The town was a trading post in Spanish days. Gen. Andrew Jackson first camped here in 1814. At the delta of Escambia River and Escambia Bay, the place served for the transshipment of goods and for the resting of travelers. King (1972) reports that Davy Crockett was here with Jackson, for in Crockett's autobiography he tells how he "went 'bar' hunting up the 'Scamby'." Floridatown was the seat of Santa Rosa County in territorial days, losing this distinction when yellow fever ravaged the community in 1842.

FOLEY • *Taylor County*
Built in 1929 by the Brooks-Scanlon Lumber Company to house employees of a sawmill. The town was named for J. S. Foley, the company's president for more than 30 years. Other milltowns named for him which still survive are in Alabama, Louisiana, Minnesota, and Washington.

FORTS •

Florida often has been called the nation's most fortified state. Many of those who use the term do not realize just how true it is. Counting the Spanish, French, and British forts of which there is recorded history, more than 300 forts, batteries, redoubts, and named camps existed in Florida, from earliest settlement to 1903, according to the meticulous research of Francis B. Heitman, compiler of the *Historical Register and Dictionary of the United States Army.*

The great forts—Clinch at Fernandina Beach, Castillo de San Marcos at St. Augustine, Jefferson in the Dry Tortugas, and Pickens and Barrancas at Pensacola—are the exceptions among the hundreds of Florida forts. Virtually all American forts of the Seminole Wars were simple defensive works, usually a combination of ditches and embankments of earth and trees to protect relatively small military units for short periods of time. Their temporary nature means that today no trace of them remains.

While the Spanish, French, and British forts usually were named for saints or members of royal families, American forts generally were named after officers of the local command. Thus, of the surviving forts, Fort Lauderdale was named for Maj. William Lauderdale, Fort Meade for Lt. George Gordon Meade (later Gen. Meade of Gettysburg), Fort Myers for Lt. Abraham Charles Myers (afterwards General), and Fort Pierce for Lt. Col. Benjamin Kendrick Pierce. But there were the usual exceptions: Fort Pleasant and Camp Lang Syne.

Seven incorporated cities retain today the names of forts: Fort Lauderdale, Fort Meade, Fort Myers, Fort Pierce, Fort Walton, and Fort White.

A number of forts survive in communities which have dropped the "fort" from their name: Maitland once was Fort Maitland, Jupiter once was Fort Jupiter, and Dade City once was Fort Dade. Still others are known now by different names: Miami was Fort Dallas, Jacksonville was founded across the river from the old site of Fort San Nicolas, and Tampa grew up on the fringe of Fort Brooke.

FORT BASINGER • *Highlands County*

Named for Lt. William E. Basinger of the 2nd Artillery, killed in the Dade Massacre. Col. Zachary Taylor, afterwards president of the United States, had a stockade built December 23, 1837, on a sandy hill on the west bank of the Kissimmee River. The fort consisted of pine logs standing upright, with sharp pointed tops. Blockhouses and lookout towers were placed at the northwest and southeast corners. The stockade was intended as a supply station for Taylor's expedition against the Indians in the Lake Okeechobee region. Visiting the area in 1972, reporter George Lane, Jr., of the *St. Petersburg Times*, could find no trace of Fort Basinger, only a historical marker at the intersection of U. S. 98 and S.R. 721. The name survives, however, in the twin communities of Fort Basinger in Highlands County and Basinger in Okeechobee County.

FORT BROOKE • *Hillsborough County*

Col. George Mercer Brooke, directed to proceed from Pensacola with four infantry companies to establish a military post at Tampa Bay, arrived in January 1824 and moved into the plantation home of the absent Robert Hackley. Erecting a log fortification, Brooke called it Camp Hillsborough for its location on the northeast bank of the Hillsborough River. But the War Department assented to the desire of Brooke's brother officers to name the fort for him and thereafter it was known as Fort Brooke. Tampa grew up on Fort Brooke's fringes.

An 1838 drawing of Fort Brooke by Nathan S. Jarvis, an Army surgeon.

FORT CAROLINE • *Duval County*

Named for Charles IX. In 1564, France sent troops to the St. Johns River, where they built the sod-and-timber Fort Caroline as a toehold in the Florida wilderness which Spain claimed. Hunger, mutiny, and Indian troubles plagued the settlement, and the Spanish executed most of the garrison in 1565. The Spanish then garrisoned the place, which they called Fort San Mateo, only to have the French strike back in 1568, hanging those who survived the assault. The first Protestant white child of the present United States was born at Fort Caroline just before 1565, according to records. The original site of Fort Caroline was washed away in the 1880s, but a replica has been erected nearby to help visitors visualize the scene. The Fort Caroline National Monument is ten miles east of Jacksonville.

FORT CLINCH • *Nassau County*

Named for Gen. Duncan Lamont Clinch, who had served with distinction in the War of 1812, the Seminole Wars in Florida, and the Mexican-American War. This beautifully restored brick fort was begun in 1847 to guard the entrance to the broad Cumberland Sound, into which flow both the

Amelia and St. Marys rivers. The fort was one of a chain of closed masonry forts on the Atlantic Coast, of which Fort Jefferson in the Dry Tortugas was another. These forts were intended to withstand the penetration of smooth-bore artillery, but after the development of rifled-bores they became obsolete. Plans for the construction of Fort Clinch were approved by Jefferson Davis, later president of the Confederacy, when he was U.S. secretary of war. The fort was far from complete at the outbreak of the Civil War. Confederates seized it in 1861, abandoning it a year later with the appearance of combined federal army and navy forces. Fort Clinch remained in federal possession for the remainder of the Civil War. Construction was discontinued in 1867. The fort was strengthened and used during the Spanish-American War and had limited use as a communications and security post during World War II. In 1936, the state acquired Fort Clinch for development as a park. Fort Clinch is situated on Amelia Island, over which have flown eight flags since the island was visited in 1562 by French Adm. Jean Ribaut. The national flags were those of France, Spain, England, Mexico, United States, and Confederate States, and the local flags of the Patriots and Green Cross. *See also* Fort Meade *and* Frostproof.

FORT DADE • *Hillsborough County*
Named for Maj. Francis Dade, it was erected in 1898 on Egmont Key at the mouth of Tampa Bay.

FORT DADE • *Pasco County*
Built in 1837 on the south bank of the Withlacoochee River at the crossing of the Fort King Road, seven miles north of today's Dade City. Named for Maj. Francis Langhorne Dade (of the Dade Massacre), it served for many years as a depot and observation post in the heart of the Seminole Indian settlement. It was here on March 6, 1837, that the Seminole leaders Jumper and Alligator met Gen. Thomas S. Jesup to sign the "Fort Dade Capitulation."

FORT DENAUD • *Hendry County*
Named for Pierre Denaud, a French Canadian who traded here with the Indians for skins and hides before the soldiers came during the Seminole Wars. This stockade guarded a crossing on the Caloosahatchee River on the military highway between Fort Meade and Fort Myers.

FORT GADSDEN • *Franklin County*
This place, affording control of commerce on the Apalachicola River, near today's Sumatra, was the site of fortifications occupied by English, free African-American, American, and Confederate forces. Built in 1814 by the British to encourage the Seminole Indians to ally themselves with England against the United States in the War of 1812, it was soon abandoned. It was occupied in 1816 by a band of free African Americans. Its location in Spanish Florida did not deter Gen. Andrew Jackson from ordering its elimination for being a threat to American commerce on the Apalachicola River. On July 27, 1816, Lt. Col. Duncan L. Clinch, with U. S. forces and 150 Creek Indians, fired on the fort. A "hot shot" cannon ball penetrated the fort's powder magazine, and the explosion killed all but 30 of the 300 occupants. In 1818 Gen. Jackson directed Lt. James Gadsden to build Fort Gadsden here in spite of Spanish protests. Confederate troops occupied the fort during the Civil War until July 1863, when malaria forced its abandonment.

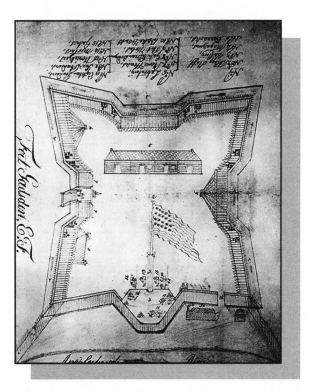

This 1820 map of Fort Gadsden was probably drawn by Major C. Hutter.

FORT GEORGE ISLAND • *Duval County*

Named for Fort St. George, erected in 1740 by Gen. James Edward Oglethorpe of Georgia and named for the patron saint of England. The St. was dropped eventually and the island simply called Fort George. Miss Dena Snodgrass of Jacksonville, an eminent Florida historian, picks up the story: "Fort George Island is the body upon which is the Kingsley plantation. This is a true island and is connected with an island at its southern tip by a man-made causeway. That connecting island is Batten Island. On it is Pilot Town. The ferry across the St. Johns River from Mayport ends at this island and town. Each is erroneously called Fort George. Mr. John F. Rollins bought the true Fort George Island in 1869. He was appointed postmaster and shortly he moved the post office from his residence to Batten Island because it was easier for river people to pick up mail there. And look what a mess he made!" Fort George Island is ". . . important because the state's history is capsuled here. From the Indian village-mission-fort period through the struggles with the British colonies and the Republic of East Florida, on through the great plantation days and the early magic of Florida as a tourist mecca. It's all here on the island where the state maintains the Kingsley plantation house, the oldest plantation house extant in Florida."

FORT KING • *Marion County*
On a knoll in the vicinity of S. E. Thirty-ninth Avenue and Fort King Road in
Ocala stood Fort King, an important military center during the Seminole
Wars. Adjacent to a Seminole agency established in 1825, the fort was named
for Col. William King and first occupied in 1827. Outside its stockade, on
December 28, 1835, warriors led by Osceola ambushed and killed Gen. Wily
Thompson and four others. In 1844, after the Seminole War ended, Fort King
became the temporary seat of newly created Marion County.

FORT LAUDERDALE • *Broward County*
Maj. William Lauderdale in 1837 was commander of the Tennessee
Volunteers. He raised five companies, a total of 500 men, from the mountain
regions of Tennessee and marched them down into Florida. On March 2,
1838, two of these companies, along with a company of pioneers under a Lt.
Anderson, were sent on an expedition that was to take them as far south as
New River. They made camp at Jupiter, and set out from there with some
artillery for their ultimate destination. On March 30, they were joined at New
River by the main body of men and established Fort Lauderdale, one of the
main bases in the Second Seminole War. In 1895, a town was established here
which took its name from the fort. Another version has it that Lauderdale
was the name of the Scottish ancestral home of Capt. William S. Maitland of
the U. S. Army, who established a fort here in 1838 during the Seminole Wars
and gave it that name.

FORT LONESOME • *Hillsborough County*
Never a fort but it is lonesome—a *Miami Herald* article by Nixon Smiley in
1971 said even the cows "sounded lonely." How the name was applied to this
crossroads, where S.R. 39 and S.R. 674 intersect, has two explanations passed
along by Mrs. James D. Bruton, Jr., of Plant City. One is that Mrs. Dovie
Stanaland, who had a store here, applied the name because there was a sense
of loneliness with only flat land as far as the eye could see. The other, which
has a martial ring to it, holds that the name was applied by a detachment of
the National Guard stationed at the crossroads during the year-long blockade
of central Florida to prevent spread of the Mediterranean fruit fly after the
infestation was discovered in Orange County on April 6, 1929.

FORT MARION • *St. Johns County*
See Castillo de San Marcos.

FORT MCNEIL • *Orange County*
A stockade with blockhouses at the diagonal corners was erected during the
Seminole War in 1837 at what today is S.R. 532, about 1,200 feet north of
Taylor Creek Bridge. It was named Fort McNeil in memory of Second Lt. John
Winfield Scott McNeil, who was killed in action on September 11, 1837. He
was the son of Gen. John McNeil and the nephew of Franklin Pierce, four-
teenth president of the United States.

FORT MEADE • *Polk County*
This site on the Peace River was at first the location of Fort Clinch, established in 1849, but the fortification was not maintained. Some three years

later, during a topographical survey of the area, the commanding officer of the party assigned to Second Lt. George C. Meade the task of finding the site of old Fort Clinch. This was not easy, because of the ambiguous description he had been given, but he found it before nightfall. Gen. Twigg, the commanding officer, exclaimed, "Here shall be Fort Meade!" Meade later gained fame at the Battle of Gettysburg. The modern town was incorporated in 1909.

FORT MYERS • *Lee County*
The name memorialized by this famous Florida city is that of Gen. Abraham Charles Myers, a distinguished officer in the U.S. Army. It was given to the fort by Gen. David E. Twiggs, federal commander in the Seminole Wars, who later became the father-in-law of Myers. The city was developed in the later years of the nineteenth century, chiefly through the initiative of Stafford C. Cleveland, a New York newspaperman. Situated on the south bank of the Caloosahatchee River, it is the county seat and largest city of Lee County. It is the location of the Florida estates of Thomas A. Edison and Henry Ford. For a while in the 1890s, Fort was dropped from the community's name, but citizenry paid no attention and Fort came back into official usage. In the Seminole War of 1835-1842, a fort was established here and named for Lt. John Harvie.

FORT PIERCE • *St. Lucie County*
The fort here was erected 1838-42 and named after Lt. Col. Benjamin Kendrick Pierce, a brother of President Franklin Pierce. It was the headquarters of the Army of the South under Gen. Jesup. A settlement began around the fort soon after its establishment. Fort Pierce is the county seat of St. Lucie County.

FORT WALTON BEACH • *Okaloosa County*
The town was named after the fort, established here during the Seminole Wars. The fort and the county adjacent to Okaloosa were named for Col. George Walton, secretary of West Florida during the governorship of Andrew Jackson, 1821-22, and secretary of the East-West Florida Territory, 1822-26. Walton was the son of George Walton, signer of the Declaration of Independence and governor of Georgia.

FORT WHITE • *Columbia County*
Named for a fort which stood here during the Seminole Wars, Fort White has no record as to the identity of the White who gave his name to the fort.

FRANKLIN COUNTY •
The seventeenth county, established February 8, 1832. Named for Benjamin Franklin.

FROSTPROOF • *Polk County*
Said to have been named by cowboys from the cattle regions just north of here who herded their cattle southward into this highland lake region during the winter months, and noted the absence of frost in the coldest seasons. Frostproof once was known as Fort Clinch. Heatherington (1928) reported a tradition that a sea serpent used to haunt adjacent Lake Clinch. "The Indians many years ago insisted there was an immense serpent in this lake. In 1907

residents of Frostproof declared they had seen the monster, and that it must be thirty feet long." When *The Miami Herald's* Nixon Smiley visited Frostproof in 1969, he commented on the unique fact that the community did not have a chamber of commerce. "But perhaps a town with the name of Frostproof doesn't need one," said Smiley.

FRUITLAND PARK • *Lake County*
Founded in 1876 by Maj. O. P. Rooks of Cincinnati, Ohio, this town was named after the Fruitland Nurseries of Augusta, Ga. There was already a Fruitland in Florida at this time, and postal authorities refused to permit the name of Fruitland Park; hence, the town was officially renamed Gardenia. But the railroad had already issued its timetables, etc., with the name Fruitland Park, and persisted in their use, so that everything except the mail was addressed in that way. Four years later, postal officials were brought round. The town was incorporated in 1925.

FRUITVILLE • *Sarasota County*
Named by the first settler, Charles L. Reaves, who came in 1876 and hoped to raise fruit.

GABRIELLA • *Seminole County*
Gabriella's namesake had a post office from 1886 until 1907, but who the girl/woman was is not known.

GADSDEN COUNTY •
The fifth county, created June 24, 1823. The county was named for James Gadsden (1788-1858), a native of Charleston, S.C., and a diplomat who served as aide-de-camp to Gen. Andrew Jackson during the 1818 campaign in Florida. Why the territorial council named the county for Gadsden is not known. However, he had been an associate of Jackson and he had been commissioned to negotiate with the Indians for their removal to then-remote peninsular Florida or completely out of the territory. Gadsden later distinguished himself nationally for what is known now as the Gadsden Purchase. For a short time, until the creation of Leon County, Gadsden was the seat of territorial government in Florida

GAINESBORO • *Orange County*
Local belief is that the community, established in the 1880s, was named after a Col. Gaines.

GAINESVILLE • *Alachua County*
Gen. Edmund Pendleton Gaines, the captor of Aaron Burr, is the man whose name lives in the name of this seat of Alachua County and of the University of Florida, but the story of its naming is not as simple as that. When De Soto marched through here in 1539, this area was called Potano Province; it was renamed Alachua when the Creek Indians took possession upon the English acquisition of Florida in 1763. A white settlement known as Hog Town grew

The second Gadsden County Courthouse was built in 1912-1913.

up around a trading post established in 1830. When the Yulee railroad was built from Fernandina to Cedar Key in 1853, it was plain that a more digni-fied name was needed. County Commissioner William I. Turner, an Indian War veteran and prosperous cattle raiser, proposed Gainesville, but a wealthy and influential planter named William R. Lewis offered his own name. Also in dispute was the location of the county seat, which had hitherto been at Newnansville. A barbecue picnic was held at Boulware Springs, where all cit-izens of the county were to settle the issue, and there was almost a rupture of the peace before dinner was served. But after all had eaten, some more peace-able negotiation and vote-swapping took place, and the present town was given both the courthouse and the name of Gainesville. The advocates of Newnansville referred in derision to their successful rival as "Gains-ville."

GALAXY • *Palm Beach County*
Galaxy was a town along the Celestial Railroad, which also served Jupiter, Mars, Venus, and Juno during 1889-1895 in what then was Dade County but now is Palm Beach County. Its proper name was the Jupiter and Lake Worth Railway, and its seven and a half miles of narrow gauge linked steamboat landings on the Atlantic Ocean and Lake Worth.

Juno's newspaper, *The Sun*, disapproved of the heavenly nickname applied by travelers, believing they were poking fun, which would obscure the worth of the area. When cold nipped the area, the editor wryly called the celestial roll—of Jupiter, Juno, Venus, Mars and the Sun—and said even Mercury had fallen there.

GALT • *Santa Rosa County*
The belief here is that Galt was the first name of the surveyor who laid out the town site. Galt gained postal status in 1890.

Toll house on the Tampa side of Gandy Bridge, 1921.

GANDY BRIDGE • *Hillsborough and Pinellas counties*
The idea of bringing together the sister cities of Old Tampa Bay—Tampa and St. Petersburg—had been in the minds of George S. Gandy and others from the time motor vehicles came into fairly general use. Gandy began making surveys in 1915 and had obtained the right-of-way and franchise for the bay bridge and causeway by 1918. The land boom of the 1920s stimulated financing, and in November 1924, the tollway was officially opened to the benefit of both Hillsborough and Pinellas counties, reducing the highway distance from 43 miles to 19. With some three miles of causeway and two and a half miles of bridge, the Gandy bridge at the time of its opening was said to be the longest motor vehicle toll bridge in the world. The tolls came off during World War II when U. S. Sen. Claude Pepper persuaded President Franklin D. Roosevelt that this was essential to the travel of war workers between Tampa and St. Petersburg.

GARDEN KEY • *Monroe County*
Garden Key is one of a group of low-lying coral and sand bars sighted first by Juan Ponce de León on his exploratory voyage of 1513 around the peninsula of Florida. He called the islands *Las Tortugas. See also* Dry Tortugas. Garden Key is the site of Fort Jefferson.

GARDEN OF EDEN • *Liberty County*
E. E. Callaway, lawyer and Bible scholar, said persuasively that the Garden of Eden was on the east bank of the Apalachicola River near Bristol. Grady Norton, once chief hurricane forecaster for the U.S. Weather Bureau, observed that the same area measured up to the Bible's specifications of the place where Noah built the ark.

GARFIELD • *Volusia County*
Settled shortly after the assassination of President James A. Garfield, who died on September 19, 1881, the town was named for the 20th president.

GASPARILLA ISLAND • *Charlotte County*
Named for José Gaspar, the renegade Spanish naval officer, real or legendary, who is said to have established a base here for his band of pirates. *See also* Boca Grande *and* Captiva.

G ATLIN • *Orange County*
The fort was built in 1836 and the town came along in 1883. Both were named for Dr. John S. Gatlin, an assistant army surgeon slain by Indians on December 28, 1835, during the Seminole War.

G EERWORTH • *Palm Beach County*
When the highway from the Palm Beaches became passable in 1921, H. G. Geer and C. C. Chillingworth developed a 16,000-acre tract nine miles east of Belle Glade, calling it Geerworth. Most of the land was sold in Britain and colonized by immigrants. This British colony, drowned in the 1922 high water, had a brief renaissance in the 1924-25 boom, but recurring floods claimed the settlement, of which no trace remains.

G EM, MARY, LAKE • *Orange County*
When attorney William Randolph came to Orange County in 1868, there was an unnamed lake adjacent to the Randolph home. He desired to honor his wife, Mary, whom he regarded as a gem, so he named the lake Gem Mary. In so doing, Randolph followed the example of a neighbor, Dr. O. P. Preston, a Texan who settled in Orange County two years earlier. He named his lake for his wife Jennie, who he said was a jewel; hence, Lake Jennie Jewel. These gems are from E. H. Gore's *History of Orlando* (1949).

G ENEVA • *Seminole County*
Because this community was situated on a pretty lake, someone was reminded of Switzerland's Geneva, lake and city.

G ENOA • *Hamilton County*
How the name of Italy's great port was transplanted here—if in fact the name derives from the overseas Genoa—seems lost to history.

G EORGE, LAKE • *Putnam, Marion, Volusia, and Lake counties*
The second-largest natural freshwater lake in Florida has an area of 70 square miles, making it second only to Lake Okeechobee. Lake George has a drainage area of 3,600 square miles. Because the lake is a part of the St. Johns River system, Lake George was likely visited first by explorers in June 1564, when members of René de Laudonnière's colony of French Huguenots ventured from Fort Caroline up the St. Johns. The name likely is a survival from the British occupation of east Florida.

Volusia bar light at the south end of Lake George, about 1930.

GEORGIANA • *Brevard County*
Dr. William Whitfield and family, of Philadelphia, settled here in 1869. The origin of the name is not known, but the community retains the flavor of old-time Florida despite its proximity to the Cape Kennedy Space Center. Nearby, on the drive once known as the Tropical Trail, are such Merritt Island communities as Tropic and Fairyland.

GIBSONTON • *Hillsborough County*
Named for founder James B. Gibson, this is the closest thing to home for the dwindling carnival folk of America. *The Miami Herald's* "Tropic" magazine section: "You'd have to think a bit before the roadside names sank in: Midway Nursery, Magic Mirror Beauty Salon, Giant's Restaurant." Here being a freak is money in the bank. The people of Gibsonton don't abhor misshape; they admire it. For example, until he died, 8-foot, 4.5-inch Al Tomaini was the town fire chief. From spring until fall, the carnival folk travel the circuit, then return to Gibsonton.

GIFFORD • *Indian River County*
The Florida East Coast Railway is said to have given this town the name of F. Charles Gifford, who in turn has been credited with having selected the site for nearby Vero Beach.

GILCHRIST COUNTY •
The sixty-seventh county, established December 4, 1925. Named for Albert Waller Gilchrist, the twentieth governor (January 5, 1909, to January 7, 1913). The legislature was about to create a new county to be known as Mellon when news came that former Gov. Gilchrist was dying in a New York hospital. By amendment during floor consideration, "Gilchrist" was substituted for "Mellon." Gilchrist was a descendant of the grandfathers of both George Washington and James Madison. He was a civil engineer, land developer, and orange grower at Punta Gorda. He was a member of the House of Representatives from De Soto County for the sessions of 1893-1895 and 1903-1905, and was its speaker in 1905. A bachelor, he provided money in his will to supply Halloween treats for the children of Punta Gorda. This was but part of Gilchrist's beneficence, for his entire estate of a half-million dollars went to charities.

GLADES COUNTY •
The fifty-eighth county, established April 23, 1921. Named for the Everglades, of which it forms a part. Bellamy (1973) recounted how the federal government in 1847 sent Buckingham Smith of St. Augustine to gather facts about the Everglades, in particular whether the land could be "reclaimed and made valuable." His report contained a lyrical description of the great marsh. At that time, the Everglades extended, unbroken, 100 miles from Lake Okeechobee to Cape Sable. Another Florida writer, Marjory Stoneman Douglas, dubbed the Everglades "the River of Grass." Ms. Bellamy said it had been described as "the widest, shallowest and strangest river in America—fifty miles wide in places, averaging around nine inches deep in fall, the

wettest season, but parched for weeks in springtime, the driest time of year." Buckingham Smith found the Everglades in 1847 to be "a vast lake of fresh water . . . studded with thousands of islands . . . which are generally covered with dense thickets of shrubbery and vines."

GLENCOE • *Volusia County*
Named for William H. Coe, who arrived some ten years after the Civil War. "Glen," meaning a pleasant valley, was prefaced to "Coe."

GLEN RIDGE • *Palm Beach County*
The name suggested by Mrs. Max Mosler at a meeting of residents of the area when they met to incorporate. Mrs. Mosler said the fact that the town is on the bank of the Palm Beach Canal gave her the idea of "Ridge." Her suggestion was accepted by majority vote.

GLEN ST. MARY • *Baker County*
Established by Miss T. M. Tilton in 1882. She owned the hotel and served as postmaster. The name was prompted by its nearness to the St. Marys River, which forms the northern boundary of Florida. (St. Marys is easier to pronounce than the Indian name of *Thlathlathlakuphka*.)

GLENWOOD • *Volusia County*
Situated in one of the earliest cleared areas under American ownership of Florida. Grants of land in this vicinity were confirmed by special acts of Congress in 1832. The railroad came through in the 1880s. Maj. George Norris of Batavia, N.Y., purchased a large tract on a high pine ridge in 1872 and may have been instrumental in selecting the name for its pleasing sound.

GOETHE • *Bay County*
Named for George Goethe, an early sawmiller.

GOLDEN BEACH • *Dade County*
As happened so often, the name originally applied by subdivision developers in the 1920s was adopted for the successor community. Golden Beach is on the Atlantic; it is an extension northward of Miami Beach.

GOLDEN GLADES • *Dade County*
Once a doorstep to the Everglades but now a bustling interchange for motor traffic pouring into Miami from the Florida Turnpike. The name bespeaks someone's hope for well-being, perhaps originally in agriculture.

GOLDENROD • *Orange County*
A settlement by the name has existed here since 1860, but the post office seems to date from 1951. Any plant of the genus *Solidago* is called goldenrod. Most species bear numerous small, yellow flowers. The wildflowers bring color to the roadside and agitation to hay fever sufferers.

GOLF VIEW, GOLF VILLAGE • *Palm Beach County*
Founded by men who had previously established Golf, Ill., and were interested in the game of golf. The communities offer the pleasing vistas of a golf course.

GOMEZ • *Martin County*
An independent community at least since 1891. The name derives from Eusobie M. Gomez, who received a Spanish land grant of 12,000 acres in 1815.

GONZALEZ • *Escambia County*
On at least three occasions—in 1814, 1818, and 1821—Gen. Andrew Jackson visited Don Manuel Gonzalez at the Don's estate, Gonzalia (known also as Fifteen Mile House because of its distance from Pensacola). King (1972) relates this anecdote: When Jackson was first about to capture Pensacola, in 1814, the general requested that Don Gonzalez have his son guide the Americans into Pensacola. Gonzalez refused, saying, "Shoot him or both of us if you must but do not expect us to betray our king and our country." Such, continues King, "was plain talk to the point that Gen. Jackson could understand and respect."

GOODBY'S LAKE • *Duval County*
See Azza Creek.

GOPHER RIDGE • *St. Johns County*
Named for the abundance of the land turtles known as gophers.

GOTHA • *Orange County*
After earning a considerable sum from a patented groin, a wedge-shaped piece of metal used to lock forms in printing, H. A. Hempel of Buffalo, N.Y., came to Florida in 1878 and established a community which he named for his birthplace in Germany, at the suggestion of H. P. Belknap of Cincinnati, a teacher in the area.

GOULDING • *Escambia County*
Established in 1889, this community derived its name from H. M. and W. J. Goulding, owners of the Goulding Fertilizer Company.

GOULDS • *Dade County*
Once called Gould's Siding, a sidetrack of the Florida East Coast Railway during the development of South Dade County.

GOVERNOR'S MANSION • *Tallahassee*
The first state-owned governor's mansion was built on the site of the present mansion in 1907 at a cost of $21,242. It was occupied for nearly 50 years by a succession of 15 governors. That first mansion was found to be structurally unsound, and was torn down in 1955.

In 1957, the present mansion was completed at a cost of $350,000 for building and furnishings. Designed by Wyeth, King and Johnson of Palm Beach, it is a Greek revival style of red brick with tall, white Corinthian columns. The central section of the exterior was designed to resemble The Hermitage near Nashville, home of Gen. Andrew Jackson, Florida's first American territorial governor.

Three flags are displayed from the balcony. The middle flag is a 27-star flag of the United States. The 27th star, representing statehood for Florida, was added to the flag on July 4, 1845.

The mansion was designed and maintained both for private living and the official entertaining of the chief executive of the state of Florida.

Upstairs is a private area with four bedrooms, four baths, and a dressing room. The south end of the main floor is also used for private living. It contains a living room, dining room, and pullman kitchen.

The center and north end of the main floor of the mansion are designated as state rooms. State rooms include an entrance hall, reception room, dining room, guest bedroom with bath, and Florida room.

Above the entrance door is a window of beveled glass etched with the state seal. West Point urns beside the door rest on small Roman bases.

The ground floor is not visible from the front of the house. Utility and boiler rooms, offices for mansion personnel, and headquarters for agents from the Florida Department of Law Enforcement, who provide 24-hour security, are all located on this level.

At the back of the house is a screened swimming pool, cabana, exercise room and a patio area that was built during the Martinez administration. This completely bricked patio is accented at both ends by pavilions of wood and brick entwined with roses. At the west end is a circular pool with a fountain that spills water into a lower pool flanked by two sets of steps.

Across the side street is a tennis court and a greenhouse. The greenhouse furnishes most of the plants and cut flowers seen at various times inside the mansion.

At this writing, eight governors and their families have lived in this mansion: governors Collins, Bryant, Burns, Kirk, Askew, Graham, Martinez, and Chiles. Each family has made some changes, reflecting their own personalities and lifestyles.

THE BATTLESHIP SILVER

The silver service of the battleship *Florida* is among the most impressive objects in the mansion and, in terms of Florida history, among the most important objects in the mansion as well. The silver service was given by the people of Florida to the battleship *Florida* in 1911. The cost was $10,000, and the amount was raised by schoolchildren and through private donations.

In 1930, in compliance with the London Naval Treaty, the battleship *Florida* was decommissioned. (It was scuttled within a few years.) The silver was returned to the state of Florida in care of the governor.

The silver was designed and made by the Gorham Company in the "Colonial" style. Each of the 26 pieces contains both the Navy seal and the seal for the state of Florida with decorations of a Florida motif. The largest piece is a 12-gallon punch bowl. On one side is an illustration of the landing of Ponce de León, and on the reverse side is a Seminole Indian. The bowl rises from a seashell supported by alligators. Its handles are pelicans. An American eagle, holding an olive branch of peace, is on the rim. The punch bowl rests on a plateau bearing the seals of the state of Florida and the Navy.

GRACEVILLE • *Jackson County*
A man named Stapleton established a grist mill here in 1824, and named the resultant town for Capt. N. B. Grace, a prominent constructor, surveyor, landowner, and officer in the Confederate Army. The old Spanish Trail passed near the site of this town; on Purcell's map it appears as Coosa Old Fields.

GRAND ISLAND • *Lake County*
Named in the 1880s by a Capt. Dodd, who had moved here from Fort Mason because he wanted to live on higher, hilly ground. Grand Island then was almost surrounded by lakes.

GRAND RIDGE • *Jackson County*
Founded by John Thomas Porter, a native of Pennsylvania, who had settled at Grand Ridge, Ill., in 1858. In 1889, he moved here, founded the town, and named it for his old home.

GRANT • *Brevard County*
Originally Grant's Farm, named for a settler on an island in the Indian River. The community's name was given by Mrs. Edwin Nelson in 1890.

GREENACRES CITY • *Palm Beach County*
Developer L. C. Swain asked his 26 associates to suggest names other than his own and then vote for the final choice. Greenacres won. The post office department suggested adding City since there was another Greenacres in Florida.

GREEN COVE SPRINGS • *Clay County*
The St. Johns River forms a curve at this point, which is sheltered by perennially green trees. Here also are located some celebrated sulphur springs, at times said to be those which Ponce de León and others were seeking. The town was established by live-oak cutters in 1830. It is the county seat of Clay County.

GREEN RIVER SWAMP • *Collier County*
Tebeau (1966) said that place names do not necessarily have any relation to natural features even when they appear to. "Green River Swamp south of Corkscrew Marsh is so named," observed Tebeau, "because of a pile of nearly a hundred Green River Whiskey bottles accumulated at a nearby hunting camp visited regularly by a party with a liking for that brand."

GREENSBORO • *Gadsden County*
In 1895, J. W. Green bought 160 acres near his birthplace in the Alamo community of Gadsden County. He moved to the place and soon secured a post office called Green's. When the Apalachicola Northern Railway was built in 1907, a depot was located on the Green farm, which was platted as a town and named in honor of Green.

GREEN SWAMP
When people started calling the Green Swamp an area of "critical state concern" in the 1970s, many Floridians first became aware of the area skirted by Pánfilo de Narváez and Hernando De Soto in the 1500s.

Tourists beside the bathing pool at Green Cove Springs, 1886.

The Green Swamp, named for its prevailing color, is situated in central Florida between Orlando and Tampa. The area contains 870 square miles, bordered by U.S. 27 on the east, S.R. 544 on the south, S.R. 28 and 301 on the west, and S.R. 50 on the north.

Despite its being avoided by Spanish explorers 400 years ago and by main highways today, the Green Swamp is not the typical low, wet land usually associated with such a label. It is a composite of many swamps distributed with fair uniformity within the area. The largest continuous expanse of swamp lies within the Withlacoochee River environs and is more than a mile in width. The Green Swamp occupies a flat plateau with elevations varying from 75 to 200 feet above mean sea level. Ridges border the swamp on the east and west, with the higher land to the east forming the Lake Wales Ridge.

GREENVILLE • *Madison County*
A town was first established here in 1850, and its post office was given the name of Sandy Ford. But during the Civil War the place was given the name of Station Five, because it was the fifth station from the capital. A women's sewing circle was organized here to sew for the soldiers in the Confederate Army, and the first box of supplies which they sent to the commissary in Richmond was designated as coming from Station Five. The quartermaster wrote the president of the society that packages would have to be given in the name of some town. The ladies met and agreed to call the town Greenville, as a tribute to Mrs. U. M. Roberts, president of the society, who came from Greenville, S.C. The Spanish missions of San Miguel de Asylo and San Mateo de Tolapato were both near here.

GREENWOOD • *Jackson County*
Established in 1824 and first called Panhandle. The final name was chosen by settlers from South Carolina in remembrance of their former home.

GREERWORTH • *Palm Beach County*
A 16,000-acre tract on the West Palm Beach canal in the Everglades subdivided for agricultural settlers, mostly from Great Britain, by H. G. Greer and C. C. Chillingworth in the 1920s.

GRETNA • *Gadsden County*
A settlement was established here in 1897 by the Humphrey Company, naval stores operators, but it was not a town in any real sense of the word, and consisted largely of a few widely scattered African-American families around the point where the railroad stopped to pick up wood. The inhabitants called the place Gritney, saying it was because there was so much sand, but this may have been a corruption of the name as now officially spelled. In time, the Humphrey Company built a turpentine still, homes for officials and workmen, and a commissary; a post office was established in the commissary and J. W. Mehaffey, son-in-law of the head of the firm, was appointed first postmaster. He decided Gritney was not a very prominent-sounding name, and changed it to Gretna, perhaps under the influence of his Scottish ancestors.

GREYHOUND KEY • *Monroe County*
The inter-city bus company had a rest stop here. When the bus company sold the key in 1966, the new owners renamed it Fiesta Key.

GROVELAND • *Lake County*
First called Taylorville, apparently after one of the original backers of the Orange Belt Railway, on which construction was begun late in the 1880s. Around 1911, the town was renamed Groveland, in reference to the large number of flourishing citrus groves in the vicinity.

GROVE PARK • *Alachua County*
A grove of great oaks grew here in 1883 as the area developed into a shipping point for truck farmers.

GRUBBS • *Holmes County*
Since Henry Grubbs was to be the postmaster when mail service began in 1902, he had an edge over other settlers when a name was chosen.

GULF COUNTY •
The sixty-sixth county, established June 6, 1925. Named for the Gulf of Mexico, which washes its southern shore.

GULF BREEZE • *Santa Rosa County*
Across Pensacola Bay from Pensacola and separated from the Gulf of Mexico by Santa Rosa Island, Gulf Breeze offers the pleasures of resort living year-round, with breezes from either the gulf or the bay. With Milton the county seat then as now, Gulf Breeze (called Town Point) was a two- or three-day round trip for the sheriff, either by land or water, in the 1800s.

GULF HAMMOCK • *Levy County*
This part of Levy County had dense hardwood stands, much of which have been timbered, and borders the Gulf of Mexico.

GULF OF MEXICO •
The name Gulf has been taken for a Florida county and a number of communities: Gulf Beach in Bay and Escambia counties, Gulf Breeze in Santa Rosa County, Gulf Gate Estates in Sarasota County, Gulf Harbors in Pasco County, and Gulf Hammock in Levy County.

GULFPORT • *Pinellas County*
The name was to have been Disston City, but because there already was a Diston (with one "s"), the community started as Bonafacio on January 5, 1885. Then the original choice of Disston City became available and was adopted in 1889. Next, Veteran City was adopted in 1906 and finally Gulfport in 1910. Bonafacio is said to have been the middle name of William B. Miranda, one of the original promoters.

GULFSTREAM • *Palm Beach County*
Derived its name from proximity to the Gulf Stream, which flows nearest the Florida mainland in this area.

GULL POINT • *Escambia County*
Situated on Escambia Bay, this was the scene of the country home of Don Juan Broshnahan. Legend says the first meeting of the Territorial Council of Florida under American ownership was held here. Because of the prevalence of yellow fever, the council later moved to the estate of Don Manuel Gonzalez. *See also* Gonzalez.

HACIENDA VILLAGE • *Broward County*
Incorporated October 29, 1949, this was originally a subdivision called Hacienda Flores. This municipality of mobile homes was notorious for its speed traps. The present-day site, a major intersection of Interstate 595 and S.R. 7, was absorbed into the town of Davie in 1984.

HAGUE • *Alachua County*
When Hague grew to post office size in 1883, it seemed natural to honor A. Hague, the postmaster and county commissioner. In 1885, Hague, on the Savannah, Florida and Western Railway, had a grist mill, steam sawmill, and cotton gin.

HAILE • *Alachua County*
On the railroad between Cadillac and Kokomo, it was named in the 1880s for a family of early settlers.

HAINES CITY • *Polk County*
A town came into being at this site in 1883 with the building of the South Florida Railroad, but the settlement was at first known as Clay Cut. It was on the railroad, but the residents couldn't get the trains to stop since the company wouldn't put a station here. When, four years later, they changed the name of the town to Haines City (in honor of Col. Henry Haines, an official

of the railroad), the railroad put up a station and made the town a stop. Haines City calls itself "The Gateway to the Scenic Highlands."

HAINESWORTH • *Alachua County*
As towns sprang up in Alachua County in the 1880s, the inhabitants were content with honoring townspeople, the Haines family in this instance, instead of searching for the promotional or image names of later years.

HALF MOON • *Alachua County*
A departure from the Alachua County custom of family names, Half Moon remains on the map, but the source of its name is unknown.

HALIFAX CITY • *Volusia County*
The Halifax in Halifax City and Halifax River derives from the second Earl of Halifax. Halifax City was chartered in 1870 and described by George J. Alden, writing in 1885, as "situated about three miles northwest and in full view of the inlet." He added that Rose Bay encircled the town east and west. Halifax took its name from the Halifax River, a tidewater lagoon whose shores were favored by British settlers during the English occupation of Florida. Later changed to Allandale.

HALLANDALE • *Broward County*
Hallandale, incorporated in 1927, owes its name to Dania and to J. E. Ingraham, Henry M. Flagler's right-hand man in the development of Florida's east coast, including the railroad. In his book *Hallandale*, Bill McGoun wrote: "After a group of Danish immigrants settled in Dania, Ingraham remarked to his Swedish brother-in-law, Luther Halland, a minister and mailman, 'Why don't you go down there and start a Swedish settlement?' Halland did; hence, Hallandale."

The Florida East Coast Railway Station at Hallandale, 1921.

H A L P A T I O K E E (Marsh and River) • *St. Lucie and Martin counties*
This Indian name, meaning "alligator water," has been superseded by St. Lucie.

H A M B U R G • *Madison County*
Carlton Smith, the Madison County historian, wrote that the Hamburg community existed in 1825 when this area still was part of Leon County. The name is said to have been transplanted by Samuel S. Hinton from his former home, Hamburg, S. C.

H A M I L T O N • *County*
The fifteenth county, established December 26, 1827. Named for Alexander Hamilton, embattled conservative and first U. S. secretary of the treasury.

H A M M O C K • *Alachua County*
Floridians usually spell it "hammock" but elsewhere the usage is "hummock." The meaning is the same, the *Random House Dictionary* defining hummock as "an elevated tract of land rising above the general level of a marshy region." The word was taken for the name of this community.

H A M P T O N • *Bradford County*
Henry Saxon, Sr., had a farmhouse at approximately the center of the present town of Hampton. When he moved to another farm, a family named Terry moved into the farmhouse. As a community formed around the tracks near the Terry farm, it was given the name of the Terrys' ten-year-old son, Hampton.

H A M P T O N   S P R I N G S • *Taylor County*
The story goes that Joe Hampton, an early Taylor County settler whose wife suffered from rheumatism, was directed by an Indian to these springs. When the water eased her pain and stiffness, Hampton obtained a government grant to the spring area for $10. A descendant built a hotel here in 1904 to accommodate visitors to the springs.

H A R B E S O N   C I T Y • *Franklin County*
Named after a family prominent in lumbering and hotel management in the Florida Panhandle.

H A R B O R •
Harbor, with the image of a safe snuggery overlooking water, has been used in the names of a number of communities: Harbor Point and Harbor Oaks in Volusia County, Harbor Bluffs in Pinellas County, Harbor Acres in Sarasota County, and Harbour Heights and Harbor View in Charlotte County.

H A R D E E   C O U N T Y •
The fifty-fifth county, established April 23, 1921. One of four counties—Highlands, Charlotte, and Glades being the others—created in a massive division of De Soto County.

Hardee was named for Cary Augustus Hardee, who was in his first year as governor when DeSoto was divided. It well may be that the promoters of county division wanted to make the legislative act more palatable to the governor possessing the veto power. But Gov. Hardee was well known and liked.

Born in Taylor County, Hardee taught school and studied for admission to the bar. Upon becoming a lawyer, he began practice at Live Oak. He served as state attorney and then was elected to the House of Representatives. His political genius may be evidenced by the fact that he was selected to be speaker before taking the oath as a member of the House. He served two terms as speaker, another rare happening, in 1915 and 1917. He was better known in later years as a banker at Live Oak than as a lawyer. He was defeated for the Democratic nomination for governor in 1932. He died at Live Oak on November 21, 1957. Plowden (1929) reports that those supporting a new county had first proposed calling it Seminole, but this was abandoned when Seminole was given to another new county. Other names suggested included Cherokee, Goolsby, and Wauchula. However, when the bill was introduced, it had the name of Gov. Hardee.

HARD LABOR CREEK • *Washington County*
About ten miles long, flowing into Holmes Creek; not an impressive waterway, but the name surely conveys a number of images of toil.

HARD SCRABBLE • *Santa Rosa County*
King (1972) recalls how the Spanish had licensed a trading firm to control the export-import business of west Florida. People seeking to evade the king's levy used the area of present-day Milton, which came to be known as Hard Scrabble, "since often these landings were made at the bluffs on the basins above town where it was a hard scrabble to get from the boat on the water to the top of the bluff."

HARMONY COMMUNITY • *Madison County*
Included places known today by such fascinating names as Friendship, Wildcat, and Eridu. In Florida's early days, the term "community" had a broader meaning than today, for a community then might cover a considerable area with a number of scattered, independent settlements.

HARNEY • *Hillsborough County*
Recalls Col. (afterwards Gen.) William Selby Harney of the Seminole Wars. Harney led a detachment that clashed with Indians in the vicinity of today's Homestead on April 24, 1838. In command of a detail to guard a trading post on the Caloosahatchee River, Harney and 13 others escaped an Indian attack on July 23, 1839, which saw 13 soldiers killed and six captured. Harney crisscrossed the Everglades, fighting the Indians on both coasts. Harney's Point in Lee County, at the Cape Coral Bridge on U.S. 41 near Fort Myers, is near the scene of the attack on the Caloosahatchee River Fort and trading post.

HAROLD • *Santa Rosa County*
Named for a son of the postmaster, according to local legend. Earlier, the community was known as Oscar.

HARPER • *Santa Rosa County*
Believed to be a family name. The post office was opened in 1907.

HARRIS, LAKE • *Lake County*
Formerly Astatula (*see also* Astatula), the name was changed to honor Col. Frank Harris, who lived with his family on its southern shore during the Seminole Wars. When word reached here of a Seminole uprising, Colonel Harris took his family to the safety of a fort at Wildwood, then returned to guard his home. In the 1880s a sawmill was set up on the shores of Little Lake Harris, a waterway looping off from Lake Harris. The availability of boards changed the character of the log cabin community and attracted other business. Kennedy (1929) relates that among the chief social events of the time were bear hunts. "Bears were so plentiful that they would steal pigs from under the cabins and out of the barns, so that the settlers organized a bear club to protect their stock. Hunts were held each week, and one day Mr. Hux killed a 400-pounder. Wild turkeys had to be killed to prevent them from destroying the crops. Mr. Hux's family were often alarmed by the howling of the packs of red wolves, while panthers screamed not only during the nights but all through the mornings until noon. Alligators were both numerous and destructive—one killing a colt of Mr. Hux, while others killed cattle that rested by the lake or would knock hogs from their wallows with a stunning blow of the tail and dispose of them. Mr. Hux used to spend his noon hour hunting alligators, and would sell the teeth to be made into souvenirs—a large 'gator being worth up to $12 for his teeth, which were sold for so much a pound."

HART BRIDGE, ISAIAH DAVID • *Duval County*
Dedicated and opened to the public on November 2, 1967, it is the fifth bridge for vehicular traffic to span the St. Johns River at Jacksonville. Its name honors the city's founder, chief proponent of the idea of a new city and leader of the landowners and settlers at Cow Ford who laid out the city in 1822. The bridge is 3,667 feet long and has a vertical clearance of 135 feet. Hart was a prominent citizen for 40 years and held many positions of trust. Following his death in 1861, his executors donated a block in the city's center for a public park in his memory. The park bears the name of Hemming, after the donor of the Confederate monument later erected there.

HARWOOD • *Volusia County*
Gold (1927) reports that a man named Harwood came here about 1883 from Minnesota and acquired much land. He enclosed about 1,700 acres with wire fence, bought several hundred head of cattle, and at one time had as many as 500 men working for him. "Before he had fully developed his ranch," continues Gold, "he is said to have been thrown from a horse and died from the effect of the injury."

HASKELL • *Polk County*
A station on the railroad to Bartow, it was a quiet little village until the Florida boom of the 1920s. The residents decided then to change Haskell to Highland City.

HASTINGS • *St. Johns County*
A famous potato-growing area, named for the H. G. Hastings Seed Company of Atlanta, Ga.

HATCHEE LUSTEE CREEK • *Osceola County*
From the Creek *hatchee*, "creek," *luste*, "black," it became Reedy Creek, visited unknowingly in most instances by the multitude attracted by the surrounding Disney World.

HATCHEE THLAKO (Hurricane Creek) • *Holmes County*
Simpson (1956) observes that the waterway's old and new names are of Indian origin. The old name is from the Creek *hatchee*, "creek," and *thlako*, "big." The present name, Hurricane Creek, is from *huracan*, name of the storm god of the Quiche Indians of Guatemala.

HATCHINEHA, LAKE • *Polk County*
Simpson (1956) says the name of this lake in the Kissimmee River system is a corruption of Creek *achenaho*, "cypress."

HAULOVER • *Dade and Volusia counties*
A haulover is a place where small boats are hauled across land from one body of water to another. The Haulover in Volusia County was where, from the earliest days of the Spanish, British, and American occupations of Florida, boats were transferred between the Mosquito Lagoon and the Indian River. Two canals were cut to eliminate this necessity, the first in 1845 and another in 1887, but the name The Haulover was retained. Similarly, in Dade County, a haulover—later cut through but also retaining the name—served for the transfer of boats between Biscayne Bay and the Atlantic Ocean.

HAVANA • *Gadsden County*
Cultivation of Cuban tobacco in this county began as early as 1829, and this town was named long afterwards for the Cuban capital as a means of honoring this remunerative crop. Stanley (1948) says a frame schoolhouse and a box-like depot were the only buildings here in 1903 when a Georgia, Florida & Alabama Railroad line was completed from Cuthbert, Ga., to Tallahassee. The railroad caused people to gravitate to the place, which was named Havana at the suggestion of Jim Mathison, a schoolteacher. The name Havana is of Indian origin, though its exact significance has been lost. The Spanish mission of Santa Cruz de Cupali stood near here.

HAVERHILL • *Palm Beach County*
A man from Massachusetts named this town after his home state's Haverhill, north of Boston.

HAWTHORNE • *Alachua County*
Calvin Waits owned land here and the settlement was first known as Waits Crossing. Adjacent land to the north was owned by James M. Hawthorn (no "e") and called Jamestown. In 1880, there was a merger and the town was named Hawthorn. But people persisted in spelling the name with a final "e" and this was adopted in 1950.

HAYDEN • *Sarasota County*
Dr. George Hayden, a traveling dentist who came here from Palmetto, founded this town.

"Havana was a tobacco town, rolling in money that came straight from the ground."

HAYNES POINT • *Lake County*

Melton Haynes built his home in 1846 on a bluff overlooking Lake Astatula and the place was known as Haynes Point. Now the area near Leesburg is called Sunnyside.

HAYWOOD • *Jackson County*

Francis P. Haywood settled here in the late 1860s. The first post office, in 1876, was called Haygood's Landing, but this misspelling was straightened out the following month and Haywood's Landing it remained until 1891, when Landing was dropped.

HELL'S HALF ACRE • *Jefferson County*

Look at a topographic map of southeast Jefferson County and you'll find a swamp with the legend "Hell's Half Acre." This swamp is unusual even among the many swamps of Florida's Big Bend for its rugged terrain. Rather than a half acre, the swamp covers approximately 1,000 acres. Tate's Hell, in the Big Bend's Franklin County, is another swamp with a fearsome reputation. The late Dr. Robert O. Vernon, state geologist, reports from personal experience that Tate's Hell is "formidable . . . frightening in its complexity."

HENDRY COUNTY •

The sixty-third county, established May 11, 1923. Honors Capt. Francis Asbury Hendry, whose fascinating history is recited in *Hendry County's Golden Anniversary Issue of the Clewiston News* (July 12, 1973).

Capt. Hendry was married at 19 and settled near Fort Meade to raise cattle. With the outbreak of the Second Seminole War, he became a dispatch bearer. Riding to Fort Harvie (afterwards Fort Myers), he became enchanted with the lands along the Caloosahatchee River. During the Civil War, he served the Confederacy as captain of a cavalry troop he recruited in Polk County. His admiration for Gen. Robert E. Lee caused him later to give Lee's name to a new county he was instrumental in creating in 1887. After the war, he moved the family home to the Caloosahatchee Valley, where cattle could be moved easily to Punta Rassa for shipment to Cuba. He platted the town site he called LaBelle, after his daughters Laura and Belle. He was elected state senator from Monroe County, which then encompassed all of present Lee, Hendry, and Collier counties. He promoted the incorporation of Fort Myers and served as one of its first city councilmen. Similarly, he promoted the creation of Lee County and served as a member of its first county commission and then six terms as state representative. He pioneered the upgrading of Florida cattle. He bought purebreds and imported grass to improve herds and pastures. With his herd containing as many as 50,000 head at a time, he was known as the "Cattle King of South Florida." He died on February 12, 1917, his life having spanned a monumental epoch in Florida's history.

Back row third from the left is Capt. Francis Hendry, an influential figure with the Seminoles who lived in the Polk County area.

HERNANDO COUNTY •

The twenty-second county, established February 24, 1843, and named for Spanish explorer Hernando De Soto. Why his first name was chosen for the county must be a historical curiosity, since his last name was selected for the county seat. De Soto's last name finally achieved county status in 1887, thus giving Florida two counties named for the same person. The name of the county seat was changed from De Soto to Brooksville. Even the name of the county was briefly lost; it was changed to Benton on March 6, 1844, to honor U. S. Sen. Thomas Hart Benton of Missouri, whose sponsorship of the Armed Occupation Act won favor among Floridians eager to evict the Indians. But Benton's moderation during the Missouri Compromise caused extremists in the legislature to switch the name back on December 24, 1850.

HERNANDO • *Citrus County*
This community, named for Hernando De Soto, is on Lake Tsala Apopka and near the place where De Soto is believed to have crossed the Withlacoochee River during his expedition north through Florida.

HESPERIDES • *Polk County*
Nine miles east of Lake Wales on S.R. 60 is the village of Hesperides, entirely surrounded by orange groves. It is another of Florida's choice classical allusions. In the Garden of the Hesperides, far in the western part of the Grecian kingdom, grew the golden apples of Hera. The Hesperides were the maidens charged with guarding this precious fruit; some say they were the daughters of the giant Atlas, others that their father was Hesperus, the Evening Star.

HIALEAH • *Dade County*
The name is of Seminole-Creek origin: *haiyakpo*, "prairie," and *hili*, "pretty." A settlement was established here in 1910 by James H. Bright, a Missouri ranchman, who transformed 1,000 acres of a 14,000-acre tract into a grazing meadow for his herd of cows, with a year-round dairy industry in view. In 1917, Glenn H. Curtiss, of Jamestown, N.Y., pioneer aviator, collaborated with Bright in building a town on the banks of the Miami Canal. The cattle were moved further north. The town was incorporated in 1925. Nowadays, the name is associated with two vastly different images: one of the nation's loveliest horse tracks (Hialeah Park), and light industry, whose numerous plants make Hialeah the industrial center of metropolitan Miami.

HIBERNIA • *Clay County*
The name refers to both a stately plantation house and a community on Fleming's Island in the St. Johns River. The cotton plantation was developed on a Spanish grant in 1790 to the Fleming family. The frame mansion, with square columns two stories high, escaped damage during the Civil War. It lasted until the mid-1900s, when the ravages of time no longer could be repaired. Bricks from its seven chimneys went into the construction of a new dwelling on the site. The Flemings came from Ireland and called their home after the poetical name for the other island.

HICKPOCHEE, LAKE • *Glades County*
From the Creek *hiyakpo*, "prairie," and *chee*, "little."

HICKS' ISLAND • *Citrus County*
The island, in Lake Tsala Apopka, recalls John Hicks, the name by which the Miccosukee chief Tokose Emathla was known to the whites. Simpson (1956) translates the name as *takosalgi*, "mole clan," and *emathla*, "leader." Hicks was friendly to the whites and for a time was able to restrain his tribesmen.

HICORIA • *Highlands County*
Founded in 1908 as a sawmill town. The name is a Latinized form of Hickory.

HIGHLAND BEACH • *Palm Beach County*
The promotional value likely suggested this name for a community which had 3,176 inhabitants in 1990.

HIGHLAND CITY • *Polk County*
Haskell was the original name of the station established on the Pemberton Ferry railroad here, but in 1924, the name was changed to Highland City.

HIGHLAND PARK • *Polk County*
Mr. and Mrs. Irwin A. Yarnell named this town after Highland Park, Ill., where they had friends.

HIGHLANDS COUNTY •
The fifty-sixth county, established April 23, 1921. The name suggests the pleasant hilliness of the area, with citrus groves marching in rows across the ridges and the bottomlands often the site of inviting lakes.

HIGHLANDS • *Lake County*
This area has been known by a number of names since the first tree was felled in April 1876. Kennedy (1929) says it first was called Highlands to distinguish the location of these homesteaders from others settling in the lowlands, then Pendryville because it was on A. S. Pendry's homestead, then Lake Eustis, and finally Eustis, which it remains.

HIGHLAND STATION • *Clay County*
First known as Highland Station, then simply Highland, this place was established in the 1870s and took its name from the plus-200-foot altitude, which was higher than the neighboring area.

HIGH SPRINGS • *Alachua County*
First founded in 1884 as Sanaffee, a corruption of the name of the Santa Fe River, near which it was located. In 1886 the name was changed to Orion, after the hunter who was transformed into a constellation. In 1889 the name was changed to its present form, because of a spring located atop a hill within the town site. The spring has since disappeared.

HIGLEY • *Lake County*
Founded in 1883 by E. E. Higley of Chicago and George W. Webb of Iowa. The area was booming as a citrus and winter tourist center until the big freeze in 1895. Some left but others remained, and gradually the groves were restored.

HILLCREST HEIGHTS • *Polk County*
So named because it lay on a hillside south of Crooked Lake. Irwin Yarnell, co-owner with F. E. Fairchild of the Southern Land Co., built a home on the crest in 1916.

HILLIARD • *Nassau County*
A trading post was established here in the early 1800s, but the present town was not founded until 1881. It was named for one of the members of the lumber company, Hilliard and Bailey, which put a mill into operation here. An airway facilities sector of the U.S. Department of Transportation is located in Hilliard.

HILLSBORO BEACH • *Broward County*
An inlet and lighthouse here gave their name to the community, and they in turn derived their name from a contraction of the Earl of Hillsborough.

HILLSBORO RIVER • *Hillsborough County*
The name appears both in the long and short forms on maps of today. The State Department of Agriculture's sectional map spells it Hillsboro, both for the river and bay, while the State Department of Transportation's highway map uses Hillsborough for the river and merges the waterways on both sides of Tampa as Tampa Bay. The U.S. Board on Geographic Names decreed that the usage should be Hillsboro River and Hillsborough County. The Indians knew the river as *locksa apopka*, or "place for eating acorns."

HILLSBOROUGH COUNTY •
The eighteenth county, established January 25, 1834. Named for Wills Hills, the Earl of Hillsborough (1718-1793), an Irish peer who in 1768 became secretary of state for the colonies. It was Lord Hillsborough's office which had the responsibility for amassing knowledge about England's possessions overseas. Those agents dispatched in Lord Hillsborough's name in turn affixed that name to places in Florida and elsewhere. Hillsborough was especially curious about Florida since he had received a large grant of land there, so he sent Bernard Romans, a surveyor and naturalist, to examine the coasts of east and west Florida. Romans regarded the Bay of Tampa as exceptionally well suited to harbor a large fleet of heavy ships, with the surrounding countryside capable of furnishing timber and water. James Grant Forbes, who navigated the waters of the west coast in 1803, confirmed Romans' opinion, writing in his *Sketches of Florida* that "Espiritu Santo, Tampa or Hillsborough Bay is the most spacious bay on the west coast of the peninsula . . . it may be justly considered the key to navigation of the British and Spanish islands to the leeward . . . ." Hillsborough appeared on some maps of the period, and later, as Hillsboro, and the shortened version may be regarded as a contraction. Lord Hillsborough, by then the first Marquis of Downshire, never saw his Florida domain. In 1956, however, a direct descendant, Arthur Wills Percy Wellington Blundell Trumbull Sandys Hills, Marquis of Downshire and Earl of Hillsborough, and his marchioness, Maureen, were Tampa's distinguished guests during the Gasparilla festival.

HILOLO • *Okeechobee County*
Simpson (1956) reports that the meaning of the modern Seminole word is "curlew."

HIRE'S LAKE • *Volusia County*
Owen Hires of Georgia settled here in the 1850s and gave his name to the adjacent lake.

HOBE SOUND • *Martin County*
The name is derived from the Indian pronunciation "hoe bay" of the Spanish *jove*. *See also* Jupiter. During the excitement of the land boom of the 1920s, Hobe Sound was changed to Olympia, which suggested the dwelling of the gods of classical Greece, but when the boom collapsed the old name was restored.

HOG MASTER'S LAKE • *Alachua County*
The obsolete name of what now is known as Lake Levy. Part of present-day Gainesville once was Hog Town, derived from the Hogmaster, a Seminole chief. The change of name for the Hog Town settlement came with the construction of the cross-state railroad from Fernandina to Cedar Key. *See also* Gainesville.

HOLDER • *Citrus County*
A family named Holder owned a hard rock phosphate mine here at the turn of the century.

HOLLEY • *Santa Rosa County*
Settled in 1893 and said to have been named for a Baptist minister, the Rev. W. D. Holley.

HOLLY HILL • *Volusia County*
Established about 1882 and probably named for the prevalence of holly trees along the ridge. One historian states that "one Mr. Fleming named the place in honor of his old home in Delaware."

HOLLY LAKE • *Broward County*
Annexed by Pembroke in 1980, the tidy oasis of landscaped lawns sits in the middle of the 14-mile Everglades buffer strip, a narrow slice of land sandwiched between U.S. 27 and the uninhabited area beyond.

HOLLYWOOD • *Broward County*
Established in 1921, this town was christened Hollywood-by-the-Sea by its founder, Joseph W. Young of California, whose visions for establishing a great new city and port seemed limitless. Collapse of the boom of the 1920s delayed the unfolding of these plans but ultimately, as with so many other developments in Florida, most of his dreams came true. Today Young likely would be delighted if he could see what he initiated. His dream of a deepwater port, Port Everglades, was designed by George Washington Goethals, who gained renown as an engineer for the Panama Canal.

HOLLYWOOD RIDGE FARMS • *Broward County*
Came into existence after the 1950 census and took its name from a big neighbor, Hollywood.

HOLMES COUNTY •
The twenty-seventh county, established January 8, 1848. Utley (1908) says the county received its name from Holmes Creek, the eastern boundary of the county. In turn, the creek was named for Holmes Valley, which received its name "either from an Indian chieftain who had been given the English name of Holmes or else from one Thomas J. Holmes, who settled in that vicinity from North Carolina about 1830 or 1834." Holmes Creek, an important tributary of the Choctawhatchee River, originally was known as Weekaywee Hatchee. Simpson (1956) interprets Creek *wekiwa*, "spring of water," and *hatchee*, "creek." A 1778 map showed *Weekaywehatchee* or Spring Creek. Simpson says the belief the name derived from that of an early white

settler cannot be substantiated. When Holmes County was created, he reports, the name already appears to have had considerable antiquity. After Andrew Jackson occupied Spanish Pensacola in 1818, he sent a raiding party under Captain Boyle to the "Uchee and Holmes old fields" on the Choctawhatchee. In the course of the raid, Boyle's men came upon Holmes and killed him. Holmes was a half-breed Red Stick, who with his band had fled to Florida after the Treaty of Fort Jackson. Red Sticks were a faction of the Upper Creeks, who had fought the Lower Creeks in the Creek War of the Alabama Territory. Substantial numbers of both groups had migrated to Florida and become known as Seminoles. The first county seat was at Hewett's Bluff, later known as Bear Pen. Cerro, Gordon, and Westville also served as the courthouse site. Bonifay, the present seat, was selected in 1905.

HOLMES BEACH • *Manatee County*
Situated on Anna Maria Island, this community derived its name from Jack E. Holmes, builder and developer.

HOLOPAW • *Osceola County*
This station on the abandoned Okeechobee extension of the Florida East Coast Railway bears a name apparently of recent Seminole origin. Moore-Willson (1928) translates *holopaw* as "walk" or "pavement." The naming has been credited to J. E. Ingraham, vice president of the FEC. A number of stations along the Okeechobee extension bore Indian-like names, among them Yeehaw, Pocatow, Nittaw, and Osowaw. Perhaps these were chosen for their sounds rather than their meaning.

HOMELAND • *Polk County*
One of the older communities in Polk County, known by that name since 1885. The settlement previously was known as Bethel for a Methodist church of the same name situated here. Heatherington (1928) reports "Jack McCormick, an Irish peddler, suggested the community's present name, noting that it impresses one who views it as the 'home land' of contented people."

HOMESTEAD • *Dade County*
Known as "the Homestead Country" around the turn of the century because the pineland was U. S. government-owned and subject to homestead entry. When the Florida East Coast Railway stretched its rails south from Miami in 1904, the abbreviated designation Homestead was tacked to the freight car first used as a station.

HOMOSASSA • *Citrus County*
This name has been given to two communities (Homosassa and Homosassa Springs), springs, a river, a bay, a point, and a group of islands. This does not include the Seminole settlement of Homosassa, which in 1836 was at or near the site of the present town. Homosassa Springs has a flow of 70,000 gallons a minute. Read (1934) defines Homosassa as Seminole-Creek *homo*, "pepper," and *sasi*, "is there," or "a place where wild pepper grows." There are others who like to think the name means "smoking creek" from the dense vapor that on cool days envelops the warm springs and river.

"Millions of dollars are being spent now building the city of Homosassa according to the most modern plan. What you see has been accomplished in 90 days—picture this city sixty days hence."

HONGRY LAND • *Palm Beach County*

Will (1964) says there's an area between Lake Okeechobee and the Jupiter Lighthouse "which has been known to cowmen and hunters for generations past as the Hongry Land." During the Seminole Wars, a starving band of Indians, their wives and children dying from the hardships of being fugitives so long, surrendered in the Everglades, asking only that they might be permitted to remain in Florida. An Army surgeon, James Rhett Motte, described the scene as the Army and the Indians waited for a reply from Washington. He said the Indians were a pitiful sight, especially the women. They wandered about the camp, picking up grains of corn dropped where the Army's horses had been fed and "were poor as snakes, with hardly enough clothes to cover their nakedness, being dressed in corn sacks which the soldiers had thrown away." Then the word came from Washington; the war must continue until every Indian was dead or deported. So they were shipped to Arkansas, leaving the Hongry Land.

HOPE

Defined by the *Random House Dictionary* as "the feeling that what is desired is also possible, or that events may turn out for the best." It has been the name or part of the name of a number of small Florida communities: Hope, Alachua County; Hopedale, Suwannee County; Hopeville, Hernando County; and Hopewell in Hillsborough and Madison counties.

HORSE CREEK • *Hardee County*

This tributary of the Peace River is a scene of the exploits of the legendary "Alligator" Platt, who in the 1880s would tackle alligators in the water, manage to run a thumb into the saurian's eyes and ride the 'gator ashore. He recommended this method since there was no expense for ammunition. Once the creek was known as Chillocahatchee, pronounced chi-loc-co-hát-chee. Simpson(1956) says the name was derived from the Seminole-Creek *cholako*, "horse," and *hatchee*, "creek."

HORSE LANDING • *Putnam County*
Capt. J. J. Dickison, Company H, 2nd Florida Cavalry, an adherent of guerrilla warfare along the St. Johns River during the Civil War, captured and sank the federal gunboat *Columbine* here. Knowing the *Columbine* had proceeded up the St. Johns for the purpose of capturing the *Enterprise*, Capt. Dickison planted the two guns of his single battery at Horse Landing to await the *Columbine*'s return. After an engagement lasting about 45 minutes, the *Columbine* surrendered and was burned by Capt. Dickison to prevent her recapture.

HORSESHOE BEACH • *Dixie County*
See Shelton.

HOWEY-IN-THE-HILLS • *Lake County*
First known as Howey, for its founder W. J. Howey, the "in-the-Hills" was adopted during the boom of the 1920s when the town was incorporated. Howey, a leader in the Florida Republican Party, was the GOP nominee for governor twice. He received 39 percent of the vote against Democrat Doyle E. Carlton in 1928 and 33 percent of the vote against Democrat Dave Sholtz in 1932.

HYPOLUXO • *Palm Beach County*
Perhaps an Indian name, but Read (1934) suggests some skepticism by writing "if this is a genuine Indian name," it may be connected with Seminole *hapo*, "mound, heap, or pile," and *poloski*, "round, circular." Hypoluxo therefore could refer to one of the numerous shell mounds along the coasts of Florida. However, Pierce (1970), writing of pioneer life in southeast Florida, says an Indian woman told an early arrival that Lake Worth was called Hypoluxo and that this meant "water all around, no get out"; in other words, the lake was landlocked. In a subsequent discussion of the spelling of the name of an island in the lake on which a group of early settlers proposed to settle, the group agreed upon "hypo" instead of "hippo" for the first syllables; they did not want everyone to call it "Hippoluxo."

IAMONIA • *Leon, Calhoun, and Jefferson counties*
A lake and community in Leon County, a river and slough in Calhoun County, and a lake in Jefferson County. Read (1934) reports Hiamonee was the name of an ancient Seminole town situated on the east bank of the Ochlockonee River five miles below the Georgia boundary. He traces the name from the tribal name *yamassee*, meaning "mild, peaceable."

ICHETUCKNEE • *Columbia and Suwannee counties*
This spring and its river gain their name from the Creek *wa*, "water," *echas*, "beaver," and *toka* or *tomeka*, "because of." The whole word means "a beaver pond."

IDLEWOOD • *Gulf County*
Another of those words with the savor of leisurely living.

ILLAHAW • *Osceola County*
A station on the now-abandoned Okeechobee branch of the Florida East Coast Railway. The Seminole vocabulary in Moore-Willson's *The Seminoles of Florida* (1928) says the word means "orange." *See also* Holopaw.

IMMOKALEE • *Collier County*
As early as 1869, trappers called this place Gopher Ridge. The first settlement came in 1884 when a sawmill was established to prepare lumber for the Episcopal mission to the Indians. The present name is Indian. Authorities differ as to whether it's Miccosukee-Seminole and means "his home" or "his people," or whether it's from the Cherokee *ama*, "water," and *kolola*, "tumbling." Tebeau (1966) says William "Billy" Allen, a Confederate veteran from Arcadia, settled there in 1872, building a log house. For 25 years it was known as Allen's Place. But when the time came for a post office in 1897, Episcopal Bishop William Crane Gray suggested the name should be a Seminole word with pleasant associations; hence, reports Tebeau, "The 'Allen Place' now became Immokalee, meaning 'my home'," although strictly interpreted the word is "his home."

INDIALANTIC • *Brevard County*
Born in the boom of 1925. Mrs. G. F. Duren won a contest to name it. Her name indicates its site—between Indian River and the Atlantic Ocean.

INDIAN (Names in Florida)
The Indian names in Florida, as elsewhere in this country, served to describe places in useful terms: Thus, "cow ford," "bloody creek," "rabbit creek," "sunning turtles," and "fallen tree."

So beware of Indian names which have been translated, as was *Itchepackesassa,* into such idyllic terms as "where the moon put the colors of the rainbow into the earth and the sun draws them out in the flowers." In Creek, *itchepackesassa,* pronounced itch-e-puck-ah-sas-sa, simply meant "tobacco field."

Stewart (1945) explained that Indian names were signposts, distinguishing one place from another but within a relatively small area. A big river seldom had the same name throughout its course. As Stewart wrote, a tribe often had no idea where its rivers came from or went to.

Too, there was no universal Indian language. "To say that a name is Indian is even less than to say that it is European, for among the tribes the languages differed much more than English from French, Dutch, or Russian," said Stewart.

The standard work for this state is Simpson's *Florida Place-Names of Indian Derivation,* edited by Dr. Mark F. Boyd of Tallahassee and critically reviewed by Robert B. Campbell of Fort Myers, both excellent scholars, before publication by the Florida Geological Survey in 1956. Simpson was an employee of the Survey and the editing and publication of the work which was his avocation was undertaken by the Survey, Dr. Boyd and Mr. Campbell as a memorial.

As observed in *Florida Place-Names,* the native Florida tribes who were numerous and powerful for a century and a half after the discovery of America have contributed little to the catalog of Florida names. They disappeared long ago, and with the exception of the Timucua, little or nothing is known of their languages.

As Simpson's book states:

"We are immediately impressed by the observation that most of the surviving Indian place-names are derived from the language of those immigrant bands from the North who moved into Florida after the decline and disappearance of the native Floridians. The newcomers were principally speakers of Hitchiti and Creek, or of other tribes whose language indicated affiliation with the basic Muskogean linguistic stock."

Simpson cautions it should be remembered that none of the old Indian languages had a written form with either an original alphabet of any description or an established orthography. The various Europeans who heard their spoken words and attempted to express them in writing followed the usage of their own language.

Another authoritative book in the field of names is Read's *Florida Place Names of Indian Origin and Seminole Personal Names* (1934). Moore-Willson, in *The Seminoles of Florida* (1928), provides a useful vocabulary of the Seminole language.

I N D I A N C R E E K V I L L A G E • *Dade County*
Incorporated in 1939, this municipality is an island in Indian Creek from which it draws its name.

I N D I A N F O R D • *Santa Rosa County*
The railroad crosses a branch of Sweetwater Creek here, as did the Indians.

I N D I A N H A R B O U R B E A C H • *Brevard County*
So named in 1955 because traces of an Indian village were found here on the shore of a sheltered cove on the Banana River.

I N D I A N K E Y • *Monroe County*
The Spanish had an Indian trading post here, although mariners feared this and nearby keys both for the many hidden reefs and for the ferocity of the Calusa Indians. The key for a time bore the name of *Matanza* (Spanish for "slaughter") because several hundred shipwrecked French were slaughtered here by the Calusas about 1755. Indian Key is remembered today principally as the place of the murder of Dr. Henry Perrine, a renowned botanist who came here with his family in the 1830s to conduct experiments in tropical plants and trees. Indians raided the key on August 7, 1840, killing Dr. Perrine and six others and looting and burning the store of Jacob Housman. Dr. Perrine's wife, son, and daughter escaped by hiding in a turtle crawl under their burning house, standing in water up to their shoulders.

INDIAN LAKE ESTATES • *Polk County*
Founded in the 1950s, this was one of the first big-scale land developments in Florida after the renewal of interest in the state following the collapse of the boom of the 1920s.

INDIANOLA • *Brevard County*
Mr. and Mrs. John E. Field, who came here in the 1880s, wanted another name but it already was in use as a post office, so they settled upon Indianola, reminiscent of the Indian mounds in the area.

INDIAN PASS • *Gulf County*
Indians are supposed to have followed this pass in traveling between the mainland and St. Vincent Island. The Spanish Mission of Cape San Blas once stood near here.

INDIAN RIVER •
A lagoon, from one to five miles wide, extending along the Atlantic coast approximately 100 miles from just north of Titusville to Stuart. The river is open to the Atlantic at several points, and for its entire length is a section of the Intracoastal Waterway. Once the Ais Indians lived on its shore. Following them were Seminoles and Creeks, who called the stream the River of Ais. The meaning of *ais* is not known, although some have felt it meant "deer."

INDIAN RIVER COUNTY •
The sixty-fifth county, established May 30, 1925. Named for the Indian River, which flows through it.

The Smith brothers homestead on the Indian River, about 1887.

INDIAN RIVER CITY • *Brevard County*
On U.S. 1 at the intersection of the old highway to Orlando, this community was first settled in 1850. It had its ups and downs until 1912, when Edgar Mills began land development. For a time, the landmark for travelers along the Dixie Highway was a filling station and restaurant owned by Frank Clark. Motorists knew the community as Clark's Corners better than by its formal name.

INDIAN RIVER SHORES • *Indian River County*
Named for its location on the shores of the Indian River.

INDIAN ROCKS BEACH • *Pinellas County*
Along the shore are a number of large red rocks, which gave the community its present name. On early maps it is known as St. Clements Point. The surrounding country has been settled since 1840.

INDIAN ROCKS BEACH SOUTH SHORE • *Pinellas County*
One of Pinellas County's smallest towns but with the longest name. It is one of eleven separate municipalities that have grown up astride the long stretch of barrier reef islands just off the Pinellas coast. It uses the phrase South Shore to distinguish it from neighboring Indian Rocks Beach. To ease the burden on everyone, residents here, in a referendum on July 25, 1973, selected a new name, Indian Shores.

INDIAN SHORES •
See Indian Rocks Beach South Shore.

INDIAN SPRINGS • *Volusia County*
Established in 1883, this community's name recalls a spring here said to have been used by Indians.

INDIANTOWN • *Martin County*
Once a trading center for the Seminole Indians.

INDRIO • *St. Lucie County*
Founded as Viking in 1898, the community in 1919 was given the name of Indrio, for the nearby Indian River, with the addition of the Spanish *rio* for "river."

INGLIS • *Levy County*
Named for Capt. John Inglis, whose family came from Glasgow, Scotland. He skippered a ship from Spain to the mouth of the Withlacoochee River during the 1800s and traded with the few inhabitants of this area. A community known as Port Inglis sprang up at the river's mouth, then the intersection of the "highways" of the Withlacoochee and the Gulf. Some time later, a new community, named simply Inglis, grew up around a chemical plant eight miles upriver from the port. Its original name was Blind Horse. Later, as roads developed and the inland population grew, ship trading declined and with it Port Inglis. But Inglis grew.

INTERCESSION CITY • *Osceola County*
Known first as Inter Ocean City, because the boom-time subdivision was midway between the Atlantic Ocean and the Gulf of Mexico, the area afterwards became the seat of a non-denominational Christian sect.

INTERLACHEN • *Putnam County*
Settled in 1872 and first known as Wilcox. The present name is Scottish, meaning "between the lakes."

INVERNESS • *Citrus County*
A Scottish settler gave the name of the ancient capital of the Scottish northern highlands to this town on the shores of 18-mile-long Lake Tsala Apopka. It is the county seat of Citrus County.

IOLA • *Gulf County*
Settled as early as 1838, and may have been a Seminole camp from 1823. Read interprets the name as *yahola*, a ceremonial cry. The name also formed part of the title of chiefs. Osceola was corrupted from *asi yahola*.

IONA • *Lee County*
John and David Bain, settling here in 1907, gave the community the name of an island off the coast of their native Scotland.

ISLAMORADA • *Monroe County*
Viewed from the sea, Upper Matecumbe Key, which this community straddles, often appears mauve or lilac-tinted, hence, *Islamorada*, Spanish for "purple island." Here the Labor Day hurricane of 1935 overturned cars of a train dispatched to evacuate veterans of World War I, remnants of the popularly called Bonus Expeditionary Force, or Bonus Army, which had been enlisted by the Florida Emergency Relief Administration to close gaps in the Overseas Highway from the mainland to Key West. After the wind and water of the Labor Day hurricane swept Windley Key and Lower Matecumbe Key, 282 of the 684 veterans encamped were dead or missing. Civilian dead were officially placed at 164, although there were higher estimates. The storm destroyed sections of the Florida East Coast Railway tracks, but the great bridges emerged undamaged and later were used to support a highway.

ISLANDIA • *Dade County*
Mrs. John Nordt of Miami writes that Islandia, on Elliott Key, was given its name by William Krome of Homestead. Mrs. Nordt said the Islandia of the ancients was identified with Ultima Thule, the highest degree obtainable or the limit of any journey. Islandia struggled for existence as an independent municipality, but the state and federal governments combined to merge Elliot, Sands, Old Rhodes, and smaller keys into the Biscayne National Monument off the lower Dade County coast.

ISLAND GROVE • *Alachua County*
A high hammock among flatlands, settled in the 1880s. Here, unusually tall cabbage palms tower over citrus groves. Island Grove is famous as the *Cross Creek* of Marjorie Kinnan Rawlings, who wrote *South Moon Under* and *The Yearling*, novels of the adjacent scrub land.

ISRAEL'S DISH • *Polk County*
The lakes from which Lakeland derived its name were named by association with people or objects, relates Heatherington (1928). Lake Parker was named for Streety Parker, who built his cabin nearby. Lake Bonny originally was Lake Boney, named for an Indian fighter. Lake Bonnet was covered with water lilies (bonnets). Lake Beulah recalled an attractive visitor. Lake Wire originally was Israel's Dish but was renamed when the telegraph line from Ocala to Punta Rassa came through Lakeland and was routed around the lake.

ISTACHATTA • *Hernando County*
A combination of Creek *iste,* "man," and *chatta,* "red," or "red man" or Indian.

ISTOKPOGA • *Highlands County*
This lake and community derive their name from the Creek *iste,* "man," and *poga,* "finished," signifying "a dead man." An 1838 map uses the name Drowned Man's Lake.

ISTO POGA YOXEE LAKE • *Polk County*
This name appears to be the Creek combination of *iste,* "man," *poga,* "finished or dead," and chee, "little," or "Little Dead Man" Lake. Another source suggests *isti,* "people," *poga,* "reside," and *i-uska,* "at the end of," or "People live at the end of it." The lake now is known as Reedy Lake.

ITABO • *Citrus County*
Read conjectures that this name, recently applied in Florida, probably is a corruption of the Creek *italwa,* "a town or tribe."

ITCHEPACKESASSA • *Hillsborough County*
From the Creek *heche,* "tobacco," *puc,* "blossom," and *sasse,* "there are," or put together, "tobacco field." The place is now Plant City. *See also* Cork.

IZAGORA • *Holmes County*
Founded in the 1880s by Whithall Curry, pastor of a church by the same name which he also founded. The meaning of the name is not known.

JACKSON COUNTY •
The third county, established August 12, 1822. Named for Andrew Jackson, who had been U.S. commissioner and governor of the territories of East and West Florida and later became seventh president of the United States.

JACKSONVILLE • *Duval County*
There has been some kind of crossing of the St. Johns River at this point as far back as history can be traced. The Timucuan Indians called it *wacca pilatka,* meaning "place where cows cross," though of course the Indians had never seen cattle until the Spaniards brought them, and *wacca* is a variant of the Spanish *vaca,* "cow." Among the Spanish names for the area were the Pass of San Nicolas (Fort San Nicolas was nearby) and the place where cows cross. When the British gained possession of Florida in 1763, the name became Cow Ford. This name was revived by American settlers of Spanish Florida in the

Andrew Jackson, for whom Jackson County is named, served as Governor of the territories of East and West Florida from March 10th to December 31st 1821.

early 1800s. In 1822, under the urging of Isaiah D. Hart, a settler from south Georgia, a town site was surveyed. Newnan, Market, Liberty, and Washington streets were laid out and named. Crossing these, Bay, Forsyth, Adams, Monroe, and Duval formed a 20-block area. Snodgrass (1969) reports John Warren, a settler who had served under Andrew Jackson as a soldier, suggested Jacksonville as the name, and this name was agreed upon without dissent. With so much known, the tantalizing fact is that so far no record has been found of the exact date in June 1822 when the city officially came into being. Probably the events were spread over a number of days. Every city must have a birthday, however, so Jacksonville has selected June 15, the date when the settlers petitioned Congress for recognition as a port of entry. Jacksonville is the county seat of Duval County.

JACKSONVILLE BEACH • *Duval County*
A seaside town about 18 miles southeast of Jacksonville and taking its name now from that city. It was at first called Ruby and later Pablo Beach. *See also* Atlantic Beach.

JAMESTOWN • *Alachua County*
See Hawthorne.

JANNEY • *Levy County*
When Janney reached the status of having a post office of its own, Louis Janney, the postmaster, was honored.

JAN PHYL VILLAGE • *Polk County*
Mr. Lesnick, a developer, had two daughters, Janice and Phyllis.

JASPER • *Hamilton County*
Fragmentary reports give record of a trading post here as early as 1830, established by families from Georgia and South Carolina. It was somewhat informally designated as Micco Town, the word thought to have been a reference to a tribe of Miccosukee Indians who lived nearby. In 1850, the town was incorporated as Jasper, in memory of the Revolutionary War hero Sgt. William Jasper, who rescued the American flag during the British assault on Fort Sullivan, now Fort Moultrie, in 1776, and who was later killed at age 29 in the siege of Savannah. County seat of Hamilton County.

JAY • *Santa Rosa County*
First named Pine Level. Two nearby post offices, which have since passed out of existence, were called Cora and Nora. When a post office was established here, it is thought to have been named from the first initial of J. T. Nowling, who owned a store here in 1900 and was appointed postmaster in 1902.

JAY-JAY • *Brevard County*
This center for the shipment of Indian River citrus took its name in 1914 from the J. J. Parrish packinghouse.

JEFFERSON COUNTY •
The thirteenth county, established January 20, 1827. Named for Thomas Jefferson, president of the United States, who had died on July 4 of the year preceding the county's founding.

JENNINGS • *Hamilton County*
Two men by the name of Jennings may have contributed the name of this town. Robert Jennings settled here in 1860, operating a farm and general store. George Jennings came to this vicinity in 1884 on a raft by way of the Alapaha River. This was an important shipping point for Sea Island cotton in the days before World War I and the boll weevil.

JENSEN BEACH • *Martin County*
Dates from 1890 and, after the promotional fashion of coastal communities, added Beach to its name in 1943.

JOHNS PASS • *Pinellas County*
An entry from the Gulf of Mexico into Boca Ceiga Bay, separating the communities of Madeira Beach and Treasure Island. Early maps called it St. Johns Pass, and it was likely named by an English surveyor. There is a belief that Pánfilo de Narváez landed his ill-fated expedition near here in 1528 and marched north in search of rich cities, but found death instead.

JONESVILLE • *Taylor County*
Near the mouth of Blue Creek on the Gulf of Mexico and known now as Adam's Beach, it was a center for salt works during the Civil War and afterwards. Taylor County's 50-mile coastline and shallow coastal waters made this ideal for manufacturing salt for the Confederacy. Trading on a barter basis, the region furnished salt for adjacent areas of Florida, including Tallahassee and south Georgia, receiving in return meat, grain, and other necessities. The salt industry escaped Union raiders and continued operations until 1868.

JULIETTE • *Marion County*
See Romeo.

JUNE PARK • *Brevard County*
Communities follow transportation. In Florida's first days, the settlements were at ports. Next, cities sprang up as railroads spread. Now, interstate highway interchanges are spawning communities. June Park, on I-95, appears to be one of those.

JUNIPER • *Gadsden County*
With Sawdust and Wetumpka, it is among the pre-Civil War communities of Gadsden County. Stanley (1948) said these communities were in "the noted small farm area of the county where 'dirt farmers' cultivate their own land, live in comfortable homes, and raise fine children."

JUNO BEACH • *Palm Beach County*
Named for the consort of Jupiter, it used to be the county seat of Dade County before Palm Beach County was organized. A tiny, narrow-gauge railroad used to run the eight miles from Jupiter to Juno. Other stations of this "celestial railroad" were Mars and Venus. Trains ran from Jupiter to Juno, then had to back up all the way to Jupiter.

JUPITER • *Palm Beach County*
A fascinating story explains how this community came to be named after a Roman god. The Indians called the place *jobe* or *jove* from the Indian names *xega, jega,* and *jeaga.* Pronounced "hoe-bay," the name stuck to nearby Hobe Sound. But English mapmakers saw Jobe and Jove and wrote Jupiter. The name inspired the names of Juno, Mars, and Venus for nearby towns. Jupiter Inlet Beach Colony and Jupiter Island in Martin County are recent communities that have adopted part of the old name. There also is a Jupiter Inlet connecting the Jupiter River to the

The keeper's house is under construction in this 1883 view of Jupiter lighthouse.

Atlantic Ocean. DuBois (1968) says the incoming tide through Jupiter Inlet brings clear, blue-green water far up the Loxahatchee River to a fork where Gen. Thomas S. Jesup's soldiers raised the palmetto log stockade of Fort Jupiter after the Battle of the Loxahatchee on January 20, 1838, in the Second Seminole War. *See also* Galaxy, Juno Beach.

KANAPAHA • *Alachua County*
This name has been given to a settlement, a prairie, a lake, and to sinks. Spelled Kanapahaw, the community appears on an 1839 map. Simpson (1956) believes this name to be a relic from the period when Timucua Indians inhabited the region. Likely from the Timucua words *cani,* "palmetto leaves," and *paha,* "house." Simpson said the Timucuans built large structures of poles thatched with palmetto leaves or bark.

KATHLEEN • *Polk County*
Heatherington (1928) reports the community was said to have been named for Mrs. Catherine Prine, who moved to that section from Hillsborough County as a small child, and died there in August 1916 at the age of 76. "The first reference to the place we find in print gives the spelling as Cathleen," wrote Heatherington. "That was in 1887." The postal register says the community first was entered as Polish in April 1886 and changed to Kathleen in July of the same year.

KENANSVILLE • *Osceola County*
Formerly a station on the Okeechobee extension of the Florida East Coast
Railway, the place in 1914 was given the family name of the third Mrs. Henry
M. Flagler, the former Miss Mary Lily Kenan of Chapel Hill, N.C. Flagler was
the builder of the Florida East Coast Railway and its affiliated hotel,
steamship, and land companies.

KENDALL • *Dade County*
A post office was established here in 1914 and named for Maj. Kendall, resident vice president of the British Land Company, which owned groves and
other agricultural land.

KENNETH CITY • *Pinellas County*
Sidney Colen developed this community and named it for his only son,
Kenneth. It was incorporated in 1957 when Kenneth was six years old.

KEUKA • *Putnam County*
Said to have been named in 1883 for a settler, W. L. Keuka, although it may
have been a transplant from New York, where there is a lake in Yates County
which has the Iroquoian name for "landing place." The word is thought by
Read to be identical with *cayuga*, a geographical name also native to New York
but now found elsewhere.

KEY BISCAYNE • *Dade County*
Known as the site of the Cape Florida Lighthouse and as a protective barrier
between the Atlantic Ocean and Biscayne Bay. Douglas (1967) said this was
the sandy cape John Cabot in 1499 had named the Cape of the End of April
and where Juan Ponce de León in 1513 had, within Cape Florida, "found the
bright nameless great bay that John Cabot had seen." *See also* Cape Florida.
The lighthouse here was completed in 1825 and remains one of the oldest
structures in south Florida. A temporary Army post, Fort Bankhead, was established here during the Seminole War of 1838. For residents of metropolitan
Miami, Key Biscayne became accessible by motor vehicle during the 1940s
with the building of the Rickenbacker Causeway and development of an out-
standing recreation area, Crandon Park. Rickenbacker took its name from the
World War I flying ace, E. V. "Eddie" Rickenbacker, and Crandon from Dade
County Commissioner Charles H. Crandon, who was the spark plug in public acquisition and development of the oceanside park. Key Biscayne became
a nationally recognized place name through the establishment here of a satellite White House during the administration of President Richard M. Nixon.

KEY COLONY BEACH • *Monroe County*
As the name suggests, this resort and development is situated in the Keys,
about midway between the mainland and Key West.

KEY LARGO • *Monroe County*
"Key Largo," a motion picture starring Humphrey Bogart and Lauren Bacall,
was filmed here and named for this lovely island. A town on the key was once
known as Rock Harbor, but developers sought to cash in on the movie's publicity by having the name of the post office changed to Key Largo in 1952.

Some seventeenth-century maps described the key as *caio de dose leguas,* "the key of twelve leagues" (Hathway, 1967). Twelve times the Spanish league of the seventeenth century would be 29 miles, roughly the length of the island. Key Largo is never more than three miles wide, and Hathaway says its Spanish name has been translated variously as "large island," "long island," and "small big island."

KEYS •
See Florida Keys.

KEYSTONE • *Hillsborough County*
During the 1880s, when many Florida communities maintained a shotgun quarantine to warn off travelers from areas affected by yellow fever, Keystone was the place where mail was left for summer campers along the Gulf coast in the vicinity of Clearwater. Straub (1929) tells how the postman would ride over, "selecting his own mail, stained with disinfectant to protect the receiver from yellow fever!"

KEYSTONE HEIGHTS • *Clay County*
New York and Pennsylvania have shared in the naming of this town. It was originally called Brooklyn. In 1922, J. J. Lawrence of Pittsburgh, Pa., settled here and was responsible for the adoption of the present name in honor of his home state, the Keystone State.

KEYSVILLE • *Hillsborough County*
A sawmill erected here in the 1870s supplied lumber for many of the pioneer homes in east Hillsborough County.

KEY VACA • *Monroe County*
Possibly the name antedates St. Augustine inasmuch as the chief of the Map Division of the Library of Congress reported (Brigham, 1957) the key appeared (as "C. d bacas") on a map that evidently was made between 1519 and 1565, since Havana is shown but St. Augustine is not. The antiquity of the place name is beyond dispute, but the meaning never has been settled. Perhaps there was a person named Vacas (or a name of that sound). Local legend attributed the English translation of *vaca* ("cow") to cattle here, but nothing has been found to substantiate this theory. Charles M. Brookfield, field representative of the National Audubon Society, once questioned the cow theory on the basis of the limited grazing area and the swarms of mosquitoes and other insects in the early days. Brookfield believes a more likely source would have been the sea cows or manatees once so prevalent in the area. Key Vaca long was the southernmost key on which freshwater could be obtained by drilling. During the construction of the Overseas Extension of the Florida East Coast Railway from the mainland to Key West, two unusual types of boats visited here—liquor boats enjoying a brisk trade among some of the workers and a "gospel boat" dispatched by Key West churches to serve the spiritual needs of the workers.

KEY WEST • *Monroe County*
One of the strangest and most amusing examples of moving names from one

language to another not by meaning but by sound—what the professors call folk etymology. Early Spanish explorers are said to have found quantities of human bones on this island, presumably the result of a battle between Indian tribes. The Spaniards called the island Cayo Hueso (pronounced "wesso")— Bone Island. It just happens that this is the westernmost of the string of islands which extends from the tip of the Florida peninsula, so it was easy to transliterate "hueso" into "west." Later U.S. settlers have tried on several occasions to give it more dignified names: for example, Thompson's Island, Port Rogers, Allentown. These were all made from the names of officials and heroes of the U. S. Navy. The last honored Lt. W. H. Allen, who, in November 1822, in command of the schooner U.S.S. *Alligator,* pursued a fleet of eight pirate vessels. He had 40 men against 125 in the pirate party; his men had muskets, swords, and pistols, while the pirates had 14 cannon. The Navy vessel took five of the pirate ships, but Allen was wounded twice and died before final victory; his name became a Navy war cry. However, neither his name nor the others stuck to the town on the island, which has remained Key West. It was first settled in 1822 by John Simonton, who purchased it from a Spaniard, Juan P. Salas, to whom it had been granted by the Spanish monarchy. The city of Key West is the county seat of Monroe County.

Key West's Last Chance bar was also the First Chance bar depending on whether you were going to the waterfront or coming from the waterfront in the 1900s.

KICCO • *Polk County*
A cattle gathering station was established here in 1918 by the Kissimmee Island Cattle Company, whose initials became the name of the settlement.

KILLARNEY • *Orange County*
The numerous lakes in the area are believed to have reminded an early settler, in the 1870s, of the famed lakes of Killarney in Ireland.

KINGSLEY • *Clay County*
The town and lake recall Zephaniah Kingsley, who in 1817 purchased the John Houston McIntosh plantation on Fort George Island, which remains of visitor interest today. Kingsley Lake once was known to aviators as Dollar Lake because its roundness resembled a silver dollar.

KINGS ROAD •
A street and highway in Jacksonville built in the 1770s by the British, then owners of Florida, and named for the king of England. This was a graded road and the first road in Florida wide enough to accommodate wheeled vehicles; other overland passageways were trails. Today the Kings Road is the principal reminder of British days in northeast Florida. The route of the old road approximates U.S. 1. It was originally planned to connect Florida, especially St. Augustine and Cow Ford (now Jacksonville), with the British colonies to the north and to encourage settlers to come into the province.

KISMET • *Lake County*
The name means "fate" or "destiny." It was founded in 1884 by the Kismet Land and Improvement Company near Lake Door in what now is the Ocala National Forest. There was a 50-room hotel for winter visitors. Kismet flourished until the great freeze of 1889 destroyed the groves and crops. Kennedy (1929) describes the fate of the hotel: It was torn down and hauled to Eustis. "Each piece was carefully preserved and the building set up on the corner of Grove Street and Magnolia Avenue exactly as it had stood at Kismet, and was named the Grand View Hotel of Eustis. Its timber was all from virgin pine and it is as good today as when it was first cut."

KISSENGEN SPRINGS • *Polk County*
The picnic area around the springs was a traditional place for political rallies in the days before the 1940s, but as the springs dried up so did the flow of oratory.

KISSIMMEE • *Osceola County*
An Indian name for which no authority has been able to find a definitive origin. This difficulty was encountered by some of the Indians, too. Even Seminoles in modern times do not seem to know the name's origin, although they say that Indians named the city. The Indians referred to were presumably the Ais Caloosas, a tribe antedating the Seminoles and slaughtered by De Soto's cavalcade about 1540. Ethnologists at the Smithsonian Institution ascribe the origin of Kissimmee to these Indians. Simpson (1946) used Kissimmee as an example of the pitfalls of trying to translate Indian words into English or any other language simply by the sound of syllables or words. Writing in *Apalachee,* the journal of the Tallahassee Historical Society, Simpson said examples of this error could be found in the popular interpretations advanced for the names Micanopy and Kissimmee. "Whereas these names do sound like 'Me-can-no-pay' and 'Kiss-him-me,' the first has no connection with ability to pay and the second has no connection with amorous activities of some early Indian maiden." The modern town, which is the

county seat of Osceola County, was founded before the Civil War by the Bass, Johnson, and Overstreet families and has long been a center of the cattle industry. In 1881, Hamilton Disston gave impetus to the town through his drainage activities and sugar-growing empire. The town is located on Lake Tohopekaliga, meaning "fort site," according to Simpson.

KNIGHTS • *Hillsborough County*
Settled in the 1880s and named for William Knight.

KOMOKO • *Alachua County*
W. W. Cummer of Cadillac, Mich., came to Jacksonville in 1896, established the Cummer Lumber Company and shipped in logs from north central counties. He named one of the company's staging areas after a Michigan Indian chief Komoka, misspelling the name with a final "o" instead of "a," according to Waldo E. Cummer, son of W. W. Cummer, who reported to Read (1934).

KORONA • *Flagler County*
Polish settlers in 1918 adopted the Latin *corona*, "crown," but with a "K" instead of a "C."

KOSTA, LAKE • *Polk County*
Known now as Tiger Lake, Kosta was derived from the Creek *katcha*, "tiger or panther."

KREAMER ISLAND • *Palm Beach County*
Really two islands in Lake Okeechobee, Kreamer Island was named for Hamilton Disston's chief engineer in the drainage of the Everglades. The postal register had trouble with the spelling. From 1918 until 1932 it was listed as Kraemer and from 1932 until discontinuance of the office in 1936 as Kreamer.

KYNESVILLE • *Jackson County*
Named for the Kynes family which settled here in the 1870s.

LA **BELLE** • *Hendry County*
The county seat of Hendry County, it was named by Capt. Francis Asbury Hendry for two of his daughters, Laura and Belle.

LACOOCHEE • *Pasco County*
A shortened form of Withlacoochee, from the Withlacoochee River. Historian John R. Swanton thinks that Chief Hurripacuxi lived somewhere in this vicinity.

LA CROSSE • *Alachua County*
Settled some time prior to 1885, by people who came from La Crosse, Wis. That town, in its turn, derived its name from the Indian ball game, to which the French had given the name lacrosse, and which was regularly played at that spot.

LADY LAKE • *Lake County*
A village near here had been named Slighville. When the railroad came through in 1884, the residents moved to this site in order to be on it. Railroad authorities wanted to call the place Cooper, but the settlers preferred a more picturesque name. The Indians had already named the lake here Lady Lake, because of an unknown white woman who drowned in it, and the town took its name from that.

LAFAYETTE COUNTY •
The thirty-third county, established December 23, 1856. Named for the Marquis de Lafayette (as was Fayette County), 1757-1834. Lafayette pleaded the cause of American independence at home, lent both his prestige and military knowledge by serving as major general in the American Revolutionary Army, and spent about $200,000 of his private fortune on behalf of the colonies. After his imprisonment and the confiscation of his estates during the French Reign of Terror, Lafayette looked to the United States to save his family from poverty. After other gifts of money and land, Congress in December 1824, appropriated $200,000 and a grant of a township of land anywhere in the unsold public domain. President Monroe was hopeful that Lafayette, then in the United States, should become a resident of Florida. As Kathryn T. Abbey (Hanna) wrote in the *Florida Historical Quarterly* (January 1932), "The General himself was keenly interested in the proposition, for while in Washington, he had come under the magnetic spell of Richard Keith Call, Florida's representative and her most ardent champion. A strong friendship grew up between the two men and before they separated, Lafayette halfway promised to visit Florida." While Lafayette did choose a township in Florida at Tallahassee, the visit never was to be. Only once was a Lafayette in Florida: in 1850, when Edmond de Lafayette and Ferdinand de Lasteyrie, grandsons of the marquis, visited the United States and conferred with their American land agent. The last of the Lafayette land was sold in 1855, although this could have been accomplished years earlier if Lafayette had not wished to experiment with the cultivation by free labor of vineyards, olive groves, mulberry trees, and silkworms. Some 50 to 60 Normans unsuccessfully tried to reproduce the agriculture of the Old World on a bluff overlooking Lake Lafayette. The Lafayette Grant, as the township is known, is formally Township 1 North, Range 1 East, bounded in today's Tallahassee by Meridian Road on the west, approximately Gaines Street on the south, and extends six miles to the east and six miles to the north. The popularity of Lafayette in the United States was such that 40 places were named for him.

LAKE COUNTY •
The forty-third county was established May 27, 1887, being taken from Orange and Sumter counties. Named for the large number of lakes within its boundaries. In 1969, Lake County had 505 lakes either named or unnamed of ten acres or more.

LAKES (of Florida)   •
With 7,712 lakes identified by the State Department of Environmental Protection, Floridians have had ample opportunity to break away from the inclination to seek names for cities which, in recent years, were intended to create the image of a good place to live, or in earlier years, honored railroad officers, postmasters and early settlers.

When it came to naming a lake or pond near a homestead or fishing spot, people usually said what they thought. Cockroach Creek in Hillsborough County is an example of some now-forgotten incident that resulted in a place name. It is easy to guess what resulted in the naming of the two Baptizing Ponds in Washington County and the Baptizing Hole in Sumter County.

Sunday picnics come to mind with the names of the six lakes or ponds called Dinner. Booze Lake in Madison County well could commemorate a pioneer family of that name rather than something alcoholic. There's a Beer Can Pond in Leon County. And there's a Polecat Lake in Polk County, a Starvation Lake in Hillsborough County, a Yankee Lake in Seminole, a Stealing Lake in Walton County, an Up and Down Lake in Putnam, a Squaw Pond in Marion County, a Lake Confusion in Polk County, a River Styx Lake in Alachua County, five lakes called Hiawatha, a Kitchen Cow House Pond in Levy County, a Camel Pond in Liberty County, a Lake Hellen Blazes in Brevard, and, wonder of wonder, a Lake Morality in Franklin County.

Repetitive names include: 37 variations of Sand Lake, including Sand Mountain Pond in Washington County; 59 names prefaced by "Little," including Little Hell Lake in Suwannee County; 29 Long Lakes or Ponds; 27 versions of Mud Lake or Pond; 20 Silver Lakes; 17 Black Lakes; 14 Buck Lakes; 15 Crystal Lakes; 12 Duck Ponds; 12 Horseshoe Lakes; five Rattlesnake Lakes or Ponds; and three Red Bug Lakes.

Sentiment likely dictated the frequent use of the names of women to identify lakes. The roll call of these include: Ada, Adelaide, Alice, Alma, Amelia, Ann, Anna Maria, Annette, Annie, Bess, Bessie, Blanche, Caroline, Carrie, Catharine or Catherine, Cathy, Charlotte, Cindy, Clara, Claire, Cloe, Cora Lee, Daisy, Dora, Effie, Elizabeth, Ella, Ellen, Erin, Fanny, Florence, Frances, Gertrude, Grace, Helen, Hettie, Hilda, Ida, Idamere, Irene, Jane, Jennie, Jessie, Jewel, Josephine, Katherine, Kathryn, Kitty, Lou, Lena, Lenore, Lillian, Lily, Lizzie, Louisa, Louise, Lucie, Lucy, Lulu, Mable, Margaret, Maria, Marie, Martha, Mary, Mary Ann, Mary Jane, Minnie, Miranda, Molly, Myrtle, Nan, Nellie, Nona, Ola, Opal, Sara, Sarah, Stella, Susan, Susannah, Sylvia, Victoria, Virginia, Violet, Violette, Wilma, and Yvonne.

Anyone not yet honored has plenty of opportunity for this to be done. The census taken in 1969 by the State Department of Conservation, itself now renamed the Department of Environmental Protection, showed literally hundreds of unnamed lakes.

NOTE: Lakes (when listed without reference to the community which takes its name from a lake) are listed in this book by their names: for example, Lake Okeechobee appears as Okeechobee, Lake.

L A K E   A L F R E D • *Polk County*
A number of less poetic names were used for this community before the present one was selected in 1913. The first of these was Fargo, after Fargo, N.D., from whence came a number of those interested in the Fruitlands Company, which developed this area. This was discarded because of postal confusion with Largo, Fla. Next came Chubb (derivation unknown), which was discarded for reasons of uneuphoniousness. Bartow Junction was tried, but Bartow was 15 miles away and folks here didn't want to be considered suburbanites. The present name was taken from the nearest large lake, which had been named for Alfred Parslow, who came to Florida in 1877 with $10,000 received from injuries in a railroad wreck at Ashtabula, Ohio. With this nest egg, Parslow and a friend, William Van Fleet, procured a charter to build the first railroad through north-central Polk County, the ambitiously named Jacksonville, Tampa and Key West, which ran between Kissimmee and Tampa. President Cleveland is said to have fished in this lake when he came to Florida for recreation.

L A K E   B U E N A   V I S T A • *Orange County*
With Bay Lake, this is one of the twin cities which serve the municipal needs of Disney World. For a while, Lake Buena Vista was called the city of Reedy Creek. There also is a Buena Vista community and a Reedy Creek in Osceola and Polk counties.

L A K E   B U T L E R • *Union County*
Named for Col. Robert Butler, who received the surrender of East Florida from the Spaniards on July 10, 1821, this community became the county seat of Union County in 1921. There is a 420-acre Lake Butler here, and the community likely took its name from the lake when the first settlement occurred in the 1840s. Continuous religious services have been held since 1844 on the site of the Mount Zion Primitive Baptist Church.

L A K E   C I T Y • *Columbia County*
The present name was bestowed in 1858 by an act of the legislature, having been selected by Mrs. James M. Baker, wife of an early Lake City attorney. The name refers to the myriad lakes which surround the city. An earlier name had been Alligator, after an Indian chief, Halpatter Tustenugee, "alligator warrior." Alligator Lake, near the city, was named for the same chief. It may have been the site of the Indian town Uriutina. When the legislature was asked to change the name from Alligator to Lake City, a puckish House member moved to amend by substituting Crocodile for Lake. Fortunately for the Lake City boosters, the amendment failed. This is the county seat of Columbia County.

L A K E   C L A R K E   S H O R E S • *Palm Beach County*
The developer named the community for the lake on which it fronts. In turn, the lake took its name from the Clarke family of Pittsburgh, Pa., which once had a fishing lodge on the lake.

Aggie Jones, a former slave, maintained a Lake City garden between 1900 and 1918 with trellises, gateways and arches of animal bones. She charged no admission but usually had flowers and vegetables for sale.

LAKE COMO • *Putnam County*
The settlement was begun in 1871 by E. C. Post and others and named Woodland. The change to Lake Como occurred in 1877 and likely because someone was reminded of the Italian lake.

LAKE FERN • *Hillsborough County*
A luxuriant growth of wild ferns by a nearby lake likely was responsible for both the lake and the settlement gaining their names. The community is said to date from 1914.

LAKE GENEVA • *Clay County*
Purcell's map of 1778 referred to the present lake as the Great Pond. The Old Spanish Trail passed nearby. The lake and community likely took their names from the Swiss lake and city. The lake, with a surface area of two and three-quarter miles, long has been a popular recreational area. There are four other lakes named Geneva in Florida: two in Lake County, and one each in Hernando and Seminole counties.

LAKE HAMILTON • *Polk County*
The origin of the name of the lake on which the town is situated, and from which it takes its own name, is obscure. It seems formerly to have been spelled "Hambleton," ruling out the obvious Alexander. The town was established in 1913. The lake itself has a shoreline of 35 miles; there are seven smaller lakes within the town site. The town is called "The Top of Florida."

LAKE HARBOR • *Palm Beach County*
Named for its location on Lake Okeechobee where the Miami drainage canal leaves the lake. Originally named Ritta in 1912, an example of how man proposes but Washington (D.C.) sometimes disposes. When the Okeechobee Fruitlands Company began to build a hotel to accommodate prospective land buyers the company was bringing into the area, a post office was needed. The community settled on the name Rita, which was understood to mean "small" and "lovely." However, "when the community sent in an application for the establishment of a post office, a careless clerk in Washington, D.C., put an extra 't' in the name and made it Ritta" (Newhouse, 1932). The misspelled name lasted until 1931, when the community was renamed Lake Harbor.

LAKE HELEN • *Volusia County*
Both the town and the lake were named by Henry DeLand for his daughter. *See also* DeLand. The town was incorporated in 1891.

LAKE JACKSON • *Leon County*
A small community on the western shore of the lake of the same name which attracts fishermen from the Tallahassee area. Jackson is named for Gen. Andrew Jackson, who marched nearby in 1818, burning 300 Indian houses, confiscating 3,000 bushels of corn, and driving off 1,000 head of cattle. Jackson did not discover the lake, which probably was given his name by his protégé and aide, Richard Keith Call, afterwards twice territorial governor, who had a plantation on the lake. The Indians called it Okaheepee, signifying "disappearing water." Lake Jackson is one of Florida's disappearing lakes.

LAKE JEM • *Lake County*
First known to the postal authorities in 1915 as Lake Gem, but changed to Jem five years later, perhaps to reduce the confusion with the other six lakes called Gem in nearby counties.

LAKE KERR • *Marion County*
Located in the Ocala National Forest, it went through several changes of name from its settlement in the early 1880s. First the name was Ker City, likely for a resident; then, in 1886, Kerr City, and finally, in 1888, Lake Kerr.

LAKELAND • *Polk County*
Named for the 19 lakes within the city limits. The name was adopted by a meeting of citizens on December 15, 1883, having been selected by a committee consisting of P. R. McCrary, E. R. Trammell, and Dr. J. L. Derieux. Abraham G. Munn, a wealthy manufacturer of Louisville, Ky., had moved here in 1881, and is credited with founding the town; with S. A. Hartwell, he formed the Lakeland Improvement Company. Incorporation of the town became effective January 1, 1885.

LAKE MAGDALENE • *Hillsborough County*
Likely commemorates Magdalena, a Florida Indian woman who served as interpreter for the Spanish expedition in 1549 which resulted in the massacre of Father Cancer and his fellow Dominican missionaries at Tampa Bay. Lake was added to the name in the 1970 census.

LAKE MAITLAND • *Orange County*
Fort Maitland was built here in 1838 and named for Capt. William S. Maitland of the U.S. Army. The lake, one of the largest in central Florida, took its name from the fort, and the town, settled some time before the Civil War, was named for the lake. The Indians had called this lake *Fumecheliga*, or "place of the muskmelons." Lake was dropped from the name in 1905.

LAKE MARY • *Seminole County*
Founded in the 1880s, the community was named for the adjacent lake, which in turn gained its name from the wife of Maj. William Randolph, father-in-law of Will Wallace Harney, Orlando poet.

LAKE MERIAL • *Bay County*
T. D. Sale, who owned much land here, named the place for his daughter.

LAKE MONROE • *Seminole County*
This community on the western shore of Lake Monroe took its name from the lake, whose name in turn honors James Monroe, fifth president of the United States. It was during President Monroe's administration that the United States acquired Florida. The community originally was named Ahern, but the name likely was changed to take advantage of the geographic location.

LAKE PARK • *Palm Beach County*
A town here was laid out in the 1920s by Harry S. Kelsey, who called it Kelsey City. After his death, residents decided to rename the town, and since it lay along the shores of Lake Worth, it was called Lake Park.

LAKE PICKETT • *Orange County*
Once a sawmill, turpentine still and cattle community, Lake Pickett and its adjacent lake recall a family that settled here in the 1880s.

LAKE PLACID • *Highlands County*
A name transplanted intact from upper New York State, when the Lake Placid Club, famous site of winter sports, chose this site for its semitropical branch. The club had been founded by Melvil Dewey, inventor of the widely-adopted system of library classification and the widely-neglected system of simplified spelling (hence the missing "le" from his first name). The Florida site was chosen for its beauty and climate. Called Lake Stearns earlier, it was founded in 1924 through a citrus development enterprise begun by A. H. DeVane, E. E. Stewart, and Ernest Morrow.

LAKEPORT • *Glades County*
Founded in 1914 on Lake Okeechobee where Fisheating Creek enters the lake. The promoters owned some 20,000 acres which they offered for sale at $50 to $100. Settlers came from as far away as Belgium to attempt the cultivation of lettuce, onions, peppers, and other vegetables. The endeavor failed and Lakeport became a fishing village.

LAKE WALES • *Polk County*
Century in the Sun, the centennial history of Polk County, gives a new but

logical version for the selection of the name of this city and its adjacent lake. *Century* reports the land around the present city was surveyed in 1879 by Sidney Irving Wailes, who changed the name of a principal lake, Watts Lake, to Lake Wailes. It is easy to understand how "Wailes" would have given way to "Wales" by 1915, when the post office was established. This is the site of the Singing Tower, a memorial to Edward W. Bok, who came to the United States from the Netherlands and became the famous publisher of *The Ladies' Home Journal*. He died at his home in Lake Wales in 1930.

LAKE WEIR • *Marion County*
Named for the lake, which is said to have been named for a Dr. Weir who lived there. Yet Taylor's 1839 map gave the name as Wares Lake. And the settlement in 1877 was known as Lake Ward. Weir, Wares, Ward: take your choice.

LAKEWOOD • *Washington County*
The proximity to an attractive lake resulted in the name. Longleaf yellow pine from the vicinity of Lakewood was used in floors of New York's Waldorf Hotel, Grand Central Station, and other well-known places. Fires, deforestation and changing tourist routes caused Lakewood to fade by the early 1940s.

LAKE WORTH • *Palm Beach County*
A town the Indians called Hypoluxo existed here as early as 1870. Later its name was changed to Lucerne, but when it was incorporated in 1913 it was named after the nearby lake, which bears the name of Brig. Gen. William Jenkins Worth, whose strategy brought the Second Seminole War to a conclusion and who went on to serve with distinction in the Mexican War.

LAMONT • *Jefferson County*
A federally-sponsored *History of Jefferson County* (1935) traces the story of Lamont from the period when the stagecoach between St. Augustine and Tallahassee made a daily stop to change horses. Mail was left at Sam Beazley's store. Later, when trains had replaced the stagecoaches, the mail went to McCain's store and the settlement was known locally both as McCains Store and Lick Skillet. A candidate for the legislature suggested neither name conveyed an image of the beauty of the tree-shaded village and urged adoption instead of Lamont, for Daniel Scott Lamont, secretary of war during the second administration of President Cleveland. Lamont recently had visited Florida and, as he was favorably remembered, the name was adopted.

LANARK VILLAGE • *Franklin County*
This community on the Gulf of Mexico has gone through a cycle of change. A resort hotel was built here in the 1890s, when the community was known as Lanark-on-the-Gulf. During World War II, it was surrounded by Camp Gordon Johnston, where tens of thousands of soldiers trained for the invasion of Europe. Now Lanark Village is a retirement community. The name is believed to be of Scottish origin: *lan*, for "land," and *ark*, for "place of refuge."

LAND O'LAKES • *Pasco County*
Known for years as Ehren, the community changed its name in 1950 to capitalize on the promotional value of the numerous lakes in this area.

LANGSTON • *Wakulla County*
Called Langston for four years in the 1890s, it gave way to Smith Creek.

LANIER • *Osceola County*
A family name for a community which first, in 1850, was called Thomas.

LANTANA • *Palm Beach County*
A tropical shrub which blooms abundantly in this locality was chosen for the name of this township in 1889.

LARGO • *Pinellas County*
Named for Lake Largo nearby. The lake itself was named by an associate of Hamilton Disston, the Philadelphia saw manufacturer whose acquisition from the state of four million acres in 1881 included a tract in this vicinity. His associate, a Mr. Livingstone, preferred *Largo*, Spanish for "long or big," to the more commonplace Big Lake by which the lake had been known. Old-timers say the community once nearly was called Luluville, in honor of the daughter of a pioneer settler, Gideon Blitch.

LARKINS • *Dade County*
Wilson A. Larkins brought his family here in 1897 and established the first store and post office. The community's name was changed to South Miami for promotional reasons during the boom days of the 1920s.

LAUDERDALE-BY-THE SEA, LAUDERDALE LAKES CITY, NORTH LAUDERDALE • *Broward County*
These neighboring communities of Fort Lauderdale (see also Fort Lauderdale) wanted identification with the big city but independence of government.

LAUDERHILL • *Broward County*
Lauderhill would be Sunnyside today but for the intervention of William Safire, *The New York Times* columnist. When developer Herbert Sadkin asked his friend Safire for advice on community names, Safire said he did not like Sunnyside because it reminded him of a neighborhood in Brooklyn. Safire voted for Lauderhill because of the wordplay of hill and dale.

LAUREL HILL • *Okaloosa County*
During the Civil War, several boys not old enough to enlist in the Confederate Army formed a unit of the Home Guards. They met here where three laurel trees grew at the top of a hill for target shooting, drill, and other military practice. The town which grew up here was named for the hill and its trees.

LAWTEY • *Bradford County*
Established in 1877 by a colony of 20 people from Chicago, Ill. The leader of the group was Col. V. J. Shipman, who had a son-in-law, William Lawtey, after whom the town was named. A Capt. Burrin donated 200 acres for a town, with the stipulation that the proceeds of the sale of lots should be used for church and school purposes.

LAYTON • *Monroe County*
This half-mile-long city on Long Key took its name from its founder, first

mayor and major landowner, Del Layton. Incorporated in 1963, it is one of only three incorporated cities on the 120-mile long string of Florida Keys.

LAZY LAKE • *Broward County*
Charles H. Lindfors acquired the land for a development in 1946 and named it Lazy Lake when a friend remarked that it looked "so lazy and peaceful." It was incorporated in 1953.

LEBANON • *Levy County*
Motorists whizzing on U.S. 19 and U.S. 98 along the west coast of Florida have an awareness of Lebanon Station, but there also was a Lebanon settlement nearby. The first post office opened at Lebanon in 1889. The name perhaps was suggested by a growth of cedar trees, which in turn suggests the cedars of Lebanon.

LECANTO • *Citrus County*
A post office has been here since 1883, but tradition says a man named Dr. Morton first settled here in 1862. Perhaps he selected the name, which combines the French *le*, "the," and the Italian *canto*, for "singing" in recognition of the numerous songbirds of the area (Federal Writers Project, unpublished, 1939).

LEE COUNTY •
The forty-first county, established May 13, 1887, and named for Gen. Robert E. Lee. *See also* Hendry.

LEE • *Madison County*
Gen. Lee also gave his name to this community, settled in the 1880s by Phillip Newland, who operated a lime kiln here. However, another settler, John Haven, is said to have suggested the name.

LEESBURG • *Lake County*
Established in 1853 by Calvin and Evander Lee but unnamed until, according to tradition, Calvin Lee went north several years later to order some goods. He realized that there was no town name to which they could be consigned. He thought up Leesburg on the spur of the moment, and it stuck.

LEIGH READ • *Almost a county*
A political duel and its chain of violent deaths from Tallahassee to Texas resulted in the flawed naming of a county. Leigh Read, a Tennessean, had been a member of the Florida Legislative Council and speaker of the House of Representatives. In the Indian campaigns, he was wounded, earned the sobriquet of "hero of the Withlacoochee Blockhouse" for leadership of a relief column, and was appointed brigadier general by President Jackson. Read also was a signer of the 1839 constitution which prohibited duels. Read's antagonist was Augustus Alston. Challenged more than once, Read, a Democrat, responded that if he must fight, he would take on Alston, whom he described as the "bulldog" of the Whigs. Read killed Alston, whose family refused to accept his death on December 12, 1839, as the chance duelers took. Alston's sister is said to have had a slug from his body molded into a bullet and sent

as a symbol of revenge to Alston's brother, Willis. Read was shot, then stabbed on another occasion. His luck finally ran out on April 27, 1841, when he was trapped in a shotgun ambush. Willis Alston, convicted of the murder, escaped from jail and fled to Texas, where a physician originally from Tallahassee denounced him as a fugitive. The physician was murdered and his friends lynched Alston. The legislature in 1842 passed a bill changing the name of Mosquito County to Leigh Read County, but a clerk kept the act from reaching the governor during the constitutional period for his consideration. There is a contemporary map showing Leigh Read County, including the present counties of Orange, Volusia and Lake, but the name never was to be.

LEISURE CITY • *Dade County*
Frank Vellenti, Sr., and Thomas E. Palmer headed the Florida Sun Deck Homes Company which started this subdivision. They wanted to attract retired people and thus chose the name, Leisure City.

LEMON CITY • *Dade County*
John Dorschner, writing in *The Miami Herald*'s "Tropic" magazine, says people began living here in the 1880s. In 1909, an area was platted as the Elmira subdivision, and what is now 68th street was designated Elmira Street, with two large stone columns marking the intersection of Elmira Street and what was then the Dixie Highway. There was the flavor of a rural community, with men and women, boys and girls strolling down to Biscayne Bay. The great land boom of the 1920s and the hurricane of 1926 ruined that and Lemon City was swallowed up by Greater Miami.

LENO • *Columbia County*
Once this area was known as Keno, for a variation of lotto gambling. To change the town's reputation as a gambling center, clergymen and others in 1876 changed the name to Leno. There was a grist mill, a sawmill, cotton gin, stores, and a hotel. But the railroad bypassed Leno and gradually the inhabitants left. The place then was spoken of as Old Leno. Now the area is bustling again as a state park called O'Leno, a contraction of Old Leno.

LEON COUNTY •
The seventh county, established December 29, 1924. Named for Juan Ponce de León, the Spanish explorer who gave Florida its name. *See also* Florida.

LEVY COUNTY •
The twenty-sixth county, established March 10, 1845. Named for David Levy Yulee, whose career and background are, as Nixon Smiley once said in *The Miami Herald*, "almost too improbable for fiction." Yulee's father, Moses, was born in a Moroccan harem. Moses was the son of the beautiful Rachel Levy, daughter of a Jewish physician living in England, and of Jacoub ben Youli, grand vizier to the sultan of Morocco. Rachel was on an English ship bound for the West Indies when captured by Barbary pirates. As a young virgin, Rachel was a prize for the slave market in Fez, where she was bought for the grand vizier. A revolution enabled Rachel and her small son to escape to

Gibraltar. In time, Moses took his mother and a sister to St. Thomas in the Virgin Islands. Moses married Hannah Abendanone, who in 1811 gave birth to a son, who was named David. When David was nine he was sent to school in Virginia and his parents moved to Florida, settling near Micanopy. Nixon Smiley observed that David was as sharp and personable as his father, and he progressed rapidly. He became a member of Florida's first constitutional convention in 1838-1839, and in 1841 was elected territorial delegate to the U.S. Congress. After Florida was admitted to statehood in 1845, he became the state's first U. S. senator. He persuaded the legislature to change his name from David Levy to David Levy Yulee. A short time afterwards, he married the daughter of Gov. Charles Wickliffe of Kentucky. Yulee developed a 5,000-acre plantation called *Margarita*, Spanish for "pearl," on the Homosassa River. His mansion there was burned by Union troops but his sugar mill escaped ruin. He headed a group which developed railroads, and fought off almost to the end of the Civil War the efforts of the Confederate government to take up some of his rails to make connections more useful to the war effort. Yulee was imprisoned at Fort Pulaski, Ga., after the Civil War, accused of aiding the flight of President Jefferson Davis and the Confederate Cabinet. After release by order of President Grant, Yulee lived in Washington with a married daughter and died in New York in 1886. Yulee has a county, Levy, and a community, Yulee in Nassau County, bearing his two last names.

LIBERTY COUNTY •
The thirty-second county, established December 15, 1855. Named for the great objective of the people who founded and built the United States. The name also has been given to communities in Glades, Liberty, and Walton counties.

LICK SKILLETT • *Jefferson County*
See Lamont.

LIDO BEACH, KEY • *Pinellas and Sarasota counties*
These areas were so named because of their presumed resemblance to the sandy islands of Italy, between the Lagoon of Venice and the Adriatic Sea.

LIGHT HOUSE POINT • *Franklin County*
Near the mouth of the Ochlockonee River at Apalachee Bay, this point was called Cape Apalachee in correspondence in 1675 and Abines Point in 1693. In Choctaw *abina* meant "an outdoor camp or lodging," and the variation may have its meaning in the Apalachee language.

LIGHTHOUSE POINT • *Broward County*
Incorporated in 1957, Lighthouse Point was named for the nearby Hillsboro lighthouse.

LIGHTWOOD • *Volusia County*
The first name of today's Paisley.

LILLIBRIDGE • *Hillsborough County*
Morton M. Lillibridge settled on 160 acres of land here in the 1880s. He

bought boards from a sawmill at Keysville and built a 16'-by-16', two-room house whose remarkable feature was the lack of ceiling over what otherwise might be called the living room. With its sister communities of Welcome, Picnic, and Cabbage Ford, Lillibridge flourished in the 1890s because of the discovery of phosphate deposits in eastern Hillsborough.

L I M O N A • *Hillsborough County*
Named for the Spanish word for lemon, it is one of the oldest communities in Hillsborough County, having been first settled in the 1830s. Its permanent settlement, however, appears to date from the 1870s.

L I P O N A • *Jefferson County*
This name is doubly fascinating because its first postmaster was Achille Murat, prince of Napoli, and Lipona is an anagram, or transposition of letters, for Napoli. Lipona was the name of Murat's plantation. The *Handbook* of the Postal History Committee of the Florida Federation of Stamp Clubs says the Lipona post office was established May 8, 1828, with Col. Murat, as he preferred to be known, in charge. Charles Louis Napoleon Archille Murat was the oldest son of the emperor's sister Caroline and her husband, the king of Naples. Exiled from Italy and France with the fall of Napoleon, Prince Murat was influenced by the marquis de Lafayette to seek a new home in Florida. The post office here was discontinued December 16, 1847.

L I S B O N • *Lake County*
A Mr. Thomas homesteaded here about 1854. He sold his claim to W. J. Alsobrook, in whose cabin the Lake Griffin post office was established as the first regular link with the outside world. But how Lisbon gained its name is not known.

L I T H I A • *Hillsborough County*
Named for the mineral lithia, found in a little spring in the area. Bryant's *Early History of Lithia* says James Alderman was the first pioneer to cross the Alafia River, in 1847. Aldermans Ford was named for him. Lithia is a strongly alkaline white powder used in ceramics and glass.

L I T T L E   R I V E R •
Gadsden County
This stream was shown on an 1684 map as *River of Sticks* and on an 1778 map as *Weeklakatchee*, or Little Big River.

Arrowroot plants decorate a motorized float for the Little River company that sold Florida Arrowroot starch.

LITTLE TORCH KEY • *Monroe County*
With its neighbor, Middle Torch Key, this island gained its name from the resinous torchwood tree. *Florida: A Guide to the Southernmost State* (1939) says the soapberry tree also flourishes here. The soapberry tree produces seed hulls which yield a soaplike substance used as a cleaner. Early settlers were said to have sprinkled the crushed seeds in small streams. The seeds stupefied the fish, which floated to the surface and were easily gathered.

LIVE OAK • *Suwannee County*
The old wagon road from the military post at Suwannee Springs to the Gulf passed a clear, deep pond here under a huge live oak tree, offering shade and an attractive camping ground. As the population increased, the spot became a sort of parking center for horses, mules, and vehicles, and when the railroad came through, workers in the vicinity would say at noon, "Let's go to the big live oak and eat." The station was given the name of Live Oak about 1855, and the town was incorporated in 1903. It is now the county seat.

LLOYD • *Jefferson County*
Walter Franklin Lloyd came from Flatbush, N.Y., shortly after the Civil War, bringing his means of livelihood, a carpenter's tool chest. He first settled at Tallahassee, then moved to what was known variously as Bailey's Mill or Number Two, the second station from Tallahassee on the Jacksonville, Pensacola, and Mobile Railroad. Lloyd opened a mercantile business and married Sallie Dry Leonard, who brought to the marriage an inheritance of farmland.

LOCHA APOPKA • *Polk County*
The former name of a lake in Polk County now called Lake Clinch. Read interprets this as from the Seminole *locha*, "turtle or terrapin," and *papka*, "eating place," thus "turtle eating place." Fond of turtles and terrapins, the Seminoles usually broil them in their shells.

LOCHLOOSA • *Alachua County*
Read says this lake and community derive their name from the Choctaw *luski*, "terrapin," and *lusa*, "black," hence black terrapin. Lochloosa is an old community dating from the 1860s.

LOCKHART • *Orange County*
David Lockhart built a sawmill here in the 1870s.

LOCKMILLER'S COVE • *Palm Beach County*
Will (1964) tells of John Lockmiller, whose Lockmiller's Cove on Lake Okeechobee now has become Bean City. "John Lockmiller," wrote Will, "a big boned man with a voice like a bull of Bashan, had arrived here from Fort Worth, Texas, though he had once been in the lumber business in Oregon. It was in the fall of 1914 that he first came to the Everglades to see the land he's bought. Well, he hasn't seen it yet. His land was ten miles down the Miami Canal and under water for twelve months of most every year. So John joined his bachelor brother Marion, who had already squatted at the western point of this Bean City cove."

LOCKSA APOPKA • *Hillsborough County*
An obsolete name for the Hillsboro River, which flows (according to the spelling of the U. S. Board on Geographic Names) in Hillsborough County. The old name was derived from the Creek *lokcha*, "acorn," and *apopka*, "place for eating." Tampa, the city beside the river, is a place for superb eating, but acorns are unlikely to be an ingredient of the recipes.

LOCKSEE • *Osceola County*
Another in the string of modern Seminole Indian names given stations along the now abandoned Florida East Coast Railway's Okeechobee Extension. Locksee is derived from *lokose*, "bear," according to Moore-Willson's vocabulary.

LOGGERHEAD KEY • *Monroe County*
Named for the loggerhead turtles which come ashore in the Keys.

LONG BEACH • *Bay County*
One of Florida's most recent cities on the Miracle Strip that is the upper Gulf Coast.

LONGBOAT KEY • *Sarasota County*
The name has probably been around since the days of the explorers. It appears on eighteenth-century maps, but its origin has been lost. A longboat is the largest boat carried by a merchant sailing vessel.

LONGBOAT KEY, TOWN OF • *Manatee and Sarasota counties*
Taking its name from the key, this community is unusual in that it straddles the boundary between Manatee and Sarasota counties. Only six cities in Florida are so split.

LONG KEY • *Monroe County*
Spanish maps called this *Cayo Vivora*, or Rattlesnake Key, because the outlet of the island resembles the spread jaws of a snake. This was the location of the Long Key Fishing Camp, where the angling attracted many famous people. Zane Grey, the Western novelist, was among those who fished here, and a saltwater creek bears his name. The Long Key Viaduct, second longest water crossing of the old railway extension from the mainland to Key West, is two miles long and has 220 arches. (Seven Mile Bridge is the longest.)

LONGWOOD • *Seminole County*
Established prior to 1885, and named by E. W. Henck for a district of his native city, Boston, Mass. Henck was instrumental in promoting construction of the South Florida Railroad from Sanford to Orlando.

LORETTO • *Duval County*
The name given to the post office that served a Roman Catholic convent established by the Sisters of St. Joseph du Puy.

LORIDA • *Highlands County*
Florida without the "F" took the place in 1937 of a name more difficult to pronounce, Lake Istokpoga. The town's former name was taken from the lake, which meant Drowned Man's Lake.

LOTUS • *Brevard County*
Named in 1894 at the suggestion of Maud Hardee, afterwards Mrs. T. G. Ronald, because of the profusion then of lotus blossoms in the shallow waterway on Merritt Island.

LOVETT • *Madison County*
Named for an early settler, Hezekiah Lovett.

LOWELL • *Marion County*
Its post office dating from 1888, this community is said to have taken its name from the Massachusetts textile milling city which, in part, used Florida cotton.

LOXAHATCHEE • *Palm Beach and Martin counties*
A river and community in Palm Beach County and a marsh that extends from Palm Beach County into Martin County. Simpson (1956) reports the name as meaning Turtle River. Will (1964) explains that the map made by an Army topographer in 1856 did not name the Loxahatchee River. "And, incidentally," wrote Will, "that name by rights was Locha-hatchee, which means Turtle Creek, but the soldiers, of course, couldn't pronounce that gutteral 'ch' so they spelled it to suit themselves, and came up with Loxahatchee, which in the Seminole lingo, would seem to mean a lying or false river, and maybe one where somebody once told a lie."

LULU • *Columbia County*
Tradition says Lulu was the sweetheat of a pioneer. In any event, she is along in years if still living, for the town was renamed in 1891 from Hagen.

LUTZ • *Hillsborough County*
Changed from Stemper in 1912 to honor a railroad official, C. E. Lutz.

LYNN • *Marion County*
Along with Lowell, also in Marion County, another of the transplanted Massachusetts textile mill city names, probably because of the use there of Florida cotton. The postal register adds an "e" to the end of the name, but the State Department of Agriculture map spells it Lynn.

LYNN HAVEN • *Bay County*
Named for its promoter, W. H. Lynn, former New Yorker and publisher of *The National Tribune* of Washington, D. C., a magazine concerned with Union veterans of the Civil War. In the early 1900s, Lynn conceived the idea of settling communities in Florida primarily for these veterans. Out of Lynn's promotional energies two communities developed: St. Cloud in Osceola County and Lynn Haven. Haven was coupled with Lynn's name to suggest this place was to be for rest and security. Lynn Haven was incorporated June 10, 1913. Later, the veterans of the Civil War were joined by those who had served in the armed forces of the nation during the Spanish-American War. In the panhandle of Florida, where monuments to the Confederacy may be expected, in 1920 a typical memorial was erected in Lynn Haven—typical except that the soldier on top is in the uniform of the North.

MacArthur Causeway • *Dade County*
The Dade County Commission during World War II honored the defender of Bataan, Gen. Douglas MacArthur, by renaming the county causeway linking Miami and Miami Beach across Biscayne Bay.

Macclenny • *Baker County*
Originally called Darbyville, this town was renamed in 1885 for its founder, H. C. Macclenny, who owned large tracts of land in the vicinity. It is the county seat of Baker County.

MacDill Air Force Base • *Hillsborough County*
Eight miles south of downtown Tampa at the tip of Interbay Peninsula, the base was activated on April 15, 1941, and named in honor of Col. Leslie MacDill, who was killed in an air crash near Washington, D. C., on November 8, 1938. MacDill, who was 48 years old, was a native of Monmouth, Ill.

Madeira Beach • *Pinellas County*
Named for Madeira, Portugal's wine-producing Atlantic island off Africa. The word itself means "wood," as the island when discovered was thickly forested. A. B. "Bert" Archibald, an early Gulf Beach developer, is credited with adopting the name.

Madison County •
The fourteenth county, established December 26, 1827, and named for President James Madison. This county drew many of its settlers from Virginia. Carved from Jefferson County, Madison originally included the present counties of Taylor, Lafayette, and Dixie. San Pedro, on the Bellamy Road about ten miles south of the present city of Madison, was the first county seat. The first courthouse consisted of a one-room log building with a big open fireplace in the south end. The county had perhaps 250 inhabitants, white and black. Carlton Smith, a Madison county historian, wrote that when Christopher Edwards, the first sheriff, found it necessary to travel to Oldtown, in the southeastern part of the county, he had to go by horseback to Charles' Ferry, some 15 miles away, then by riverboat to Fort Fanning, then by horseback or foot for the remaining six or eight miles to Oldtown. Justice in those days relied upon the people of the community for whatever immediate action was required.

Madison • *Madison County*
Established May 2, 1838, as the county seat of Madison County this town was first called Hickstown, after the Seminole Indian chief John Hicks; later it was known as Newton. But mail kept arriving addressed to Madison C. H., meaning the courthouse of Madison County—which had been named after James Madison, the fourth president of the United States. After the Civil War the "C. H." was dropped. A little northwest of Madison stood the Spanish mission of Santa Helena de Machaba. The site is on the route of De Soto and on the upper route of the Old Spanish Trail.

MAGNOLIA • *Wakulla County*
It requires imagination to stand today on the west bank of the St. Marks River, eight miles above the confluence of the St. Marks and Wakulla rivers, and realize a town once existed here. Peering into the greenery on either side of the river, it is far simpler to imagine Indians concealed by the underbrush than to think of sailing ships able to take Magnolia's cotton to New York and New Orleans, and of a town with four warehouses, a cotton press, three stores, a bank, a newspaper, and dwellings. But that was the scene in 1833. Now all that remains are graves, concealed from strangers by trees and underbrush. Gravestones recall the founding Hamlin family of Augusta, Maine. Magnolia failed, in part, because an obstruction in the river limited the size of ships. This encouraged the building downstream of Port Leon, which was destroyed by the gale and tidal wave of September 13, 1843. Magnolia and Port Leon—two lost towns.

MAGNOLIA SPRINGS • *Clay County*
Even before the Civil War, this was a popular resort on the St. Johns River. In later years, a large riverfront hotel had President Grover Cleveland among its guests. There is a story that the president found the spring water so much to his liking that he had bottles sent to the White House. Between the springs and highway is a small stone shaft memorializing Union soldiers who died during Florida campaigns of the Civil War.

MAITLAND • *Orange County*
Fort Maitland, named for Capt. William S. Maitland, was built here in 1838. Until 1905, the name was Lake Maitland. *See also* Lake Maitland.

MAJETTE • *Bay and Gulf counties*
Both communities are believed to have derived their name from a family that conducted turpentine and other naval stores operations in the woodlands of these adjoining counties.

MALABAR • *Brevard County*
One of the older places on Florida's east coast, the settlement dates from 1875 and its post office from 1883. C. W. and E. A. Arnold of New York and George U. Damon of New Hampshire are regarded as the founding fathers. The name likely was taken from the Malabar on the coast of India which, while it suggested the wealth of the Indies, means "bad bar" in Spanish.

MALONE • *Jackson County*
Established in 1911 and named after its developer, John W. Malone.

MANALAPAN • *Palm Beach County*
The name of this town is an Indian word meaning "good bread" or "good country."

MANATEE COUNTY •
The thirty-first county, established January 9, 1855. Named for Florida's manatees, or sea cows, now an endangered species. Manatees were once found as far north as the Carolinas and all around the Gulf of Mexico. Now they

survive only in isolated pockets of Florida, with man their only natural enemy. When Columbus thought he saw mermaids in 1493, he likely had sighted manatees. Science has preserved a vestige of the mermaid legend, for a nineteenth-century taxonomist gave the order the scientific name Sirenia, from the Spanish *sirenas* or "mermaids." The common name manatee came from the Spanish *manati*. Manatee eat submerged aquatic plants. They usually stay submerged about five minutes, but will surface once a minute when swimming because of the need for oxygen. The typical manatee is ten feet long and weighs 1,000 pounds. Manatees are both friendly and harmless. The reproduction rate of one calf for each adult female every three years explains the reason why the manatee has been unable to cope with man through loss of feeding areas, by hunting, and through injury resulting from the propellers of powerboats.

MANATEE • *Manatee County*
Two rivers and a community of the same name.

MANAVISTA • *Manatee County*
Coined from Manatee, the county, and the Spanish *vista*, or "view."

MANDALAY • *Taylor County*
The name is likely derived from Kipling's *Road to Mandalay*.

MANDARIN • *Duval County*
Known as San Antonia when Spain possessed Florida, and St. Anthony under English rule, the community changed its name to Monroe in honor of President Monroe when the United States acquired Florida. There was another quick but lasting change in 1841 when the town became Mandarin, presumably because Ebenezar Eveleth, an Oriental traveler, settled here. Mandarin is a variety of Chinese orange. The place became widely known after the Civil War as the winter home of Harriet Beecher Stowe, author of *Uncle Tom's Cabin*. Mrs. Stowe and her husband, a Presbyterian minister, spent their winters in Mandarin from 1868 until 1884. She wrote while there, continuing to be the main support of her family. One of her works, *Palmetto Leaves*, likely attracted tens of thousands of persons eager to see the semitropical land of which Mrs. Stowe wrote. Her brother, the Rev. Charles Beecher, served as Florida's superintendent of public instruction from March 18, 1871, until January 23, 1873. A memorable picture in the Florida State Archives photographic collection shows Mrs. Stowe standing with the governor and other officials and citizens on the steps of the Capitol at Tallahassee, an unlikely place indeed for the woman whom President Lincoln called the little lady who hastened the Civil War.

MANGO • *Hillsborough County*
The name derives from the mango, quantities of which were at one time grown here. A settlement has been here at least since 1884.

MANGONIA PARK • *Palm Beach County*
Subdivided by lawyer A. R. Roebuck, this town resurrects a name that had died. The original Mangonia was on the northwest shores of Lake Worth. It

was settled by a family of Kansans, and named because a parson interested in horticulture started cultivating mangoes there. The original Mangonia was absorbed by West Palm Beach.

MANHATTAN • *Manatee County*
From the Algonquin Indian "island of hills," this name is a frequent transplant, appearing in six states other than New York and Florida.

Manhattan's general store, 1926.

MANHATTAN BEACH • *Duval County*
A stretch of beach. Why the name was applied is not known.

MANNSFIELD • *Citrus County*
Sen. Austin Shuey Mann was a prime mover in the creation of Citrus County in 1887, but those who had prepared for Inverness becoming the county seat were startled to discover that the legislature had situated the seat at Mannsfield. This was a settlement mainly of homesteaders from Tennessee, Alabama, Georgia, and other Southern states, while Inverness was the center of the so-called old-timers. It took a contested election to wrest the seat from Sen. Mann and Mannsfield, and today Mannsfield is gone but Inverness remains.

MANNS SPUR • *Baker County*
Settled in the early 1900s, it bears a family name.

MANVILLE • *Putnam County*
When the settlement needed a post office in 1882, W. M. Mann became postmaster and the town took his name.

MARATHON • *Monroe County*
Midway on the Overseas Extension of the Florida East Coast Railway from the mainland to Key West, Key Vaca became the food supply depot for the 3,000 to 4,000 construction workers. Tradition says someone volunteered the opinion that by the time the railroad had reached Key Vaca, the task had become "a marathon," or endurance contest, and the name stuck to the place.

MARCO ISLAND • *Collier County*
The northernmost of the Ten Thousand Islands of the Florida west coast. The first post office here was known as Malco, as postal authorities thought there already was a Marco in Florida. In 1895, there was unearthed here by accident one of the richest collections of carved and painted ceremonial and utilitarian aboriginal objects found in Florida. *See also* Collier City.

MARGATE • *Broward County*
Jack Marqusee, one of the principal developers of this community, selected the name because it contained the first syllable of his name. He liked the "gate" because it is a gateway to the coastal area from the western part of the county. He liked the idea, too, that there were Margates in New Jersey, England, and South Africa.

MARIANNA • *Jackson County*
Established in 1823, this town was named by the original owners of the site, Robert Beveridge and wife, for their two daughters, Mary and Anna. It is the county seat of Jackson County, and was the scene of the Battle of Marianna in 1864, when federal forces were resisted by old men and boys.

MARIETTA • *Duval County*
Florida's Marietta was an organized settlement as long ago as 1885 and earlier had been in the path of both Union and Confederate armies maneuvering about Jacksonville during the Civil War. The source of the name is not known, but possibilities exist elsewhere. In Pennsylvania and Oklahoma the name was coined from Mary and Etta, while in Ohio and Minnesota it is an Italian or Latinized form of Marie Antoinette, queen of France.

MARINELAND • *Flagler County*
The site of the famous Marine Studios, where sea creatures of many kinds may be viewed and photographed through portholes in the walls of large pools where they are kept under native conditions. Marineland has grown up around this unique enterprise on the coastal highway just south of St. Augustine.

MARION COUNTY •
The twenty-fourth county, established March 14, 1844, and named for Gen. Francis Marion, the Swamp Fox of the Revolutionary War. This county drew many of its early settlers from South Carolina, the hero's native state.

MARTIN COUNTY •
The sixty-fourth county, established May 30, 1925, and named for John W. Martin, governor at the time. There is a belief that the promoters insured

themselves against a gubernatorial veto by giving the proposed new county the name of the chief executive. Martin was three times mayor of Jacksonville and governor from 1925 to 1929.

MARTIN • *Marion County*
Founded in the 1880s by Col. Martin and named for him. In all likelihood, he was an ancestor of Gov. Martin, a native of Marion County.

MARY ESTHER • *Okaloosa County*
A certain Professor Newton, a Presbyterian minister and teacher who had come to Florida from Pennsylvania, passed through here in a boat on his way to settle in Walton County and found it so lovely and peaceful that he marked it in his mind as a place where he would like eventually to have a home. In Walton County he established Knox Hill School, where he taught for a number of years, but true to his promise to himself he came back to this spot. One version of the naming says that the two names were those of his wife and daughter; another that they were the names of his two daughters. Both could be true if one daughter had been named after her mother.

MASARYKTOWN • *Hernando County*
Named for Tomas G. Masaryk (1850-1937), first president of Czechoslovakia, this agricultural colony was founded in 1924 by Joseph Joscak, editor of a Czech newspaper in New York.

MASCOTTE • *Lake County*
Established in 1885 by J. W. Payne of Boston, after a ship that sailed a route from Boston to St. Petersburg. The word is the French spelling of mascot, meaning a person, animal, or thing supposed to bring good luck.

MATANZAS • *St. Johns County*
In 1565, some 300 French Huguenot castaways, under Jean Ribaut, were massacred here by Spaniards, crushing the French attempt to occupy at least some of Florida. The French ships, sailing from Fort Caroline to attack St. Augustine, were driven ashore by a storm. At this place near the south end of Anastasia Island, close to Matanzas Inlet, most of the survivors were put to the knife by Don Pedro Menéndez, "not as Frenchmen but as Lutherans." *Matanzas* in Spanish means "slaughter or massacre." The present community is said to date from 1829, when Abraham Dupont settled here.

MATECUMBE • *Monroe County*
A corruption of the Spanish words *matar hombre*, "to kill a man." Here crews of shipwrecked sailing vessels were said to have been killed or enslaved by Indians. There are two keys by the name, Upper Matecumbe and Lower Matecumbe. This was the area swept by the Labor Day hurricane of 1935, which resulted in the death by drowning of more than 400 people.

MATHEWS BRIDGE, JOHN E. • *Duval County*
This bridge over the St. Johns River at Jacksonville is a memorial to John E. Mathews, chief justice of the Florida Supreme Court when he died on April 30, 1955. He was born at Gray's Landing, Ga., on July 19, 1892. He served as

Monument at Islamorada on Matecumbe Key dedicated to those
who perished during the September hurricane of 1935.

a member of the House of Representatives for the sessions of 1929 and 1931, and in the Senate for two four-year terms beginning in 1942. He was appointed justice of the State Supreme Court in 1951. He was a leader in a long campaign for construction of bridges across the St. Johns River at Jacksonville. The Mathews Bridge is 7,382 feet long and has a vertical clearance of 148 feet.

MATOAKA • *Manatee County*
The Algonquin name of Chief Powhatan's famous daughter we know as Pocahontas.

MATTLACHA PASS • *Lee County*
Simpson (1956) opines Mattlacha may be an Indian corruption of Ponce de León's name for neighboring Big Pine Island in Charlotte Harbor. Ponce de León called the island *Matanza* for the number of Indians killed in an attack on his party. More likely, continues Simpson, Mattlacha was derived from the Creek *imatha* or *ematha*, "leader or chief," and *lako* or *thlako*, "big."

MAXVILLE • *Duval County*
After 1790, Americans began settling in Spanish Florida. With Spanish grants having taken up the land on the St. Johns River, the remote areas of Duval County offered settlers their only opportunity. One of the important settlements at that time was a colony of Georgians who clustered at Maxville. Another community by the same name existed in Bay County during the 1890s.

MAUD • *Hardee County*
At the turn of the century, there was a community named Maud near Fort Meade.

MAXIMO POINT • *Pinellas County*
Florida: A Guide to the Southernmost State (1939) says the first white settler of record for the peninsula known as Pinellas County was Antonio Maximo, who set up a fish *rancho* in 1843 on a point of land at the southern extremity. The area, now called Maximo Point, was swept by a hurricane five years later and Maximo disappeared.

MAYO • *Lafayette County*
This county seat of was established in 1874 by John B. Whitfield and named after James Micajah Mayo, who had been a colonel in the Confederate Army. In charge of a survey crew working nearby, Col. Mayo had occasion to deliver a Fourth of July speech which so impressed settlers that they named their community for him. Col. Mayo was the father of Nathan Mayo, longtime Florida commissioner of agriculture, and grandfather of William T. Mayo, a member of the Public Service Commission, 1966-1981.

MAYPORT • *Duval County*
The St. Johns River was called the River of May by the French in the 1560s and that name is recalled in this community, a base for the pilots who guide ships in the great river. Mayport also is a landing for the St. Johns River ferries, a big U.S. Navy base, and the center of a seafood industry.

MAYSLAND • *Madison County*
There have been Mays in this area since 1835.

MAYTOWN • *Volusia County*
This May was May Cook, honored in 1886.

McALPIN • *Suwannee County*
Named by railway officials for Daniel M. McAlpin, who represented Suwannee County in the Florida House of Representatives during the 1870s.

McCAINS STORE • *Jefferson County*
See Lamont.

McCULLOUGHS CREEK • *St. Johns County*
Named for a family that homesteaded here.

McDAVID • *Escambia County*
First known as Regia, this community's name was changed in 1883 to honor Joel McDavid, a member of a family here.

McINTOSH • *Marion County*
The best account of the origin of this place name is given by Neil S. Meffert, staff writer of the *Florida Times-Union,* in an article in that paper on February 13, 1955, which is quoted directly: "The name of the town came, not from absentee owners, but from a squatter who came from Georgia and made himself to home, thank you, on the VanNess acreage. According to the twice-told tale related by Mrs. Annette Gist Haden, the squatter set up a sugar mill on what is now known as the Belk Place. Palatka, 60 miles away, was the nearest source of provisions. On his last shopping trip, the squatter was waylaid by Indians and scalped. A companion (either a Negro slave or a friendly Indian)

got away and warned the victim's wife, who fled with her children. Though many years gone from the scene by the time the township was formed, the squatter had managed to identify himself so indelibly with the area that it was henceforth known by his name—McIntosh."

M c I N T Y R E • *Franklin County*
A family name. This community, near the confluence of the Ochlockonee and Crooked rivers, first was known as Curtis Mills.

M E C C A • *Pinellas and Seminole counties*
Mecca, as a place reached after a pilgrimage, seemed just the right name for these communities in Pinellas and Seminole counties—at least that was the thought of E. T. Woodruff, who persuaded a railroad in 1912 to establish a stop in Seminole County for his farm products.

M E D L E Y • *Dade County*
Named for Sylvester Medley, who settled here in 1905. He farmed here until his death in 1950. His name was chosen in a vote of citizens, not only to honor the man who had brought his cow up the creek 45 years before, but also because it was a pretty name.

M E D U L L A • *Polk County*
Settlements in rural Florida were more mobile than we think of cities today. Often they consisted of a post office operating within a general store that served customers from outlying homesteads. When the general store proprietor felt he would do better a few miles away, the post office and the settlement moved with him. That's what happened at Medulla, which prior to 1881 was known as Spring Hill. After the railroad came through in 1883, L. M. Ballard packed up his merchandise at Medulla, including postal fixtures, and, without a by-your-leave to the U.S. government, moved to Lake Wire, which shortly became Lakeland.

M E L B O U R N E • *Brevard County*
Two accounts give slightly different dates for the founding of this town, and ascribe its naming to different persons, but they agree it was named after Melbourne, Australia. One account says that C. I. Hector sailed into the harbor here in 1872 and the settlement was named after his former Australian home. Although Hector himself preferred the name of Park Ridge after the Illinois home of a local girl he evidently admired, she sought to return the compliment, and in a drawing of straws, she won. Another says the town was founded in 1878 by Thomas Mason, a London schoolteacher, and that the name was given later by John Hector Cornwaith, a former resident of the other Melbourne. A number of satellite communities have grown up in the vicinity of Melbourne and some of these have incorporated Melbourne in their names.

M E L L O N V I L L E • *Seminole County*
Sanford is an outgrowth of Mellonville, a trading post established in 1837 on the fringe of Fort Mellon, a frontier fort which was a base for Army campaigns during the Seminole Wars.

MELROSE • *Putnam and Alachua counties*
Straddling the line separating Putnam and Alachua counties, about halfway between Palatka and Gainesville, stands a small and quiet village with the highly conventional name of Melrose. Not many of those who pass through it or see its name on a map would know that it once bustled and thrived as a resort center, or that it once went by the proud name of Shakerag.

The activity which brought this community to birth and gave it its first and most poetic name was pony racing. Pony owners from miles in every direction brought their racers here on Sunday afternoon, for a fine track had been built. But they didn't let the starter waste perfectly good bullets. They gave him a large white cloth to wave to get the ponies off; hence, Shakerag.

In 1882 a Scottish resident, thinking Shakerag was a bit crude and yearning for the poetry of his homeland, renamed the community Melrose. Seven years later, two Canadian women came to Melrose, decided it had a future, and invested their money in the building of a 125-room wooden hotel. Three years later, both of the original investors had died and the structure had become the property of C. P. Huffman.

How profitably Huffman operated the hotel for the next decade and a half is not recorded, but in 1908 a man named George C. Looney rented the building for use as a military college. He was from Georgia, where he had had a similar school. This one he named Phi Sigma College. The college enrolled 180 students and put them into glamorous uniforms, but 18 months later the building burned to the ground and the light of learning went out.

Shakerag certainly got off to a good start when they shook that rag.

MERRITT • *Brevard County*
From the 1880s, this community was known as Merritt, but in 1934 the name was stretched to Merritt Island. Merritt was among the off-the-highway Florida communities of the old Tropical Trail.

MERRITT ISLAND • *Brevard County*
Once called Stony Point, but in documents as early as 1808 it is referred to as Merritt's Island, or Marratt's Island. The name may have come from a Capt. Pedro Marratt, a surveyor for the Spanish government in east Florida. But there was also a Mr. Merritt who had planted crops here before 1823.

MEXICO BEACH • *Bay County*
Two developers, Gordon U. Parker of Blountstown and W. T. McGowin, Sr., of Panama City, are credited with giving the community its name in 1948 by reason of its location on the Gulf of Mexico.

MIAKKA • *Sarasota County*
A variant spelling of Myakka and Mayaca, all thought to be the same as Miami, translated by Professor William A. Read as possibly being a compound of Choctaw *maiha* and *mih*, "it is so," and applied in Florida to Lake Okeechobee. (*See* Myakka City.)

MIAMI • *Dade County*

The derivation of the name Miami is a mystery which has engaged the attention of many authorities in this field. The commonly accepted story is that it is an Indian word meaning "sweet water." That was the meaning understood by founding fathers, however wrong they may have been linguistically. Some wanted to name the new city Flagler in honor of Henry M. Flagler. But Miami is not a Seminole word, phonetically, and no words have been found in the Seminole language with this meaning and sound. Another version translates it as "big water," said to refer to Lake Okeechobee, of which the present Miami River was once an arm.The Chippewas, a group of Algonquin Indians, have a word *miami* in their language which means "people who live on a point," and these Indians lived on a peninsula. Their word is the origin of the name of Miami, Ohio, and *The Miami Herald*'s John Pennekamp said research indicates Indian trade routes could have brought the Chippewa word into Florida. There are numerous speculations involving various Indian dialects as well as the Spanish language. One goes through Choctaw and arrives at "it is so wide," referring to Lake Okeechobee. Another uses Spanish to reach "place of complete contentment." Still another quotes an Indian chieftain as having said to an Indian maid, "You are my beautiful." To which she replied, "My, am I?" None is authoritative, but all seem to afford some pleasurable conjecture. In the language of the United States, Miami means a place of relaxation, subtropical warmth, luxury, and diversion. It is, among other things, the county seat of Dade County.

Fort Dallas, established by the Army in January 1838, occupied a strategic place near the meeting of the Miami River and Biscayne Bay. The fort was abandoned in June 1858. Remnants have been moved to a park upstream but still near the river.

Today's Miami was chartered in 1896 with the coming of the Florida East Coast Railway. A number of satellite cities use Miami in their names.

The Miami Chamber of Commerce van, October 1926.

MIAMI BEACH • *Dade County*
Much of the first part of Miami Beach to be reclaimed from mangrove swamp and Biscayne Bay was known as Alton Beach. Redford (1970) reports that Carl G. Fisher, the developer, took that name from a passing railway freight car marked Chicago & Alton Railroad. Fortunately, that same whimsicality did not prevail when the three developing companies put their territories together in a new city they called Miami Beach. It was agreed that Fisher's friend, James Whitcomb Riley, the Hoosier poet, should plant a tree symbolic of how the developers hoped their town should grow and flourish. The tree, now lost to history, was planted on what was to become Lincoln Road, and Riley recited:

> We plant this tree beside the sea
> In trust, that it yet may wave
> Through shower and shade
> In sunny hours
> For other eyes as glad as ours.

The developers were ambivalent in their feelings toward the older city across Biscayne Bay. While tied to Miami in many ways, the boosters of Miami Beach desired separate identification. When Julius Fleishmann, of the yeast family, dropped dead during a polo game, Steve Hannegan, the city's publicist, telegraphed the news services of Fleishmann's passing, then added, "Don't forget the Miami Beach dateline!"

MIAMI LAKES • *Dade County*
Former *Miami Herald* reporter Jeanne Bellamy writes, "A remarkable family carved Miami Lakes, a totally planned community, from a 3,000-acre dairy farm."

The patriarch, Ernest R. "Cap" Graham, a former gold miner in the Black Hills of South Dakota, moved to Florida in 1919 to start a sugarcane plantation in the Everglades for the Pennsylvania Sugar Co. (Pennsuco). When the sugar project failed, Graham turned the sugar mill into a vegetable canning plant and started a dairy, which prospered for two decades. Graham served two terms as a state senator, and raised a family that would add luster to the Graham name. His only daughter, Mary, was married to prominent Miami mortgage broker Lon Worth Crow, Jr., for several years. She died in 1985. His eldest son, Philip, married Katharine Meyer, and is credited with revitalizing the newspaper owned by her family, *The Washington Post*. His third child, William, minded the farm and led in the development of Miami Lakes. Four of his five children run various facets of the family business, the Graham Companies, which span residential, commercial and industrial property development, and a hospitality division which runs Don Shula's Hotel and Golf Resort and several restaurants.

The youngest son is Bob Graham, who was elected to the Florida House of Representatives in 1966, state senator in 1970, governor of Florida in 1978 and U.S. senator from Florida in 1986.

An in-law, Mrs. Ina S. Thompson of DeFuniak Springs, served as state motor vehicle commissioner during the six years LeRoy Collins was governor, thus becoming the first woman in the "little cabinet" of gubernatorial departmental appointees.

It was the sons of "Cap" Graham who foresaw that their father's land would not remain forever a dairy. They hired architects and city planners to draft a master plan for a new town with man-made lakes, winding streets, parks, and plenty of trees.

MICANOPY • *Alachua County*

Mikanope was the chief of the Seminole Indians at the beginning of the Seminole War of 1835. The name itself signifies chief of chiefs. He was the leader of the Indians who perpetrated the Dade Massacre, December 28, 1835. *See also* Dade City. Earlier that year a Dr. Payne, a Virginian, had established a settlement here, and in 1837 the government established a military post here. Near this site had stood the Spanish mission of Santa Ana. White colonists reached the area in 1817 to settle on a land grant of 290,000 acres owned by Don Fernando de la Maza Arredondo of Cuba. There is a folklore account which names the community for a slow-paying Irish merchant—Micky-no-pay. Still another twist on the name is that the trader told an Indian creditor, "Me can no pay."

MICCO • *Brevard County*

Settled in 1884. Believed named after a Seminole known simply as Chief since the Seminole-Creek word for "leader" was *miko*.

MICCOSUKEE • *Leon and Jefferson counties*

A community in Leon County and a large lake in Jefferson County. Simpson (1956) concludes the name means *nikasuki*, "hog-eaters."

MIDDLEBURG • *Clay County*

Formerly spelled Middleburgh and first known as Carey's Ford, it was a hub in the early nineteenth century, with ships traveling Black Creek to and from the St. Johns River and overland routes both to Tallahassee and the peninsula. Thus, it was the middle, but whether that had anything to do with the name is not known. Because of the deep-water port on the river and of the land routes, this location was important during the Seminole War, 1835-1842. Fort Heilmann was constructed here.

A student pageant at Concord School in Miccosukee, 1960.

MIDWAY • *Gadsden County*
Midway is halfway between Tallahassee and Quincy. According to Tom and Ray Magliozzi, or Click and Clack the Tappet Brothers, of Public Broadcasting's "Car Talk," this is one of 66 communities in the United States that bears the name Midway.

MILES CITY • *Collier County*
Named for Miles Collier, youngest of the three sons of Barron G. Collier. *See also* Collier.

MILLVIEW • *Escambia County*
A sawmill area since before the Civil War.

MILLVILLE • *Bay County*
The post office was established in 1899, but there were sawmills in this vicinity even earlier.

MILTON • *Santa Rosa County*
Formerly known by the eloquent names of Scratch Ankle and Hard Scrabble, it was established as a trading post about 1825. As pioneer hardships gave way to modern culture, the poetic names gave way to a respectable one. Just which Milton was honored by the final name is a dispute. Some say it is a contraction of an earlier Milltown; others that it was Milton Amos, a pioneer and ancestor of the present Amos family; still others that it was John Milton —not the English poet but the Civil War governor of Florida.

MIMS • *Brevard County*
Likely named for a family. The community's post office dates back to 1886.

MINERAL CITY (Ponte Vedra) • *St. Johns County*
In 1916, two young chemical engineers from Harvard University are said by the Federal Works Progress Administration to have sailed along the Atlantic coast from Brunswick, Ga., to Cape Canaveral, landing at intervals of 10 miles to take samples of the beach. Their analysis revealed many useful minerals in the vicinity of today's Ponte Vedra. During World War II, the federal government took over the holdings and produced ilmenite and rutile, both used in the manufacture of munitions. Also produced were zircon, monasite, and a silicate of aluminum. The mill and adjacent works were no longer used, and in time all traces vanished. Ponte Vedra now occupies the site of Mineral City.

MINNEHAHA, LAKE • *Lake and Orange counties*
Some reader of Longfellow's *Song of Hiawatha* took for these lakes the name of the heroine, Minnehaha. This name first was used in Mrs. Mary Eastman's *Life and Legends of the Sioux* (1849), in which she translated *minnehaha* as "laughing waters." Etymologists disagree.

MINNEOLA • *Lake County*
A settlement was established here in 1870 by William A. Smith, but was given no name. In 1882, George W. Hull, a Canadian by birth, came here from Duluth, Minn.; he made a survey and map of the town. At the instigation of

his wife, he named it Minneola, a name which is found in several states and is a Dakota Indian word meaning "many waters." The name was also applied by the Hulls to the lake here. Minneola was originally in Sumter County, but the boundary was moved.

MINORVILLE • *Orange County*
A family named Minor came here in 1900 to farm and grow citrus.

MIOMI, LAKE • *Sumter County*
This doesn't mean what it seems to mean (my-oh-me)—or does it? It appears at first reading to be one of the cuteisms that people apply to their ponds. But Simpson (1956) says Miomi may be a corruption of Seminole *wyoma*, "bitter water or whiskey." So maybe it really is my-o-me.

MIRAMAR • *Broward County*
It is odd that it is not by the sea, but a founder, Abe Mailman, took the name from the Cuban community of Miramar ("see the sea"), where he owned a vacation home.

MODELLO • *Dade County*
As the Florida East Coast Railway built southward from Miami at the turn of the century, its officials gave a contraction of the FEC's Model Land Company to what at first was a siding.

MOHAWK • *Lake County*
Stewart (1958) says Mohawk spread to many states because the tribe, as the most easterly tribe of the Iroquois, gave their name to the river and valley of New York and because the Mohawks were so well-known. As people from New York fanned out in the country, they applied Mohawk as a name for places without really thinking of the tribe. Florida's Mohawk was named in 1888 by Dr. C. H. Stokes of Lee Center, N.Y., in commemoration of New York's Mohawk River. Professor William Read says *mohawk* means "they eat things," that is to say, cannibals.

MOLINO • *Escambia County*
Molino is the Spanish word for "mill," and there was a mill situated here before the American acquisition of Florida from Spain in 1821.

MONROE COUNTY •
Established July 3, 1823, as the sixth county, and named for James Monroe, fifth president of the United States. His administration has become known as the Era of Good Feeling. Among other achievements of his eight years as president was obtaining the Floridas from Spain.

MONROE, LAKE • *Seminole and Volusia counties*
The St. Johns River widens at the town of Lake Monroe into a lake by the same name with a surface area of 9,406 acres, draining 2,420 square miles. The lake's name also honors the president.

MONTBROOK • *Levy County*
Unlike the mythical bird which is the symbol of immortality, this Phoenix, founded in 1891, changed its name to Montbrook after eight years.

M O N T C L A I R • *Lake County*
This could have been a transplant from Montclair, N.J., or it could have meant "lovely view" to a settler who was charmed by the greenery of the hills. Through confusion of Spanish, English, and Italian words, *mont* often is taken for "mountain" when *monte*, "wood, forest, thicket" is meant.

M O N T E V I S T A • *Lake County*
Spanish for "forest view," the name was bestowed in 1905 by Capt. R. D. Milholland, when he erected a log house on Lake Crescent and it became the site of the post office which had formerly been on Lake Nellie. The name was suggested by the Thlauhatka Hills, which can be seen from here.

M O N T I C E L L O • *Jefferson County*
This county seat of Jefferson County is named for the historic Virginia home of Thomas Jefferson. The post office here received the name in 1827. Near here stood the Spanish mission of La Concepcion de Ayabuli.

M O N T V E R D E • *Lake County*
Established in 1885 and incorporated in 1924. The name, taken as meaning "green hill," referred originally to the hills of citrus groves near the site, although this is now a grape-growing region.

M O O R E H A V E N • *Glades County*
Named for its founder, James A. Moore. It is the county seat of Glades County.

M O S E L E Y H A L L • *Madison County*
During the 1850s, numerous fine homes were built in Madison County. Like "Tara" in *Gone with the Wind*, these mansions had names and personalities. There was Maj. Livingston's "Peachy Orchard," and Lewis H. Moseley's "Mosley Hall." Settlements grew up around many of the plantations, and one of these was Moseley Hall.

M O S Q U I T O • *Once a county*
Many places in Florida are named for the promotional value of a pleasant name. But Mosquito County was stuck with just the reverse. There were some 700 settlers, excluding Indians, in the huge territory embraced by Mosquito County at the time of its creation by the territorial council on December 29, 1824, and it does not appear that those people were consulted about the name. The county, taken from St. Johns, embraced virtually all of peninsular Florida, being 190 miles long and 60 miles broad. New Smyrna was designated the county seat in 1835, so it appears the county was without a seat for about ten years. Even then, the county records remained at St. Augustine until 1843. The county was given the name by which the Spanish had known the coast. Mosquito Inlet had been named by the Spanish prior to 1573 and the land in the area was called *Los Mosquitos*. While the name means "gnat," it is certain that what the Spanish had in mind by mosquito was the insect that plagued the saltwater marshes of the coasts until the comparatively recent draining and spraying of these. Yet there was considerable cultivation of the coastal area in the period prior to the destruction during

the Seminole Wars. There was an abortive effort in 1842 to change the name of Mosquito to Leigh Read (*see also*), but finally on January 30, 1845, Mosquito disappeared from the map as the territorial council approved the substitution of Orange. Meantime, another county, St. Lucie, had been carved from Mosquito so the old county had fewer people—around 175—than when it was created.

M O S S   B L U F F • *Marion County*
First settled a century ago. The name likely was suggested by the Spanish moss which grows in profusion from the trees here and from an elevated view of the Ocklawaha River.

M O S S D A L E • *Volusia County*
Another old-timer, this community first was settled in the 1850s. Again, the name probably resulted from the attractiveness of the Spanish moss dropping from the trees.

M O U L T R I E • *St. Johns County*
Named for John Moultrie, lieutenant governor of Florida during the English occupation, 1763-1783, who lived nearby in a stone mansion on his planta-tion, Belle Vista. He joined other English settlers in going to the Bahamas when Florida was returned to Spain.

M O U N T   C A R R I E • *Columbia County*
There was a post office here from 1878 until 1885, but who Carrie was is unknown.

M O U N T   D O R A • *Lake County*
A settlement here was first known as Royellou, from the names of Royal Ella and Louis Tremain, who were among the pioneer residents who established the community in 1882. During the resurvey of the boundaries of Orange County, the U. S. government surveyors (of whom John W. Weeks, later sec-retary of war in the Coolidge cabinet, was one) ran their lines through this section and Mrs. Dora Ann Dowdy offered them camping hospitality on her homestead. In appreciation, they named the lake here Lake Dora, and the town was later renamed after the lake. Mount refers to the fact that the town is on a plateau 266 feet above sea level.

M O U N T   P L E A S A N T • *Gadsden County*
Occupying a high ridge in this hilly region of Florida, the view here is pleas-ant indeed, as some early settler doubtless felt. Mount Pleasant is a pre-Civil War community.

M O U N T   V E R N O N   A R S E N A L • *Gadsden County*
Andrew Jackson was responsible for building an arsenal here when he was president of the United States. His knowledge of this area of Florida may have influenced his approval of the strategic site near where the Chattahoochee and Flint Rivers converge to form the Apalachicola River. On November 3, 1832, the president ordered the Tallahassee Land Office to withdraw 1,500 acres from the public domain. The small community adjacent to the arsenal site was given the name of Mount Vernon in 1832, although another arsenal

site in Alabama had the same name. The resultant confusion in mail delivery caused the legislative council to change the name of Mount Vernon in 1834 to Chattahoochee. There are remains of the arsenal on the grounds of the Florida State Hospital.

MUD LAKE • *Polk County*
The legal site of the county seat for about a year in 1860-1861.

MULAT • *Santa Rosa County*
A contraction of mulatto. Took its name from nearby Mulatto Bayou, beside the Spanish land grant to the son of a Spanish nobleman and his slave-wife.

MULBERRY • *Polk County*
There are four large phosphate plants in the immediate vicinity of this town, and at a point convenient to all four there stood a large mulberry tree. Freight for one of the plants was frequently marked "put off at the big mulberry tree," and when a regular railroad agency was set up about 1889 it was given the name Mulberry.

MUNSON • *Santa Rosa County*
Named in 1913 for a lumber company manager, Capt. Charles Munson.

MUNYONS ISLAND • *Palm Beach County*
This island in Lake Worth was named in 1903 for Dr. Munyon, who had his winter home here and also grew and shipped King oranges and cultivated papayas, which he used in part for medicinal purposes.

MURDOCK • *Charlotte County*
Vasco Peeples of Punta Gorda, knowledgeable about Charlotte County, reports that Murdock was named in 1911 for a settler, but now even the sign on the depot has been changed to Port Charlotte. This may be poetic justice, for Murdock originally was called Charlotte.

MUSCOGEE • *Escambia County*
Said to be a transplant from Muscogee, Ga., Muscogee is the name of the Creek and related Indian tribes of the Southeast. Read (1934) defined the word as meaning "swamp" or "swamp Indian."

MYAKKA CITY • *Manatee County*
Variously spelled Myakka, Mayaca, Mayaco, Miakka, and Miaco and applied to communities, a lake, and a river in Manatee, Sarasota, and Martin counties. The name is of obscure Indian meaning. McDuffee (1961) says Myakka City adopted the changed spelling to distinguish the new community from old Miakka (*See also*).

NALCREST • *Polk County*
A retirement community for postmen sponsored by the National Association of Letter Carriers (NALC-rest), which has a bronze statue that reached its town square after standing for a quarter-century in front of the William Penn

Post Office Annex in Philadelphia. Nixon Smiley told of the statue's travels in *The Miami Herald*. The statue is of Richard F. Quinn, a "thick-set, broad-shouldered and sawed-off Irishman with a Grover Cleveland mustache." There is a letter pouch hanging from one shoulder and a raft of letters in his left hand. Quinn was immortalized in bronze because he was one of the organizers of the NALC and its first president, from 1881 until 1895. When the Philadelphia post office was rebuilt, Quinn's statue disappeared. In 1942, William C. Doherty, then president of the letter carriers, went searching and eventually found the statue, crated and on its back in an attic of the new post office. Smiley says Doherty had Quinn resurrected and placed in the NALC's building in Philadelphia until 1963, when he was crated again and shipped to Nalcrest.

NAPLES • *Collier County*
This beautiful resort town on the Gulf coast was named for another beautiful city, Naples in Italy.

NARANJA • *Dade County*
Established in 1905 by M. L. Albury. When the post office department rejected the suggested name of Silver Palm because of another Silver Palm, the residents agreed on *Naranja*, Spanish for "orange," because of the many groves nearby.

NARCOOSE • *Osceola County*
Derived from the Creek *nokose*, "bear." Among the first settlers in the mid-1880s were three groups from England: retired professional and military men, who came to Florida because of the climate and their limited incomes; a younger category of people, including sons of well-to-do families who had been sent abroad for various reasons and were supported by remittances; and workers, some employed as servants by the other groups. All expected to find comfortable living and cash for their cultivation of oranges.

NASSAU COUNTY •
The tenth county, established December 29, 1824. Named for the Nassau River and Nassau Sound which, in part, separate Nassau and Duval counties. The river and the sound here and elsewhere in the United States and the capital of the Bahamas were named for the Duchy of Nassau, a former state in the western part of Germany whose seat was Wiesbaden. The line of William the Silent and his descendants, the princes of Orange-Nassau, became extinct when King William III of England died in 1702. The name was brought to Florida during the English occupation of 1763-83.

NATURAL BRIDGE • *Leon County*
Florida has a number of natural bridges where streams either go underground or emerge. Arch Creek in Miami was one. But the best-known place is Natural Bridge, five miles east of Woodville in Leon County. Here on March 6, 1865, cadets from the West Florida Seminary (now Florida State University) joined Confederate regulars and home guards to halt the advance of Union forces seeking primarily to cut off St. Marks, Newport, and maybe Tallahassee. In

the battle at the Natural Bridge, Union losses were eight dead, 105 wounded, and 35 missing. The Confederates had three killed and at least 30 wounded. "They had saved the capital, and indeed at the end of the war it was the only confederate capital east of the Mississippi River that had not been captured" (Dodd, 1959).

N AVARRE • *Santa Rosa County*
The French wife of an army colonel who came here in the 1900s gave the community its name. The ancient kingdom of Navarre was a buffer state between France and Spain. Now Navarre is a province of Spain with Pamplona, its capital, famous for the yearly running of the bulls. At Florida's Navarre, there is a 2,640-foot bridge crossing Santa Rosa Sound to link Santa Rosa Island and the mainland.

N EEDHELP • *Collier County*
Tebeau (1966) tells of C. G. McKinney, who came to Chokoloskee in 1886 to farm. He named his place Needhelp after discovering that the soil, however black and rich in appearance, lacked certain minerals essential to the growing of good crops.

N EPTUNE BEACH • *Duval County*
One of a group of seaside communities about 18 miles southeast of Jacksonville, it takes its name from that of the king of the sea. *See also* Atlantic Beach.

N EW BERLIN • *Duval County*
The post office opened here in December 1875, but a Dr. von Balson is said to have bestowed the name on the community in the 1860s.

View from the St. Johns River of New Berlin, in 1900.

N EWBERRY • *Alachua County*
The first post office, established March 1894, was called Newton, but on August 1, 1894, it was changed to Newberry, for Newberry, S.C. Phosphate deposits were discovered here about 1890, and by May 1895 there were seven phosphate plants in the vicinity. Newberry was the southern terminus of the Jacksonville & Southern Railway.

N E W B U R N • *Suwannee County*
When Henry H. Platt homesteaded here, the area was known as Platt. Later, R. L. Millinor purchased the land and changed the name to Newburn.

N E W F O U N D H A R B O R • *Brevard County*
Divides the southern end of Merritt Island into two tongues of land.

N E W N A N S V I L L E • *Columbia County*
Formerly Dell's, it was a center of trade and plantation life for some 30 years from 1826. It served as the seat of Alachua County until Columbia County was created and Newnansville was included in the new county. A decline was accelerated by the decision of the Cross-Florida Railway to run its tracks through the area then known as Hog Town but later as Gainesville. The freeze of 1886 destroyed the extensive citrus plantings. Lake Newnan, in Alachua County, likely derived its name from the same person, Col. Daniel Newnans.

N E W P O R T • *Wakulla County*
Founded in October 1843, the fifth and last town started on the St. Marks River while Florida was a territory. As W. T. Cash suggested, in an article in the Tallahassee Historical Society's *Apalachee* (1944), Newport was just that, a new port reestablishing storm-ravaged Port Leon on another site. The port was intended to draw shipments of cotton, tobacco, lumber, naval stores and furs from the Tallahassee Railroad. Newport became the seat of Wakulla County on February 1, 1844; by the end of 1843 it likely had a newspaper, a drugstore, and some 1,500 inhabitants. The town began to decline in 1860 because St. Marks kept the railroad and was five miles nearer the sea. Among Newport's residents was the Rev. Charles Beecher, brother of Harriett Beecher Stowe and state superintendent of public instruction from March 18, 1871, to January 23, 1873.

N E W P O R T R I C H E Y • *Pasco County*
Named for Old Port Richey, which had been located about a mile north of here, and which had been settled by A. M. Richey, merchant and postmaster.

N E W R I V E R • *Bradford County*
Perpetuates the original name of the county.

N E W R I V E R • *Once a county*
The thirty-sixth county, established December 21, 1858. It was created with Suwannee County in a division of Columbia County. New River took its name from the river of the same name. New River's name was changed December 6, 1861, to Bradford, honoring Capt. Richard Bradford, the first Florida officer killed in the Civil War.

N E W S M Y R N A B E A C H • *Volusia County*
In 1767, Dr. Andrew Turnbull obtained several thousand acres of land from the British Crown under the English Occupation Act and established a colony of Greeks and Minorcans on this site. He named the place for Smyrna, his wife's former home in Asia Minor. The location is said to have been occupied for nine months by Menéndez in 1565, after which his group abandoned it

An 1890s New Smyrna group posed under a large live oak tree.

for St. Augustine. Near here stood the Spanish mission of Atocuimi. Seven miles south of here is Turtle Mound, said to be the only large Indian shell heap to survive to the present day with relatively little damage.

NICEVILLE • *Okaloosa County*
Formerly called Boggy Bayou. A group of citizens—including postmaster B. P. Edge, B. H. Sutton, George Parrish, S. S. Spence, John Allen, and G. B. Anchors—met and submitted a list of names to the Post Office Department. Portsmouth was the name preferred by the group, but this was rejected by the postal authorities because of its similarity to Portland, only 21 miles east. The name Niceville, suggested by Mr. Edge, was assigned.

NITTAW • *Osceola County*
Another of the Indian names sprinkled by railroad officials along the right-of-way of the extension of the Florida East Coast Railway from New Smyrna southward into the interior near Lake Okeechobee. One source interprets this name as Creek for "day" while another says it is Indian for "lone eaters." The word likely was chosen for the sound rather than the meaning.

NIXIE • *Marion County*
The postal clerk's designation for an improperly addressed letter or parcel was the name of this community for six months in 1883-1884. The reason is unknown.

NIXON • *Bay County*
A community in Bay County bore the name of the country's thirty-seventh president, Richard M. Nixon, but no honor to him was intended, since Florida's Nixon was established before the president was born.

NOCATEE • *DeSoto County*
Again, euphony may have dictated the choice, for the Seminole Indian word *nakiti* means "what is it?"

NOKOMIS • *Sarasota County*
Longfellow's poem *Hiawatha* doubtless inspired the name. The Ojibway Indian word means "grandmother."

NOMA • *Holmes County*
Named for the Noma Mill Company. Noma could be pronounced No Ma, but the town had two "pa's" in Drew Morris and Ira Hutchinson, who together operated a sawmill here at the turn of the twentieth century. Who or what was Noma remains unanswered.

NORTH PORT • *Sarasota County*
Unlike many Florida communities which have enlarged their original names, North Port Charlotte's voters in 1974 lopped off Charlotte. Their reason was a closer identification with Sarasota County than with Charlotte County and its Port Charlotte. They were not deterred by the fact that a few canals are the city's only claim to being a port.

NORUM • *Washington County*
It has been said, perhaps in jest, that this name designated a dry community, where alcohol was not sold, but there must be some other explanation, yet unfound. The community had a post office from 1908 to 1921.

OAKDALE • *Jackson County*
The great oaks here gave the place its name.

OAK GROVE • *Okaloosa County*
John F. Thomas opened a general store here in the 1870s and the live oaks suggested a name when the post office was opened in 1878. There also was an Oak Grove in the Mt. Horeb community of Madison County.

OAK HILL • *Volusia County*
Established about 1866 and named for an oak tree that grew on a shell mound near the home of J. D. Mitchell, the first settler.

OAKHURST • *Pinellas County*
There is something majestic about oaks, and that appealed even here in this community of large citrus groves.

OAKLAND • *Orange County*
Established in 1884 by settlers from South Carolina. Its name refers to the live-oak trees in the vicinity. It became a busy and thriving site of sawmills, sugar mills, and cotton gins. In 1889, it became a junction for the Orange Belt and Florida Midland railroads, and hotels, stores, and blocks of workmen's shanties sprang up with the establishment of large railroad shops. When the Midland Railroad went bankrupt, the shops were removed, and

later a disastrous fire swept the business district. Today, Oakland's livelihood comes from the raising of citrus fruit and winter vegetables.

OAKLAND PARK • *Broward County*
The first permanent white settlers were Mr. and Mrs. Thomas Whidby, who came from Georgia in 1901. In 1922, the Skipdull Improvement Company of Miami subdivided the area and named it Oakland Park after a large stand of oak trees along the banks of the north fork of Middle River. In 1925, the American British Improvement Association bought a large tract. The association had among its members such notables as the countess of Lauderdale, an ex-king of Greece, and Mrs. Horace E. Dodge. The Oakland Park area merged with adjoining land and it was incorporated as Floranada in December 1925. The 1926 hurricane stopped development. In 1929, Floranada was officially reduced in size and reincorporated as Oakland Park.

O'BRIEN • *Suwannee County*
Once known as Dod's Hole from a sink on the homestead of John F. White, O'Brien was given its name in 1884 to honor an official of the Savannah, Florida and Western Railroad.

OBSERVATION ISLAND • *Glades County*
Observation Island in Lake Okeechobee was named on a map made in 1856 by Lt. Ives of the Army's Topographical Corps.

OCALA • *Marion County*
The literal meaning of this Indian word is heavily clouded—perhaps beyond discovery. *Ocali* was the name of an ancient Timucuan province through which De Soto almost certainly passed in 1539. It later was used by the

Ocala's Fourth of July parade, 1899.

Indians to refer to the whole area of middle Florida, and there was at least one Timucuan chief who bore the name. During the Seminole War, Fort King, the principal fort in the state, stood on the present site of this town. The name was changed to Ocala in 1847, presumably by someone familiar with the history of the Indians and the Spanish in Florida. Some of the literal meanings which have been suggested for the name are "water margin," "lay on the fire," "kingdom," "fertile soil," "abundant," "green," "fair land," and "big hammock"—as wide a choice as any hobbyist of name origins could ask for. Read (1934) flatly states: "Ocala cannot be translated." Ocala is the county seat of Marion County.

O C E A N P O N D • *Baker County*
For a state with a boundary of several hundred miles on the Atlantic, ocean appears in few place names—Ocean Breeze in Martin County, Ocean City in Okaloosa, Ocean Ridge in Palm Beach, and Oceanway in Duval—but the best-known of all the Oceans is far from the Atlantic. It is Ocean Pond, a lake of some 1,700 acres in Baker County near the place where troops fought the major engagement of the Civil War in Florida. Better known as the Battle of Olustee, the clash of arms on February 20, 1864, resulted in Confederate casualties of 93 killed, 847 wounded, and six missing. The Union losses were so great—203 killed, 1,152 wounded, and 506 missing—that in federal camps the battle was spoken of as the second Dade Massacre. For the remainder of the Civil War, Union forces in Florida were confined to Jacksonville, St. Augustine, and Fernandina.

O C E A N R I D G E • *Palm Beach County*
Originally the land east and west of the inland waterway here was named Boynton. In 1932, the property owners east of the inland waterway separated from Boynton, setting up their own government and taking the name Boynton Beach. About 1937, some of the residents wanted to give up the name Boynton altogether. Several names were offered for their selection, and they chose Ocean Ridge. This derived from the fact that for many years, until 1925, there had been a hotel on the high coastal ridge at Boynton and several homes built by people who had earlier stayed at the hotel. In describing their location, these residents always said, "We live on the ridge."

O C E A N U S • *Brevard County*
Founded in 1893, it has disappeared from the map of Merritt Island. Oceanus was god of the stream in Greek mythology.

O C E A N W A Y • *Duval County*
The developer of this community, S. E. Gillespie, said in 1928, "We will call it Oceanway because it is on the way to the ocean."

O C H E E S E • *Calhoun and Jackson counties*
The name of a village in Calhoun County, a landing on the Apalachicola River in the same county, and a lake in Jackson County also known as Cypress Lake. Ocheese seems derived from the Hitchiti *ocheesulga*, meaning "those of a different speech" or "other tribes."

O CHLOCKONEE • *Gadsden, Liberty, and Franklin counties*
A river forming a bay of the same name to enter the Bay of Apalachee after flowing southward from Worth County, Ga., through Gadsden, Liberty, and Franklin Counties.

From Hitchiti *oki,* "water," and *lagana,* "yellow." The river was known to the Spanish in 1693 as the *Amarillo* and to the English in 1720 as the Yellow. Today the river bears the melodious Indian name.

O CHOPE • *Collier County*
A dot on the Tamiami Trail in the Big Cypress Swamp, it lies 35 miles from Naples or 60 miles from Miami. It is said to have the smallest U.S. post office. The area at one time had a sizable population for Collier County. The county was flush with tomato fields and packinghouses. Then the population dwindled as the federal government authorized the National Park Service to acquire land. "They're killing Ochopee," said Forest Harmon, a tall Kentuckian who moved there in 1962 and began to buy most of Ochopee along the Trail to create a retirement community.

O CITLOTA FUNKA • *Taylor County*
Simpson (1956) lists this small stream in Taylor County by another Indian name, *Achenahatchee,* which he translates as compounded from the Creek *achena* and *hatchee,* "creek." Nowadays the river is known more commonly as Spring Warrior.

O CKLAWAHA • *Marion County*
A tributary of the St. Johns River, a town in Marion County, and the lake formed by the Rodman Reservoir of the Cross-State Barge Canal. For a river 79 miles long, the Ocklawaha has achieved much notice as a result of the efforts of naturalists to preserve the river from the digging of the Cross-State Canal. The name is a corruption of the Creek *ak-lowahe,* "muddy." The Rodman Reservoir was named for a small community on the site. A congressional resolution gave the name Lake Ocklawaha to the body of water formed by the reservoir. In 1992, these entities regained the "c" in their names. The "c" mysteriously changed in 1892 and old-timers labored to persuade the United States Board of Geographic Names to restore the "c." Finally, in response to "a ton" of local requests, the name was again officially Ocklawaha.

O COEE • *Orange County*
Platted and named in 1885 by R.B.F. Roper. The name was taken from that of a small town in Polk County, Tenn., from which Roper's wife had come. It is a Cherokee Indian word which has been anglicized. Its original spelling was *uwagahi* and it means "apricot vine place." This Florida town was the site of the pioneer work of Capt. B.M. Sims in budding wild orange trees. Here he started the first commercial citrus nursery in the United States and supplied many of the old groves in Florida with their first trees, as well as shipping many young trees to California. For several years Ocoee was known as Starke Lake for Dr. J. D. Starke, who had a camp on the lake here.

OCTAHATCHEE, LAKE • *Hamilton County*
This is either Sand Creek or White Sand (Creek).

OJUS • *Dade County*
When Richard La Penta came to Florida he asked how Ojus got its name. He said people responded, when asked where they were from, "Oh just Florida." Not satisfied, he inquired of *The Miami Herald*'s "Action Line," which told him "Ojus is the Seminole word for plenty, and Ojus was a plenty important place when Miami was only a wide space in the road. Ojus is one of the oldest settlements in Dade County. It had the railroad when Lemon City was the southern terminal, and that was a year or so before Henry Flagler extended the tracks to the little riverside trading post called Miami. Ojus ceased to be a town back in 1936 when it was abolished by an act of the state legislature. Boom debts did Ojus in—plenty of 'em."

OKAHUMPKA • *Sumter and Lake counties*
The name of a lake in Sumter County and of a community in Lake County. It is freely translated as Hitchiti *oki*, "water," and Creek *hamken*, "one," or single lake. There was an Indian town where the modern community now stands. The present community was founded in 1880 by the Rev. Edmund Snyder of Germantown, Pa. Kennedy (1929) says: "Okahumpka is the English word for the Indian word *Okeehumpkee*, meaning Deep Waters because of a spring of unknown depths that lies near the town of Old Okahumpka. This spring, whose depths have never been sounded, was named Bugg Spring because a man of that name was drowned there. Old Oka-humpka was on Lake Dunham and was the last landing place of the steamboats coming up the Ocklawaha."

Tourists on the Okeehumkee *made a day-long trip from Palatka to Silver Springs.*

OKALOACOOCHEE SLOUGH • *Collier and Hendry counties*
The name means "little bad water." This slough is in the Big Cypress Swamp of Collier and Hendry counties.

OKALOO • *Okaloosa County*
Obviously a shortening of the name of the county.

OKALOOSA COUNTY •

The fifty-second county, established June 13, 1915. Read (1934) says that the word is Choctaw *oka*, meaning "water" and *lusa*, meaning "black." Thus, the name likely referred to the Blackwater River in the same county. The county was taken from Santa Rosa and Walton counties.

OKEECHOBEE COUNTY •

The fifty-fourth county, established May 8, 1917. The name means, as might be expected, "big water," and is derived from two Hitchiti Indian words, *oki*, meaning "water" and *chobi*, meaning "big." The word Miami is thought to have the same meaning in another Indian dialect, and to apply to the same body of water. *See also* Miami.

OKEECHOBEE • *Okeechobee County*

The first settlement was called Tantie, after Tantie Huckabee, a redheaded schoolteacher who came here from Carolina. Early in the second decade of the twentieth century, the Florida East Coast Railway took over the settlement and laid out a model town. It was then named for Lake Okeechobee.

OKEECHOBEE, LAKE • *Okeechobee, Martin, Palm Beach, Hendry, and Glades counties*

The second-largest freshwater lake entirely within one state. It has an area of about 730 square miles. Alaska has the largest, Lake Iliamna, of 1,033 square miles. Utah's Great Salt Lake covers 1,500 square miles. Lake Okeechobee is the fourth-largest natural lake entirely within the United States. Lake Michigan, which touches Wisconsin, Illinois, Indiana, and Michigan, is the largest, with 22,400 square miles. Lake Okeechobee is a remnant of a shallow sea, known as the Pamlico Sea, which once occupied what is now the Everglades–Lake Okeechobee basin. This basin formed when the Florida plateau emerged from the Atlantic Ocean as a result of movement of the earth's crust. Although large in area, Lake Okeechobee is shallow, and probably contains less than two cubic miles of water. Simpson (1956) reports the lake appeared as Mayaiami on the Solis de Meras map of 1565-1567, Macaco on the Searcy map of 1828, and Wethlacco on the Poinsett map of 1838. "The spelling on the Poinsett map, *We Thlacco*, is from the Creek *we*, 'water,' and *thalka*, 'big,' and its present name is from Hitchiti *oki*, 'water,' *chubi*, 'big.' The entire synonymy apparently resolves itself into an expression of its size."

OKEELANTA • *Palm Beach County*

Situated on the North New River Canal, about six miles from Lake Okeechobee. The name was coined from those of the lake and the Atlantic Ocean. Once there was an Okeelanta and a New Okeelanta, but since the first existed only on paper, the New of the second was soon dropped.

OKEFENOKE OR OKEFENOKEE • *Baker and Columbia counties*

A swamp extending from Georgia into northeastern Florida. Hitchiti *oki*, "water," and Creek *fenoke*, "trembling," or trembling water. The swamp also was known by the Creek *ekan*, "land," and *fenoke*, "trembling," or trembling land.

OKHAKONKONHEE, LAKE • *Polk County*
This lake has two names of recent application, either of which—Lake Caloosa or Crooked Lake—appears a less formidable pronunciation. Read (1934) suggests the original name to be a derivative of Hitchiti *oki,* "water," Seminole-Creek *lako,* "big," and Seminole-Creek *yanahi,* "crooked," or crooked big water.

OKLAWAHA • *Gadsden County*
A creek in Gadsden County. *See also* Ocklawaha.

OLD SALEM • *Gadsden County*
When the Georgia, Florida and Alabama Railroad completed its line from Cuthbert, Ga., to Tallahassee, a small depot was placed in 1903 at a spot about three-quarters of a mile from Old Salem, a pre-Civil War community. The railroad exerted a magnetic influence and soon most of Old Salem's businesses had moved to the new town, which was called Havana because of the principal crop of the region: shade tobacco.

OLDSMAR • *Pinellas County*
Established in 1907 by the Reolds Farm Company, headed by R. E. Olds, a Michigan automobile manufacturer. In 1925, to gain identification value during the land boom, the name was changed to Tampa Shores, but the old name was restored in 1937.

OLD TOWN • *Dixie County*
Inhabited by the Upper Creeks, Old Town, often called Suwannee Old Town, was one of the largest Indian villages in northern Florida. Old Town was captured by Gen. Andrew Jackson on a punitive expedition in April 1818. Among those trapped was Robert Chrystie Armbrister, a former British officer suspected by Jackson of fomenting Indians to warfare in Spanish territory. Jackson had Armbrister shot. Another Britisher, Alexander Arbuthnot, captured at St. Marks, was hanged by Jackson for the same reason. When the Indians were pushed out during the Seminole Wars, the Americans took over Old Town. There has been a post office here since 1857.

OLD TOWN • *Hendry County*
Maps bear the intriguing legend "Ruins of Sam Jones Old Town." *See also* Sam Jones Old Town.

OLGA • *Lee County*
A Norwegian sea captain with a long red beard, Peter Nelson came up the Caloosahatchee River in the early 1880s. There were stories that he was an offshoot of the Norwegian royal family—that he was, in fact, a prince. He fell in love with the Caloosahatchee and in 1883 founded two waterside towns, Olga and Alva. Miss Margaret Verdier Jones, niece of the first schoolteacher upriver, is quoted as saying Olga was named by Captain Nelson for a "Russian princess then in the news."

OLIVE BRANCH • *Osceola County*
A community beginning in 1894, but with its period of greatest activity

between 1904 and 1910. The town was established by the religious group known as Shakers, the United Society of Believers in Christ's Second Appearing. Olive Branch was one of some 20 Shaker communities in the United States. The Florida communal establishment was involved in farming, cattle raising, commercial fishing, and timbering.

OLUSTEE • *Baker County*
Read (1934) translates Olustee as corrupted from the Seminole-Creek *oklasti,* "blackfish." It was here that federal and Confederate troops fought the major engagement in Florida of the Civil War. *See also* Ocean Pond.

OLUSTEE CREEK • *Columbia and Union counties*
This stream forms the boundary between Columbia and Union counties. *See also* Olustee.

ONA • *Hardee County*
Named for a daughter of the Whiddon family, among the original settlers.

ONECO • *Manatee County*
An Indian name, but did it come from Oneka, oldest son of Uncas, a Mohican sachem? Or did it come from Onaka, the fortune-teller and Seminole chief? Sources differ.

ONOSHATCHEE RIVER • *Monroe County*
May have taken its name from Onasa Island, or the Fortune Teller's Island, in the Everglades. Creek *onaka,* "the saying or the word," or Seminole *onasa,* "seer or fortune-teller."

OPAL • *Okeechobee County*
The name of a station on an abandoned branch line of the Florida East Coast Railway. The name was derived from Creek *opa,* "owl."

OPA-LOCKA • *Dade County*
The Indian name of this town refers to a hammock nearby. The word is Seminole and is made up of *opilwa,* meaning "swamp," and *lako,* meaning "big." That may have been a short form of *opatishawaukalocka*; roughly, "hammock in the big swamp." The community was started by Glen H. Curtiss, pioneer of the aviation industry, and James H. Bright during the 1920s land boom. They also produced Hialeah and Miami Springs on the doorstep of Miami. Curtiss is credited with having selected the name Opa-Locka, because the original buildings were reminiscent of a city from the *Arabian Nights.*

ORANGE •
Because of its identification with Florida, Orange has been given to many communities, among them: Orange Dale in St. Johns County, Orangedale in Polk and St. Lucie counties, Orange Hammock in Clay and Flagler counties, Orange Heights in Alachua County, Orange Hill in Washington County, Orange Lake in Marion County, Orange Mills in St. Johns County, Orange Park in Clay County, and Orange Springs in Marion County.

ORANGE COUNTY •
The eleventh county, established December 29, 1824, under the name Mosquito. *See also* Mosquito. Renamed on January 30, 1845, for the many orange groves in the vicinity.

ORANGE BEND • *Lake County*
The post office here dates from 1884 when the railroad came through. Said to have been named for wild orange trees cut down by John Bentley, Joseph Baught, and Armlain Bryan in the 1850s to plant sugar cane.

ORANGE CITY • *Volusia County*
Established in 1876 by Dr. Seth French and a number of others from Wisconsin. By 1850, there were some 175 citrus groves blooming on about 1,000 acres of land, and when, in 1882, the town was incorporated, a name was chosen to reflect that fruitfulness. Prior to that, the community had been known simply as Wisconsin Settlement.

ORANGE PARK • *Clay County*
A community was founded here in 1876, and during the 1880s was the center of considerable wealth. It was named for the orange groves which flourished here during that period. Previously, it had been known as Laurel Grove, the name of the old Kingsley plantation.

ORCHID • *Indian River County*
One of the older communities in this area. The post office dates from 1887 and the settlement likely was here earlier. It is surmised that the name was derived from wild orchids in the trees here.

ORIENT PARK • *Hillsborough County*
Appears to have been known previously as Bunchville and Hancock. There is some feeling that the Orient was taken from the mystical luster perceived as the sun sets over nearby Hillsborough Bay.

ORION • *Alachua County*
Buchholz (1929) says this community, first settled in 1847, had grown sufficiently by 1884 to be named Santafee (San-taffy) after the Santa Fe River. The name was changed to Orion in 1886 and finally to High Springs in 1898. Buchholz comments that High Springs was derived "after a spring on top of a hill—the spring has long since disappeared but the name still remains."

ORLANDO • *Orange County*
Several legends elbow one another in the effort to explain the origin of the name of this central Florida city. One says that Judge James G. Speer, who came here from South Carolina in 1854 and became a state senator, took the name from that of a character in Shakespeare's *As You Like It*. Support is given this by the fact that the city has a Rosalind Street. Another account says that a certain Mr. Orlando was leading an ox caravan to Tampa when he was seized by colic (now appendicitis) at this spot, passed away, and was buried where he fell; later passersby were said to have remarked, "There lies Orlando." What has become the official version concerns Orlando Reeves,

The Orange County Courthouse at Orlando, 1904.

who was on sentinel duty for a camping party while his companions slept. An Indian stealthily approached in the guise of a rolling log; Orlando saw him for what he was and fired his gun, waking the other campers and saving their lives, but not before the Indian had launched an arrow which took Orlando's life. In 1939, students of Cherokee Junior High School at their own expense erected in Eola Park a tablet which says:

> *Orlando Reeves*
> *In whose honor our city*
> *Orlando was named*
> *Killed in this vicinity by*
> *Indians September, 1835*
> *"How sleep the brave who sink to rest*
> *By all their country's wishes blest!"*

> —William Collins

Wherever and by whomever the name was chosen, the community was earlier known as Jernigan, after Aaron Jernigan, who came from Georgia and settled here in 1842. The first post office was opened in 1850, and the name was changed to Orlando in 1857. The city is the county seat of Orange County and has 30 lakes within its limits.

ORLOVISTA • *Orange County*
A combination of Orlando and the Spanish *vista*, "view" or "scene."

ORMOND BEACH • *Volusia County*
A group came here in 1873 or 1875 from New Britain, Conn., where its

members had been associated with the Corbin Lock Company. They included Daniel Wilson, George Millard, and Lucius Summers. At first they called
the Florida community after their old hometown. Later settlers wanted a
name more closely associated with local history, and Ormond was chosen on
April 22, 1880. Strickland (1963) tells a story about the change of name that
is reminiscent of the "Dr. Livingston, I presume?" meeting of Stanley and
Livingston in Africa. A New Britain settler, John Anderson, was recovering
from fever in 1880 when he heard a knock on the door of his log cabin. A
distinguished-appearing stranger extended his hand and said, "My name is
Ormond." He was James Ormond III, third in a line of Ormonds identified
with this area. Capt. James Ormond I settled Damietta, a 2,000-acre plantation on a Spanish land grant. He was killed about 1815. James Ormond II
died in 1829 on the plantation, and his grave, which still may be seen near
Ormond Beach, bears the legend, "An Honest Man." Anderson joined in
proposing Ormond as a substitute for New Britain.

ORSINO • *Brevard County*
Said to be derived from Orsino, the Duke of Illyria, in Shakespeare's *Twelfth
Night.*

ORTEGA • *Duval County*
Here at the junction of McGirts Creek (renamed Ortega River) and the St.
Johns, in the city of Jacksonville, is the residential suburb whose land
belonged for a decade after 1804 to the president of the Republic of East
Florida, John Houston McIntosh, whose headquarters were at Fernandina.
The republic existed in 1812-1816 as a phase of American efforts to push out
the Spanish. This point of land was once known as McGirts Point, after the
infamous brigand Dan McGirt, and as Sadlers Point, after a son-in-law of
McIntosh. Ortega could have been derived from the Spanish word meaning
"grouse or quail" or from a Spanish family name. But family members of
developers of the modern suburb, according to Miss Dena Snodgrass, believe
that those who named Ortega simply had heard the name and liked it, and
nothing more.

ORTONA • *Glades County*
An Italian established a subdivision here in the 1920s and gave it a name,
understood to mean "garden spot," which he believed would appeal to fellow countrymen. Little remains.

OSCEOLA COUNTY •
The fortieth county, established May 12, 1887, and named for the famous
chief of the Seminoles. Osceola was imprisoned by Gen. Thomas S. Jesup after
having been captured under a flag of truce. Osceola was first locked up at Fort
Marion (Castillo de San Marcos) in St. Augustine, but when some Indians
escaped from there, he and other prisoners were transferred to Fort Moultrie
at Charleston, S.C. Osceola died there on January 30, 1838. Weakened by
chronic malaria and quinsy, he lost the will to live in captivity. As Tebeau
(1971) opines, "Had he not been captured under a flag of truce and sent away

to die in prison, he might have died as ignominiously as many of his brethren. As it is, his place as the most romantic if not the most heroic figure in the annals of the war seems secure." Twenty years after the incident the criticism still was so great that Jesup found himself trying to explain his actions. Osceola was born on the Tallapoosa River in Creek Country about 1803. Osceola is derived from the Creek *asi-yahola*, "black drink cry." The Creeks and later the Seminoles prepared a ceremonial black drink from the leaves of the yaupon. Research indicates Osceola was part Creek Indian, part Scotch. A Seminole leader of present days was quoted as saying that for the Seminoles, Osceola is a George Washington or an Abraham Lincoln because of his unquenchable determination to keep the Seminoles free and to retain possession of the Indian lands (Hartley, 1974). Moore-Willson (1935) states that credit for naming the county belongs to State Sen. J. Milton Bryan, who represented Orange County when Osceola was split away. The senator lived near Kissimmee, seat of Osceola. Mrs. Moore-Willson quotes Judge Bryan's daughter, Mrs. C. A. Carson, as saying: "When my father came home from Tallahassee there was a great celebration; every one in town (Kissimmee) turned out to meet him at the train and they carried him on their shoulders in celebration of the new county."

O S C E O L A • *Lake County*
Crow's Bluff on the St. Johns River first was named Osceola by E. H. Crow, who opened a store and post office here. Because of confusion with Ocala, with shipments for each going to the other place, Crow changed the name of Osceola to Hawkinsville. Now, it is Crow's Bluff and notable for a bridge across the St. Johns, connecting highways in Lake and Volusia counties.

O S C E O L A • *Orange County*
From 1858, when the first log cabin was build by David Mizell, until 1884, when Winter Park became its name, there was a community here known as Osceola. As the story goes, the Indian chief had a camp here overlooking the lake which today bears his name.

O S C E O L A • *Seminole County*
The Osceola Cypress Company, establishing a mill here in 1925, changed the name from Cook's Ferry.

O S C E O L A P A R K • *Broward County*
Named after the Seminole Indian chief.

O S K I N • *Okaloosa County*
Seminole-Creek for "rain."

O S L O • *Indian River County*
Believed to be a transplant from Oslo, the capital of Norway, a belief supported by the fact that Oslo's neighboring community on the Florida coast is Viking.

O S O W A W • *Okeechobee County*
Another station with an Indian name on the abandoned Okeechobee extension of the Florida East Coast Railway. *Osowaw* is Seminole-Creek for "bird."

O S P R E Y • *Sarasota County*
An old community, said to date from John Webb's settlement in 1867, with
the name of the hawklike bird found here.

O S T E E N • *Volusia County*
Known first as Saulsville for George Sauls, whose home was here in the 1850s,
the town changed its name in the 1880s to honor a pioneer cattleman, H. E.
Osteen.

O T A H I T E • *Okaloosa County*
Simpson (1956) says this name may have been derived from the Creek *otahi-
ta*, "damp place," and may relate to the seepage springs common here.

O T T E R   C R E E K •
There are Otter Creeks in Bay, Levy, Lafayette, and Wakulla counties, and an
Otter Island in Sarasota Bay of Manatee County, all named for the abundance
of otters at some time. There also is a community known as Otter Creek in
Levy County, taking its name from the stream.

O V E R S E A S   H I G H W A Y • *Monroe County*
The drive from Miami to Key West on U.S. 1 is as close to driving on water as
most people will ever experience. The scenic, 150-mile drive carries motorists
over a series of 37 bridges linking the Florida Keys before ending in Key West.
Getting there is most of the fun.

Today's U.S. 1, known as the Overseas Highway in the Florida Keys, sits on
an embankment originally developed by Henry Flagler's Florida East Coast
Railway. The single track line, completed to Key West in 1912, was an engineering marvel. For 23 years, the railroad carried travelers to and from Key
West. After World War I, the dream started to fade and Flagler's crowning
achievement turned into "Flagler's Folly." The Key West extension of the

*A view of the longest bridge of the Overseas Highway, Seven Mile Bridge, looking east from
Bahia Honda Key.*

Florida East Coast Railway never made a profit. But the railway's board of directors did not decide to abandon it; nature did.

The 1935 Labor Day Hurricane destroyed the railroad. Storm winds gusting to nearly 200 miles per hour sent waves crashing over the tracks, sweeping away large sections of the line. A 17-foot tidal wave claimed hundreds of lives near Islamorada. The storm washed away more than 40 miles of track between Key Largo and Key Vaca.

With the effects of the Depression still lingering, financing for the rebuilding of the railway was hard to come by. Finally, the railroad sold portions of the line to pay its debts.

In March of 1938 local headlines proclaimed the opening of the Miami-Key West Overseas Highway. However, this was only a beginning, as there was still more work to be done. Until 1941, there were still "more than one hundred miles of narrow, poorly aligned, winding roads in the Florida Keys and many obsolete wooden bridges . . . ," according to the *Journal of the Historical Association of Southern Florida.*

With the outbreak of World War II, movement of military traffic to and from Key West became a priority. Funding appeared and the second phase of the Overseas Highway reconstruction started. Engineers completed work in 1944.

O V I E D O • *Seminole County*
A settlement was begun here in about 1869, and in 1879 a post office was established. A name was sought which would not duplicate any other in the United States. Andrew Aulin, one of the early settlers, selected the name of the capital of the Spanish province at Asturias, largely because of its euphonious sound. However, the Spanish pronunciation of Ove-yay-do has long since been altered by Floridans to O-vee-do.

O X F O R D • *Sumter County*
The first name of this community was Sandspur, but in 1879 a group of town officials met to decide on a new name. W. J. Borden, later a state senator, submitted the name of Oxford. He thought it appropriate since there were several Oxfords in the United States. There is another story that the town got its name because during rainy seasons there was a pond on the road south of town. Sometimes ox teams pulling heavy log carts would get stuck in the pond. Thus, Ox-ford.

O Y P A S • *Clay County*
Local legend links this to an Indian word *oypatukla,* "potato-eating people."

O Z O N A • *Pinellas County*
First known as Yellow Bluff, after being settled by Walton Whitehurst in 1870 under the Homestead Act, the name was changed in 1878 to Bay St. Joseph and then in 1889 to Ozona. The story goes that Yellow Bluff was discarded because of the unpopularity then of any name suggestive of yellow fever. Two physicians, Whitford and Richardson, are said to have suggested Ozona because of the invigorating Gulf breezes.

PACE • *Santa Rosa County*
Named in 1909 for a prominent lumberman, James G. Pace, Sr.

PAHOKEE • *Palm Beach County*
Incorporated in 1922 and named from a Hitchiti Indian word meaning "grass water," a term applied by the Indians to the Everglades. On Taylor's map of 1839, the name of the Everglades is given as Pay-ha-o-kee.

PALATKA • *Putnam County*
Established in 1821 as a trading post on the St. Johns River and said to have been known variously in its earliest years as Buena Vista, Gray's Place, Bush Post, and Fort Shannon. Its current name derives from a Seminole Indian word, *pilotaikita*, meaning "ferry," "food," or "crossing." The Indians had long regarded it as an important place on the river; they held canoe races at this point. The first contraction of the Indian word used as the town's name was spelled Pilatka, but postal authorities complained that this spelling was too easily confused with Picolata, farther down the river, so the "i" was changed to an "a." The settlement was burned in 1836 during the Seminole War. In 1838, the Army established Fort Shannon to serve as a garrison, supply depot, and hospital for the forts in the peninsula. Among the officers stationed here were Winfield Scott, Zachary Taylor, and William T. Sherman. During the Civil War, the community was occupied by Union troops. In the post-Civil War period, Palatka, because of its location on the St. Johns River, became one of the state's leading tourist centers. Palatka is the county seat of Putnam County.

PALATLAKAHA CREEK • *Lake County*
This has been translated as "swamp-big-site."

PALM •
Palm, as a word of identification with Palm Beach and with Florida, has become part of the name of many communities: Palm Bay and Palm Shores in Brevard County; Palm Beach Gardens and Palm Beach Shores in Palm Beach County; Palm City in Martin County; Palm Harbor in Pinellas County; Palm River in Hillsborough County; Palm Springs in Dade, Palm Beach, St. Johns, and Seminole counties; Palm Valley in St. Johns County; and Palm Villa in Seminole County.

PALMA SOLA • *Manatee County*
A lone palm, for a single palm on a nearby offshore island, suggested the name of this community, settled in 1880 by W. S. Warner.

PALM BEACH COUNTY •
The forty-seventh county, established April 30, 1909. The name quite logically was taken from the profusion of coconut palm trees on the Atlantic Ocean beach.

PALMETTO • *Manatee County*
Established prior to 1885. Its name was suggested by the abundant growth of

small palms in this vicinity. The word derives from the Spanish word *palmito*, meaning "little palm tree."

PALM VALLEY • *St. Johns County*
See Diego Plains.

PANACEA • *Wakulla County*
Panacea derived its name from the ancient Greek goddess of healing because of the springs here, which were believed to be a remedy for ills. Some of the old families still do not accept Panacea. The story is that after the Civil War, a Northerner with political influence had the name changed to promote a real estate development. The old-timers prefer King's Bay, and this name appears on some signs. People at the coast refer to their community as Ochlockonee Bay.

The tram road ran between Sopchoppy and Panacea, ca 1911.

PANAMA CITY • *Bay County*
George W. West, the original developer of this town, gave it this name because it is on a direct line between Chicago and Panama City, Canal Zone. Panama City, Fla., is on St. Andrews Bay and is the county seat of Bay County. Panama City Beach is a satellite community in Bay County.

PANAMA PARK • *Duval County*
A suburban town established in 1881 three miles north of Jacksonville at Trout River. Although it is now a part of the city, it is still known as Panama

Park. It was popular with bicycle riders, and a club and cycledrome were built here. Also, the Cummer Lumber Company built a large mill here. The area claims earlier fame as the birthplace in 1841 of Francis P. Fleming, fifteenth governor of Florida and one of three natives of Duval County to fill that office.

PANASOFFKEE • *Sumter County*
A lake in Sumter County which discharges into the Withlacoochee River and a community on the lake. Creek *punne*, "valley or ravine," and *sufkee*, "deep," derived from the high banks of the outlet stream.

PAOLA • *Seminole County*
Paola has had a post office since 1880, so the first settlers likely came earlier. The name appears to be a transplant.

PARADISE • *Alachua County*
Jesse Davis of Gainesville, Alachua County historian, says Paradise was a bustling community with a post office between 1885 and 1908. The town was named when the landowner, negotiating with a railroad for right-of-way, remarked that the track "would go right through Paradise." There are other Paradises in Florida: Paradise Park in St. Lucie County, Paradise Point in Citrus County, and Paradise Key in the Everglades National Park.

PARKER • *Bay County*
Named for W. H. Parker, who settled here many years ago. Other communities named Parker are in Escambia and Hillsborough counties, and likely derived their names from residents.

PARKLAND • *Broward County*
Founded by Bruce B. Blount, this agricultural community of less than 400 acres prides itself upon the resemblance to a park, hence the name.

PARKLAND • *DeSoto County*
Founded in the 1880s and named for L. H. Parkland.

PARRAMORE • *Jackson County*
Gained its name in 1892 from a family here.

PASCO COUNTY •
The forty-fifth county, established June 2, 1887, and named for Samuel Pasco of Monticello, speaker of the Florida House of Representatives at the time the county was created. Pasco was elected by the legislature on May 19, 1887, as U.S. senator and served until December 4, 1899.

PASS-A-GRILLE BEACH • *Pinellas County*
This resort on Long Key, an island in the Gulf of Mexico, was incorporated in 1911, but maps dated as early as 1841 show the original form of the name as *Passe-aux-Grilleurs*. This referred to the fact that fishermen using this point to cross over the island would stop here to cook or grill their meals. In time, and through use by Americans unfamiliar with the French language, the name became shortened to its present form.

PAXTON • *Walton County*
A longtime resident, Mrs. G. W. Pittman, reports a sawmill was erected here around 1910 and among the investors in the area was John Paxton of Chicago.

PEACE RIVER • *Charlotte, Desoto, Hardee and Polk counties*
A river of two names: Peace and Peas. Old maps and accounts called the river *R de la paz, Sur el rio de la Paz,* and *F. Pacis.* The oldest name that we know, therefore, was Peace. But the Seminoles called the stream Peas, from cowpeas or black-eyed peas, which grew in wild profusion along the river. On the Taylor military map of 1839, the stream was shown as Talakchopko or Pease Cr. The Summerlin family, whose cattle in this area numbered in the thousands in the years between the Civil War and the Spanish-American War, knew the river as Peas. Modern usage, however, has been Peace.

PEMBROKE • *Polk County*
Named in 1910 for an adjacent Pembroke mine of a phosphate company.

PEMBROKE PINES • *Broward County*
Named by Walter Seth Kipnis, who suggested at an incorporation committee meeting in 1960 that the development take the name Pembroke Pines. Pembroke came from the main access road, Pembroke Road, and Pines from the large number of those trees in the area. Pembroke Pines spawned adjacent Pembroke Park in 1957.

PENIEL • *Putnam County*
Genesis 32:30, "And Jacob called the name of the place Peniel: for I have seen God face to face, and my life is preserved."

PENNEY FARMS • *Clay County*
This unusual community, eight miles west of Green Cove Springs, was founded by J. C. Penney, chain store magnate, for retired ministers, gospel workers, and their wives, in memory of his father, a minister, and his mother.

PENNSUCO • *Dade County*
Established about 1919 by the Pennsylvania Sugar Company, for sugarcane plantations. The name is formed from the first letters of the three words of the company name.

PENSACOLA • *Escambia County*
The Smithsonian Institution indicates that the most likely derivation of this name is from that of a tribe called *Pansfalaya,* meaning "long-haired people." Other authorities suggest derivation from the same meaning but by a different route: Choctaw *pansi,* means "hair" and *okla,* means "people." Note that the "o" and the "k" in the latter word have been transposed. Still another meaning from the Choctaw is given as "bread people." In the Pansfalaya or Pensacola tribe, the men as well as the women wore their hair long. Whatever the source of its name, the city was established by the Spaniard d'Ariola in 1698. Here was arranged the transfer of the Floridas to the United States from Spain, and here also was located the first capital of the territory of West

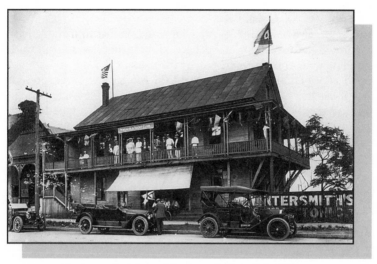

Members on the balcony of the Pensacola Yacht Club, 1913.

Florida. Pensacola is the county seat of Escambia County. Pensacola Bay has been given a variety of names. Simpson (1956) says the bay was called Achuse by Ranjel, Achusi by Garcilaso, and Ochus by Elvas in 1540. In 1559, it was called Polonza by de Luna, and in 1693, Adm. Pez named it the Bay of Santa Maria de Galve. Across Pensacola Bay from today's city, Tristan de Luna established a colony in 1559. This settlement, abandoned two years later after a storm wrecked de Luna's fleet, antedated by six years the founding of St. Augustine. The colony also antedated by five years the French settlement at Fort Caroline. It is likely that the first Catholic white child born in the United States was born in de Luna's colony.

PERDIDO RIVER • *Escambia County*
Forms the western boundary of Florida. It appears to have derived its name from the word for ruin or destruction. There is a mountain by the same name in the Pyrenees of northeast Spain.

PERKINS • *Leon County*
Believed to date from 1860 and to have taken its name from a Tallahassee family.

PERKY • *Monroe County*
A weatherbeaten monument to man's fight against the mosquito stands on this tropical isle like a Dutch windmill without its blades, as Frank Eidge of United Press International described it. An inscription scratched in concrete says: "Dedicated to good health at Perk, Florida by Mr. and Mrs. R. C. Perky, March 15, 1929." Righter Clyde Perky sought to combat the clouds of mosquitoes and salt-marsh sandflies through the bats he hoped to entice by building a tower and using a special bait. No bats ever turned up, but the tower still stands. Perky no longer exists; the island now is called Sugar Loaf Key.

PERRINE • *Dade County*
Named for Dr. Henry Perrine, a physician and botanist to whom the government granted a township of land here in 1838 for his use in conducting experiments with tropical plants. This township ran from today's Coconut Grove, in suburban Miami, through the Cutler Ridge area to the present community of Perrine. He was killed by Indians on Indian Key, where he was living with his family. Dr. Perrine, a native of New York City, had decided while serving in 1827-1838 as U.S. consul at Campeachy (now Campeche), Mexico, to devote the remainder of his life to introducing useful tropical plants into semitropical Florida. Offspring of some of the plants he brought to the vicinity of Biscayne Bay are to be found there now, in particular a species of vanilla (Walker, 1926). The site now called Perrine was chosen by the Model Land Company when the railroad was opened. The Perrine heirs retained some of the grant, but as Perrine Palmer, Jr., former Miami mayor and great-great-great-grandson of Dr. Perrine, ruefully recalled in 1973, "all of the land was taken for taxes during the Depression."

PERRY • *Taylor County*
Research by Mrs. Ed Brannon has established that Perry existed in 1859 and the name therefore likely commemorates Gov. Madison Starke Perry (1857-1861) rather than Gov. Edward A. Perry (1885-1889) as previously assumed.

PERSHING • *Taylor County*
Dating from the end of World War I, this settlement likely honors Gen. John J. Pershing, commander-in-chief of the American Expeditionary Force in France during that war.

PETERS • *Dade County*
A community in the farmlands of south Dade County named for Tom Peters, who was known as the "Tomato King" in the early 1900s.

PICNIC • *Hillsborough County*
A community on Hurrah Creek where S.R. 39 and S.R. 674 intersect. Nixon Smiley (1971) talked with Mrs. Bernice West, who was born "right here at Picnic" too long ago to remember. She did recall that when she was a child the settlement was known as Hurrah. People used to meet for a picnic or a fish fry at a "pretty prairie" where Hurrah Creek runs into the Alafia River. In time, the name of the settlement was changed from Hurrah to Picnic. "Hurrah isn't for what you think it is," Mrs. West told Smiley. "It's an Indian word, and it means something different from the word hurrah that most people think of." Mrs. West lived in a little cottage on a narrow, rutted road that was shaded by moss-laden live oaks. "That's the original road—the main road through Picnic when I was a girl," she said. "It's Picnic Road." When she was a girl, her father, traveling by wagon out along the Picnic Road, took two days to go to Tampa and two days to return.

PICOLATA • *St. Johns County*
Spanish for "broad bluff," which suggests the strategic importance of the place. Here, where the St. Johns River narrows, a natural crossing was used by

Indians and later by the Spanish, who built forts on both sides of the river to protect the trail to the west in the Apalachee country around present-day Tallahassee. The English, under Gen. James Oglethorpe, captured this place in 1740. William Bartram, the naturalist, had an indigo plantation here in 1766. Actors in the cast of *Honeymoon* were waylaid in 1840 while en route to St. Augustine from Picolata by stagecoach. One actor was killed, and Indians wore the captured costumes for a while, an incongruous sight in the Florida wilderness.

PIEDMONT • *Orange County*
Settled at the turn of the century. The name is believed transplanted from the Piedmont of Carolinas, although the Florida community hardly was at the foot of the mountain.

PIERSON • *Volusia County*
Established in 1876 by Peter Pierson and his family, who gave it their own name. The woodsy rural town calls itself "The Fern Capital of the World."

PIGEON KEY • *Monroe County*
Known even in Spanish days as Pigeon Key, this islet was named for the white-crowned wild pigeon native to the West Indies and fairly numerous among the Florida Keys. This pigeon has bluish-black plumage. The upper part of its head is white, edged with deep brown at the sides of the crown. James John Audubon, the naturalist, noted the presence of the pigeons in the Keys in 1832.

Pigeon Key beside the Seven Mile Bridge on the Overseas Highway, 1938.

PINE •
Florida's pine tree, as a natural distinguishing feature, has become part of the names of many communities, just as orange and coral are used to identify communities with Florida. There's Pine Barren (once Piney Barren), Pineville,

and Pine Forest in Escambia County; Pine Log in Bay County; Pine Top in Baker County; Pine Shores and Pinecraft in Sarasota County; Pine Hills in Orange County; Pinewood in Santa Rosa County; Piney Point in Manatee County; Pinecrest in Hillsborough County; Pineland and Pine Island in Lee County; and Pine Level in DeSoto County

PINECASTLE • *Orange County*
In 1870, on the western shore of Lake Conway, Will Wallace Harney, Kissimmee editor, promoter and poet, built a "castle" of pinewood constructed with vertically applied boards and overlapping weather strips. The main part was octagonal and designed with a high peaked roof flanked on either side by conical turrets or towers, giving it a castle-like effect. In 1894 the castle, in which Harney had grieved over the untimely death of his young wife, was razed by fire, but its memory lives on in the town's name.

PINECRAFT • *Sarasota County*
A small community within the city of Sarasota, this is the winter home of Amish and Mennonite families from Pennsylvania, Ohio, Michigan, and Indiana.

PINEDA • *Brevard County*
Named in 1891 after having been established as Hartland. Local legend says Pineda was named for a Spanish officer. Because the change of name was recent, this seems questionable. However, it is interesting to find in Kjerulff (1972) a reference to Pineda in an interview with Mrs. Lucille Peck Berg about her family's homestead here in the 1890s. Mrs. Berg said the family had built a big house in view of the railroad tracks. Before the Spanish-American War, the house unfortunately had been painted the red and yellow of Spain. As troops passed en route to Miami and the Spanish-American War, soldiers fired shots at the house.

PINE LEVEL • *DeSoto County*
On April 29, 1866, the legislature designated Pine Level as the new county seat for Manatee County, an area that now comprises seven counties and 5,000 square miles—one tenth of the state. When DeSoto County was created from Manatee, on May 19, 1887, Pine Level was DeSoto's county seat for the next 18 months.

PINELLAS COUNTY •
The forty-eighth county, established May 23, 1911, being separated from Hillsborough County by Old Tampa Bay. The peninsula which forms the larger part of the county was known to the Spaniards as Punta Punal, said to mean "point of pines," and the present name was fashioned from that. A number of its communities—Pinellas Park and Pinellas Point—have taken their name from the county.

PITHLACHASCOTEE • *Pasco County*
A river in Pasco County. Creek *pithlo*, "canoe," and *chaskita*, "to chop out," known also as Boat Building River.

PITHLACHOCCO, LAKE (Newman's Lake) • *Alachua County*
From the Creek *pilo* or *pithlo*, "boat or canoe," and *chuko*, "house," and the present name from Col. Newnan of the Georgia Volunteers in the Seminole Wars.

PITTMAN • *Lake County*
Another of the towns whose progress was retarded by the big freezes of the 1890s, Pittman was named in 1883 for George T. Pittman of Louisville, Ky., one of the three men who furnished the land for the town site.

PLACIDA • *Charlotte County*
Apparently an Americanized form of the Spanish *placido*, "placid," for the pleasantly calm, tranquil waters of this noted fishing area on the Peace River.

PLANTATION • *Broward County*
Most of this city is on land that used to be known as the Frederick C. Peters plantation. Development of the city began in the 1910s with platting and sales by the Florida Fruitlands Company of one-acre suburban sites usable for truck gardening and called plantation homes. So, Plantation was selected as the name of the city when it was incorporated. Peters, whose family operated a shoe manufacturing company in St. Louis, came to Miami and began land development in 1934. He died in 1964.

PLANTATION KEY • *Monroe County*
Once there were pineapple and banana plantations here, but marketing proved a problem. Adjacent to the key is Cowpens Anchorage, a reminder of the enclosures built in the water long ago to hold manatees, or sea cows, until they were needed for food.

PLANT CITY • *Hillsborough County*
The first Anglo-Saxon community here was established in 1846 at the site of the Indian village Itchepackesassa, meaning "tobacco field." On Taylor's map of 1839 it is designated as Fort Fraser. The name was changed to Cork by an Irish post office official who fancied the conciseness. When the Sanford-to-Tampa section of the Atlantic Coast Line railroad was graded in 1883 by

Plant City's first rural mail carrier, M. F. Tillman, in 1903.

Henry B. Plant, the line passed through this district. J. T. Evers purchased a large portion of what is now Plant City, laid it out and readily disposed of business and residential lots. He might have named the town Eversville, but insisted that it should be named after the railroad-builder who had freed the community from isolation. The town was incorporated as Plant City in 1885.

PLANTER • *Monroe County*
Key Largo's first settlement was for years the site of activity by pirates, Bahamians, and Indians. Only a pier remains of the once-bustling community about a mile north of Tavernier. Planter's agricultural base was undercut by Caribbean islands producing the same crops more cheaply; the hurricanes of 1906 and 1909 finished it off.

PLAYALINDA BEACH • *Brevard County*
Pseudo-Spanish and a redundancy translating as "beach pretty beach."

PLUMMER • *Duval County*
Daniel Plummer settled here in 1801 and his name has been given to this community, Plummer's Point, and Plummer's Cove on the St. Johns River.

PLUM NELLY • *Putnam County*
A lumber mill settlement outside Palatka has one of the most charming names in Florida. Someone described the place as "plum out of town and ne'ly in the country." Thus, its name: Plum Nelly.

PLYMOUTH • *Orange County*
Settled in the 1880s by English immigrants, the community first was known as Penryn and then as Plymouth, both old-country names.

POCATAW • *Orange County*
Another of the stations with modern Indian names on the abandoned branch line of the Florida East Coast Railway, Pocataw is defined in the Moore-Willson vocabulary as meaning "twins."

POCOMOONSHINE • *Dade County*
Before Miami stretched out its boundaries in 1925, there was a prairie to the northwest of the city known as Pocomoonshine. The land became too valuable during the boom for continued use by farmers and dairies. Streets and buildings changed the nature and caused the disappearance of the prairie. The name (but spelled Poke-O-Moonshine) long has been known in New York and New England. Stewart (1970) says Poke-O-Moonshine derives from an Algonquian original, "but so completely reworked by folk-etymology as to be obscured; 'broken-off-smooth' is the conventional translation, but cannot be considered certain. The opening *Pok-* is common in Algonquian names, with various meanings."

POINSETT, LAKE • *Brevard County*
This 4,334-acre lake is named for Joel Robert Poinsett (1799-1851), special envoy to Mexico in 1822 and American minister to that country in 1825. He discovered here and introduced to this country the plant with the brilliant scarlet, pink or white leaves known as the poinsettia.

POINT OF REEFS • *Brevard County*
Another early name for the oldest landmark on Florida's Atlantic coast, Cape Canaveral.

POINT WASHINGTON • *Walton County*
Situated to look down a long stretch of Choctahatchee Bay, this is the setting for a modern Eden, a mansion built in 1895 which has become a state-owned showplace. Washington derives from the county which once included the point.

POLK COUNTY •
The thirty-ninth county, established February 8, 1861, and named for James Knox Polk, eleventh president of the United States (1845-1849). Polk had the political distinction of twice being rejected for reelection as governor of Tennessee, the last time in 1843, a year before his election as president as the first dark horse nominee of the Democratic Party. He was chosen over Henry Clay and Martin Van Buren because he demanded control of Oregon and annexation of Texas.

POLK CITY • *Polk County*
Established in 1922 by Isaac Van Horn and named after its county.

POMONA PARK • *Putnam County*
Pomona was the Roman goddess of fruit trees, usually depicted as holding fruits and a pruning knife.

POMPANO BEACH • *Broward County*
An interesting story is that a survey party from the Florida East Coast Railway was treated by local folks to a pompano dinner. To let future survey teams know about the delicious fish, they jotted the word pompano on their charts. Those who followed thought it the name of the settlement. The name stuck. Another version credits Franklin Sheehan, a surveying engineer with the Model Land Company, with naming the town after the fish. At any rate, the Beach was added after 1940.

PONCE DE LEON • *Holmes County*
Established in 1875, this community was named for the Spanish explorer.

PONCE INLET • *Volusia County*
Named not for the explorer but for Antonio Ponce, who received a Spanish grant in 1790.

PONTE VEDRA • *St. Johns County*
Once known as Mineral City, for the ilmenite, rutile, and other heavy minerals associated with beach and dune sands. The National Lead Company wanted a Spanish-sounding name in the 1930s when the area was changed to a seaside development, and accepted a New York architect's suggestion of Ponte Vedra, for the city in Spain.

PORT BOCA GRANDE • *Lee County*
Boca grande, Spanish for "large mouth," long was an important shipping point, being situated on a large natural harbor. Port Boca Grande offers shipping facilities nearer the point of Gasparilla Island than its parent community.

PORT CANAVERAL • *Brevard County*
This port, developed to serve Cape Kennedy Space Center and the Bahamas, took the ancient name of its area.

PORT CHARLOTTE • *Charlotte County*
Named in 1955 for the county where it is located.

PORT EVERGLADES • *Brevard County*
The dream of a deep-water port had stirred people here as early as 1912, but Port Everglades was a boom-time project brought to fruition in February 1928. President Calvin Coolidge pressed a button in Washington to set off the final charge of dynamite to open a channel connecting the port to the Atlantic Ocean, but the electrical impulse did not reach Florida, so engineers touched off the blast locally. The port was dedicated as Bay Mabel Harbor, since it was developed from a shallow, natural body of water known as Lake Mabel. The port was the result of an unusual tripartite agreement: two cities, Fort Lauderdale and Hollywood, joined J. W. Young, the promoter of Hollywood, in financing the initial dredging.

PORT INGLIS • *Levy County*
The western terminus of the aborted Cross-State Barge Canal. Inglis is a family name. *See also* Inglis.

PORTLAND • *Walton County*
On Alaqua Creek near the Choctawatchee Bay, this community, its post office dating from 1884, seems by its name to advertise its land-water location.

PORT LEON • *Wakulla County*
Devastated by a hurricane and tidal wave in September 1843, just as the community was achieving stability and prosperity after having been incorporated in 1841 as the competitor of two other ports, Magnolia (*see also*) and St. Marks. The port took its name, as did its county, from Ponce de León. In its heyday, Port Leon had eight or ten business houses, three or four warehouses, a hotel, and one or two taverns. It was the seat of Wakulla County after Wakulla was created on March 11, 1843. A bridge across the St. Marks River tied the port to the Tallahassee Railroad. After the storm, Port Leon was never rebuilt.

PORT MAYACA • *Martin County*
A variant of *mayaimi*, "big water," with Port prefixed.

PORT ORANGE • *Volusia County*
The Dun-Lawton plantation, with its sugar mill, was the first occupant of this site. The naturalist John James Audubon was here in 1826. In 1861, Edward Archibald McDaniel established a plant here for making salt, boiling water from the Halifax River in kettles formerly used by the sugar mill. The salt was sold to the people of the interior during the Civil War. In 1866, the Florida Land and Lumber Company purchased state land adjoining the north of the property of Bartola Pacetti on Mosquito Inlet, established a village and named it Port Orange because of the citrus culture.

PORT RICHEY • *Pasco County*
Situated on a point between the Pithlachascotee River and the Gulf of
Mexico, this community was established in 1883 and named for its first post-
master, A. M. Richey.

PORT ST. JOE • *Gulf County*
The first town established here, known as St. Joseph, was the scene of the
convention which wrote Florida's first constitution in 1838. It was destroyed
by a yellow fever epidemic and a tidal wave in 1841. The site is on St. Joseph
Bay, which was named by the Spaniards for the husband of Mary, the
mother of Jesus.

*The Constitution Convention Monument in Port St. Joe marks the site where Florida's
first constitution was signed.*

PORT ST. LUCIE • *Martin and St. Lucie counties*
Designed largely to attract retirees, this community straddles the boundary
between Martin and St. Lucie counties, taking its name from the latter.

PORT SALERNO • *Martin County*
Named for an older, nearby community of Salerno.

PORT SEWELL • *Martin County*
Named for a pioneer resident, Capt. Henry E. Sewell. It has been a center for
sports fishermen since the turn of the century.

PORT TAMPA • *Hillsborough County*
The port city for Tampa, located on Tampa Bay. It was founded in 1885 by
Charles W. Prescott and Capt. James W. Fitzgerald and boomed when the
South Florida Railroad made Port Tampa its terminal in 1877. Port Tampa
once was the headquarters of the Honduras National Lottery.

POSTAL COLONY • *Lake County*
A colony of retired postal clerks was established here in 1923.

POWELL • *Hernando County*
Enjoyed postal recognition for ten years beginning in 1912.

PRINCETON • *Dade County*
The Model Land Company established a town here in 1904 and named it Modello. In 1905, Gaston Drake, with a group of Princeton University alumni, came to the community and named it for their alma mater.

PROSPECT BLUFF • *Franklin County*
See Achackweithle.

PROSPERITY • *Holmes County*
This name must have expressed a hope, not necessarily fulfilled with the passage of time.

PROVIDENCE • *Gadsden, Polk, and Union counties*
Florida has three communities named Providence, although the name is rare elsewhere. Stewart (1970) suggests the name probably was rare because it was thought "overly pious or even pretentiously so." He reports a few habitation names were taken from country churches so named. Providence in Gadsden County antedates as a settlement the creation of the county in 1823, while Union County's Providence is said to date from 1830.

PULL-AND-BE-DAMNED CREEK • *Monroe County*
The name of this stretch of waterway at Key Vaca likely refers to someone's efforts to row against a swift current. There were Indians on the shore of Pull-and-be-Damned Creek for many years. Colonists in 1818 built on an Indian kitchen midden the beginning of the town now known as Marathon. The naturalist John James Audubon was here in 1826.

PUNTA GORDA • *Charlotte County*
Peeples (1967) tells of a squabble over the community's name. Early in 1883, Isaac H. Trabue, a middle-aged attorney from Louisville, Ky., purchased a 30-acre tract on the south side of Charlotte Harbor. "Now as for naming the place," Trabue wrote, "if we want to bring the place into notice—we must give it a name that will give it notority (sic). I know of no name that will advertise it better than ours—will therefore name it Trabue." Alas, a squabble developed, which resulted in the town's incorporation under the name Punta Gorda, explained by an anti-Trabue leader as having been "chosen almost unanimously because it was the original historical and geographical Spanish name." Trabue claimed that leader was the person who had counted the votes. He thereafter referred to the town he had birthed as "Trabue, alias Punta Gorda." The Spanish had applied the name Punta Gorda, "wide point or fat point," to an arm of land jutting into Charlotte Bay near the present city.

PUNTA RASSA • *Lee County*
Translated from the Spanish as "flat point" or "raveling point." The coastline of Sanibel Island, opposite Punta Rassa, is felt by some observers to present a

The Punta Gorda hotel in the 1880s.

ragged or raveled appearance. Fort Delaney was extablished here in 1837, abandoned, then reoccupied in 1841. It was occupied again during the Civil War. Cable communications between the United States and Cuba were established at Punta Rassa in 1866, and it was here that the first news was received of the sinking of the battleship *Maine* in Havana harbor. This was a shipping point of cattle to Cuba at the turn of the century.

PUTNAM COUNTY •

The twenty-eighth county, established January 13, 1849. Named for Benjamin A. Putnam, a prominent St. Augustine lawyer and officer in the Second Seminole War. He was the first president of the Florida Historical Society on its organization in 1856.

PUTNAM HALL • *Putnam County*

Settled in 1850 by Elijah Wall and likely named for the same person as the county.

Q UAY • *Indian River County*

The first name for the community known now as Winter Beach. Will (1964) says mail for the Okeechobee country "in 1902 come [sic] weekly by horseback from Quay (they call it Winter Beach now, up Vero way) by way of Fort Drum."

QUINCY • *Gadsden County*

Founded in 1825 when John Quincy Adams was secretary of state of the United States. Later, on February 15, 1828, Adams, as sixth president, signed a deed for the town site of Quincy, further establishing his relationship with the community named in his honor. An act of the Legislative Council to incorporate the town of Quincy was approved by Gov. William P. DuVal on November 19, 1828.

QUINTETTE • *Escambia County*
The fifth station north from Pensacola.

RAIFORD • *Union County*
Named for a pioneer settler, Raiford has become synonymous for Florida's "big house," as the state's main penitentiary and prison farm are located nearby.

RAINBOW SPRING • *Marion County*
Four miles northeast of Dunnellon, it is among the state's top three first-magnitude springs (depending upon how you rank Wakulla Spring) whose water emerges from a single outlet.

RAMROD KEY • *Monroe County*
Said to be named for a ship wrecked nearby.

RANDS • *Seminole County*
This first was a switchyard for the Atlantic Coast Line Railroad and the name likely was that of a company official.

RASTUS • *Alachua County*
Still on the State Department of Agriculture's sectional map but not shown on highway maps, this likely was a siding of the Atlantic Coast Line Railroad for the shipment of farm products.

RATTLESNAKE • *Hillsborough County*
For a number of years in the 1930s, the throng of motorists crossing the Gandy Bridge between Tampa and St. Petersburg passed a store, snake pit, and post office called Rattlesnake, Fla. This story is told in *The Tampa Tribune* of November 30, 1958: The site at the east end of the approach to the Gandy Bridge had been purchased by George End, a Connecticut Yankee who came to Arcadia with his family during the boom of the 1920s. When the boom exploded, End was among the thousands of Floridians who cast about for some way to make money. End met Guy (Rattlesnake) Johnson of Nocatee, who confided (1) he had orders for live rattlesnakes for medicinal purposes and (2) they were living in an area with unlimited raw material. End decided to join in the snake catching. His boys brought in a dead six-footer. "Well, boys," he is quoted as having said, "we will skin him and maybe we can sell the hide." The meat revealed by the skinning looked sufficiently inviting that the family cooked and ate some. Ultimately, this led to a business of canning rattlesnake meat and, because of publicity which End engineered as a former newsman, to the purchase of the Gandy site for public display of snakes and sale of canned meat. *The Tribune* reports End died from the bite of a snake which for several years "had been very docile and gentle." James A. Clendinen, editor of *The Tribune*, who turned up the 1958 story, added that when the territory containing Rattlesnake was annexed to Tampa in the 1950s "the name of the Rattlesnake community disappeared—without any mourning from the residents." The name, however, still appears on the state's sectional map.

The Elks Magazine Good Will Tour makes a stop at Rattlesnake.

RATTLESNAKE ISLAND • *St. Johns County*
An island in the Matanzas River, on which the Spanish in 1736 built Fort Matanzas to ward off enemy ships seeking to move against St. Augustine. The fort still stands.

RAVENWOOD • *Lake County*
Laid out in the 1880s by Maj. John S. Banks of Scotland and named for his home there. The community, consisting of a hotel, stores and homes, was virtually destroyed by a fire in 1888.

REDBLUFF • *Escambia County*
Settled in Spanish times, the area took its name from the bluffs of red clay.

RED BUG • *Polk County*
Heatherington (1928) speaks of a little country store in a locality known as Red Bug near Lake Gibson. In the 1870s, Heatherington reports, "fifty cents would buy a quart of first-class rye whiskey, and the people from the Socrum and Combee settlements would gather there on Saturday and engage in horse-racing and otherwise have what they considered a good time."

REDDICK • *Marion County*
Established in 1882 and named for its first postmaster.

REDINGTON BEACH • *Pinellas County*
Named for Charles E. Redington, a developer of this area.

REDLANDS • *Dade County*
Farmland south of Miami, named for the reddish tinge to the soil.

RED LEVEL • *Citrus County*
Settlers believed there was reddish tinge to the soil after plowing. And the land was level.

RED OAK • *Madison County*
A magnificient red oak tree shaded Andrew J. Aman's general store. When a post office was authorized here in 1902, it seemed to be the natural, distinguishing name.

REEDY CREEK • *Orange County*
Reedy Creek, with Bay Lake the twin cities of Disney World, had its name changed to Lake Buena Vista.

REFORM • *Gadsden County*
Reform, sad to say, was short-lived, from April 1846 until December 1848.

RELAY • *Flagler County*
Once the relay station on a stagecoach line.

REMINGTON • *Clay County*
English colonists in the 1890s gave this place a family name.

REMLAP • *Hillsborough County*
The name spelled backwards identified holdings here as being part of those belonging to Mrs. Potter Palmer of Chicago and Sarasota.

RHODES • *Leon County*
Down the St. Marks road from Tallahassee was the Rhodes community, known to picnickers in the old days for its four springs shaded by large water oaks and to others for the naval stores and lumbering operations. Likely named for G. W. Rhodes.

RIBAUT RIVER • *Duval County*
Jean Ribaut, an ardent Calvinist, commanded three French ships which arrived at the St. Johns River on April 30, 1562, with 150 people. Ribaut named the waterway River of May, planted a stone pillar with the arms of France, and sailed south to confront the Spanish at St. Augustine.

RICHMOND HEIGHTS • *Dade County*
Named for a Dr. Richmond who lived in the area before the turn of the century.

RICKENBACKER CAUSEWAY • *Dade County*
This causeway linking Miami and Key Biscayne was named for Capt. E. V. "Eddie" Rickenbacker in the 1940s in recognition of his leadership in the development of commercial aviation. The Miami area had benefited in particular because Rickenbacker established the main overhaul base of his company, Eastern Air Lines, here. Capt. Rickenbacker was the United States' "Ace of Aces" in World War I, shooting down 26 German aircraft while battling Baron Manfred von Richtofen's planes over the fields of France.

RIVER JUNCTION • *Gadsden County*
This community, at the junction where the Chattahoochee and Flint rivers become the Apalachicola, appears on maps as early as 1824 as McCulloch's Ferry, possibly for Briant McCulloch, one of the first five people to receive land grants from the federal government. A post office was established there in 1884 and the town was incorporated in 1921. Growth of the nearby town

of Chattahoochee overtook River Junction, and the River Junction post office was consolidated with the Chattahoochee post office in 1951.

RIVER OF REEDS •
The Suwannee River as the Timucua and the Apalachee knew it.

RIVER OF THE DEER •
In diaries of the expedition of Hernando De Soto in 1539, the Suwannee River was called River of the Deer because "there the messengers from Ocachile brought hither some deer, of which there are many fine ones in that land."

RIVERVIEW • *Hillsborough County*
On a stream leading into Hillsboro Bay.

RIVIERA BEACH • *Palm Beach County*
Judge A. E. Heuser, an early resident, named this town Oak Lawn, but a visitor's casual remark, "This is the Riviera of America," brought about a change of name.

RIXFORD • *Suwannee County*
Founded in 1873 by George C. Rixford.

ROACH • *Taylor County*
There was a settlement by this name for four years, beginning in 1922, near Hampton Springs.

ROBISON'S • *Jefferson County*
John G. Robison and his wife Fanny were the first settlers in the vicinity of Monticello. A post office was established on May 10, 1827, at Robison's. On December 26, 1827, the name was changed to Monticello.

ROCHELLE • *Alachua County*
First called Gruelle, the town changed its name in 1884 to Rochelle, derivation unknown. It is near the former plantation of Madison Starke Perry, who was governor when Florida withdrew from the Union on January 11, 1861.

ROCK •
Rock has been prefixed to some other word to form the name of numerous Florida communities. Only one, Rockledge, has achieved the distinction of being included in the 1990 federal census. Among the Rock settlements, past and present, are: Rock Bluff, Liberty County; Rock Creek, Jackson and Okaloosa counties; Rockdale, Dade County; and Rocky Point, Alachua County.

ROCKET CITY • *Orange County*
This area of scrub and swamp was touted as both retirement area and home for the thousands of workers serving Cape Canaveral. Many land purchasers found the lots were too small, oddly shaped or under wetlands. Today Rocket City has a new owner and a new name, Wedfield. The original lots were what county planners described as "bowling-alley" lots, 75 feet wide and 600 feet long. Since 1962, the rules have changed and the county does not allow lots that are less than 110 feet wide.

ROCKLEDGE • *Brevard County*
Established about 1875. Its name is derived from the formation of coquina rock which crops out in ledges along the shore. Coquina rock, from one to 30 feet deep, is a substratum of the soil.

Meeting the Florida East Coast Railway train at the Rockledge station, 1902.

RODMAN RESERVOIR • *Marion County*
Named for a small community on a site that was flooded when the reservoir was created.

ROLLESTOWN OR ROLLSTON • *Putnam County*
On the St. Johns River about a mile from today's San Mateo, the town was established in 1765 by Denys Rolle, English philanthropist and member of parliament. He named it Charlotia, after Charlotte, queen of George III. Rolle "brought a motley crew of men and women from the slums and streets of London, intending to rehabilitate these unfortunates, create a Utopia, and make Charlotia its capital. Disease, dissatisfaction, and desertion soon decreased the ranks of the colonists. Undaunted, Rolle purchased additional land until he controlled 80,000 acres; he worked his plantations with slave labor, and struggled along for several years shipping rice, corn, beef, lumber, and naval stores. In one season he exported 1,000 gallons of orange wine. When Florida was returned to Spain in 1783, Rolle abandoned his plantation and removed with his slaves to the Bahamas" (Federal Writers Project, 1939).

ROMEO-JULIETTE • *Marion County*
In the northwest corner of Marion County, just below where U.S. 41 comes

into the county on its way from Williston to Dunnellon, you'll find yourself passing through a little place called Romeo. Don't ask a smart question like "Wonder where Juliet is?"—because 7.3 miles later you'll find out: right where you are. But she has taken to spelling her name Juliette. The story is that there were actually two Florida lovers whose families didn't get along. The boy lived in what is now Romeo, the girl in what is now called, by an inadvertent misspelling, Juliette. It is said the Florida story ended as tragically as the Veronese, though details are not to be had.

ROSE •
Used as the name or part of the name of a number of communities, particularly in the later years of the nineteenth century. There was Rose in Leon County, Rosebud in Madison County, Rosedale in Gadsden County, Rose Head in Taylor County, Rosehill in Citrus County, Roseland in Indian River County, and Rosewood in Levy County.

ROSALIE • *Polk County*
Likely named for nearby Lake Rosalie which, in turn, may have been named for a wife or daughter.

ROSEWOOD • *Levy County*
Once a breakfast stop on the Cross-Florida railroad. The name is believed to have been taken from the red cedar trees which made nearby Cedar Key famous as a center for milling the slabs of wood for pencil factories.

ROUND LAKE • *Jackson County*
Settled in the 1890s, the community took its name from a circular lake here.

ROYAL PALM BEACH • *Palm Beach County*
Located a few miles west of West Palm Beach, and contrived to use the words Palm Beach. Similar examples are Palm Beach Shores, Palm Beach Lakes, Palm Beach Gardens, Palm Beach Isles, North Palm Beach and, indeed, West Palm Beach. Palm Beach has a magic to its name!

ROYELLOU • *Lake County*
Known now as Mount Dora, the settlement first was called Royellou, from the names of Royal, Ella, and Louie Tremain, who pioneered here in the 1870s. *See also* Mount Dora.

RUSKIN • *Hillsborough County*
Dr. George McA. Miller, president of Ruskin College in Glenn-Allen, Ill., sought a more temperate climate and moved the college to this site around 1910. The town was named for the college, which in turn was named for John Ruskin, English author and socialist.

RUTLAND • *Sumter County*
When the post office was established in 1884, the community was given the name of a family here.

RYE • *Manatee County*
Developed in the 1880s by a Mr. Mitchell, who is believed to have given it the name of the English seaport.

A Ruskin cucumber field, October 11, 1947.

SADLER • *Taylor County*
Settled in the 1900s and named for a townsman, C. J. Sadler.

SAFETY HARBOR • *Pinellas County*
First settled by Dr. Odet Phillippi in 1823. It was first known as Espiritu Santo, "holy spirit." Later it was called Green Springs, and finally it was incorporated as Safety Harbor in 1917. The name indicates that it is a shelter for seamen and vessels.

ST. ANDREWS BAY • *Gulf County*
Presumably named by the Spanish for the saint on whose feast day the bay was discovered. The town of St. Andrews Bay dated from 1845. In 1902, the name was shortened to St. Andrew.

ST. ANTHONY • *Duval County*
Known as San Antonio in Spanish times and St. Anthony in English, this place first was called Monroe in honor of President James Monroe after the American acquisition and then Mandarin because of a variety of oranges brought from China. *See also* Mandarin.

ST. ARMANDS • *Sarasota County*
On Lido Key across Sarasota Bay from Sarasota, it has been a fashionable shopping center since the 1950s.

ST. AUGUSTINE • *St. Johns County*
The oldest continuously settled city in the United States, having been founded in 1565 by Pedro Menéndez de Avilés, and named by him for St. Augustine, Bishop of Hippo, on whose feast day, August 28, he sighted the coast. It is situated between two salt-water rivers, the San Sebastian and the

Matanzas. Its history is not only longer but perhaps richer and more colorful than that of any other in our nation. In or near St. Augustine were the missions of Nombre de Dios, San Sebastian, Nuestra Senora de la Leche, and San Diego de Salamototo. St. Augustine is the county seat of St. Johns County.

Governor William S. Jennings (right) posed in a "gatormobile" near the St. Augustine city gate.

ST. CATHERINE • *Sumter County*
First known as Hiawatha in 1884, it changed the next year to Massacre, doubtless because the scene of the Dade Massacre was but a few miles away. In 1902, it became St. Catherine.

ST. CLAIR • *Lake County*
A short-lived town, existing for a year in the 1880s.

ST. CLEMENTS POINT • *Pinellas County*
Marked on a 1792 map as St. Clements Bay, this stretch of Boca Ciega Bay now is known as Indian Rocks.

ST. CLOUD • *Osceola County*
Originally the site of a sugar plantation established by the Hamilton Disston Company in 1882. In 1909, Raymond Moore of New York City succeeded in making this settlement a semi-official residence for veterans of the Union Army. It was named for the suburb of Paris which was the location of the great palace occupied by Marie Antoinette, Napoleon, and other French sovereigns.

ST. DIEGO • *Duval County*
This Yamassee mission existed in 1726 on the Diego plains just south of the present Jacksonville Beach. *See also* Diego Plains.

ST. FRANCIS • *Lake County*
On the St. Johns River, it was founded in 1887 and flourished until the big freeze of 1889. The town, developed by L. H. Harris of Pittsburgh, supported a weekly newspaper, post office, general store, hotel, a warehouse with wharves, and residences.

ST. GEORGE ISLAND • *Franklin County*
Now linked to the mainland by a bridge, this island is thought to have been named for the patron saint of England.

St. Helena • *Columbia County*
Settled in 1857, St. Helena passed out of existence in 1867.

St. James Island • *Franklin County*
Relatively isolated, St. James Island has been a summer center on a Gulf beach for residents of Tallahassee since the turn of the century. During World War II, this was a part of Camp Gordon Johnston, where tens of thousands of soldiers trained for the invasion of Europe.

St. James City • *Lee County*
Founded in 1887 by a group of New Englanders who constructed buildings of spruce and white pine shipped from Maine. For a time before Flagler developed Palm Beach, St. James City was one of the most popular resorts in south Florida.

St. Johns County •
St. Johns was paired with Escambia on July 21, 1821, as Florida's first two counties. The county was named for the St. Johns River. *See also* St. Johns River.

St. Johns Bluff • *Duval County*
Rising about 75 feet above the river, it was the site of sod-and-timber Fort Caroline, built by the French in 1564 and named in honor of Charles IX. The fort was captured the next year on Saint Matthews Day by the Spanish, who called the fort San Mateo for the saint. English, American, and Confederate troops occupied the area because of its strategic value. The site of Fort Caroline was washed away in the 1880s when the St. Johns was deepened. The *Handbook* of the Postal History Committee of the Florida Federation of Stamp Clubs says the first post office here was established January 30, 1828.

St. Johns River •
Miss Dena Snodgrass of Jacksonville, biographer of the St. Johns, says five names have been applied to the river in its entirety and several others to portions of the river. From Miss Snodgrass we learn that the Indians gave the river its first name, *Welaka* or *Ylacco*, two spellings with much the same pronunciation. A Spanish explorer called it *Rio de Corrientes*, "river of currents," in recognition of the spectacular way the currents at the river's mouth clashed with the surf. France's Jean Ribaut entered the St. Johns on the first day of May and hence named the river *Rivière de Mai*, "river of May." Spain's Pedro Menéndez captured France's Fort Caroline and renamed both fort and river San Mateo. About 1590 the Spanish mission *San Juan del Puerto*, "St. John of the harbor," was established and ultimately gave its name, in shortened form, to the river. For a time in the mid-1700s, both San Mateo and San Juan were shown on some Florida maps as two names for the one river. It was during the 20-year period of British ownership of Florida, 1763 to 1783, that San Juan finally became St. John's and since has remained save for the dropping of the apostrophe.

St. Johns Town • *Duval County*
The English established a settlement near St. Johns Bluff in 1782, naming it

St. Johns Town. It was a place of refuge for Tories from Southern colonies during the Revolutionary War. The town declined when England returned Florida to Spain, and no vestige remains today.

S T .   J O S E P H • *Gulf (then Franklin) County*
The most notable of Florida's lost towns. It was here that Florida's first constitution was written in 1838-1839 in anticipation of the statehood which came in 1845. This seaport city was known as the richest and wickedest city in the Southeast. The Spanish and the French had fortified this landlocked bay, but the Americans came in throngs after the U.S. Supreme Court in 1822 invalidated land titles in Apalachicola, 30 miles away. St. Joseph was built fast and big. There were wharves and warehouses, brick store and office buildings, and mansions regarded then as palatial—all supported by a forest of spars and masts as vessels crowded the port. What happened then is described in *Florida: A Guide to the Southernmost State.* "In 1841 a ship from South America brought in yellow fever, and within a few weeks three-fourths of the town had succumbed. Panic-stricken survivors abandoned their homes and fled; ships avoided the port; hotels and business houses closed. For three years the town remained deserted. Fear of the plague was so great that only a few venturesome fishermen dared to approach the spot. In 1844 a hurricane and tidal wave swept in from the gulf, leveling empty buildings and floating many out to sea. Devastating storms followed at intervals, and bit by bit all remains of the town were effaced." By 1854, the place was gone. Today, the tangible reminders of St. Joseph are a cemetery and a state park with a constitution memorial and museum, both situated about a mile and a half from the landward limit of St. Joseph.

S T .   J O S E P H • *Pasco County*
Settled in 1893.

S T .   L E O • *Pasco County*
Four Benedictine monks from Germany were sent in 1886 from the Belmont Abbey in North Carolina to minister to the spiritual needs of Seminole Indians and of German-Americans in the area. The monastery and subsequent college community were named for St. Leo, Leo the Great, who was Pope Leo I, 440-461.

S T .   L O U I S • *Bradford County*
Established in 1858, it passed out of existence within a year.

S T .   L U C I E   C O U N T Y •
First established as the twenty-fifth county on March 14, 1844, and recreated as the forty-sixth county on May 24, 1905. The original St. Lucie County was given the name of Brevard County on January 6, 1855. The county was named for St. Lucie of Syracuse. The name of St. Lucie was first given in the area to a fort built by the Spanish near Cape Canaveral in 1565.

S T .   L U C I E • *St. Lucie County*
Settled in 1868.

ST. MARKS • *Wakulla County*

The first community on this site was established in March 1718, by José Primo de Rivera, probably on the feast day of St. Mark. A wooden stockade had been erected by the Spanish in 1680. A Spanish masonry fort, San Marco de Apalache, was built here in 1759 and was captured in 1799 by William Augustus Bowles and his band of Indians. The Spaniards recaptured the fort and made a prisoner of Bowles. The fort was taken by Gen. Andrew Jackson in 1819. Nearby was the Spanish mission of Santa Maria de Apalache. Before the Civil War, the town of St. Marks was an important shipping port.

ST. PETERSBURG • *Pinellas County*

The sunshine city, but its name comes from that of one of the coldest great cities in the world—Russia's St. Petersburg, formerly known as Leningrad. When the Orange Belt Railroad was extended down to this part of the coast in 1887, its president was Peter Demens, a Russian by birth who had changed his own name from Dementief. Tales differ as to just how he got the privilege of choosing a name for this town—whether by straw-drawing, coin-flipping or courtesy—but he chose the name of his native city. Some of his associates objected, but consoled themselves with the thought that the town would never amount to anything anyway. Its green benches and balmy breezes make it—among other things—a most pleasant haven, causing it to be almost as famous as the arctic city of Peter the Great.

A 1920s aerial view of St. Petersburg showing the airport, Al Lang baseball field, the boat basins and the "Million Dollar Pier."

ST. TERESA • *Franklin County*

Settled in 1873, the area has been a way of life for some Tallahassee families for generations. When they speak of "The Coast," they mean the summer homes along a two-mile stretch of Apalachee Bay. The resort was named for Teresa Hopkins. Nobody remembers why and when the "St." was added. The late Mrs. R. B. "Miss Annie" Sensabaugh of Tallahassee remembered going to St. Teresa by horse and carriage, train, and boat. It was a day's journey then, an hour by automobile now.

S T. V I N C E N T I S L A N D • *Franklin County*
Off the coast and surrounded by the waters of Apalachicola Bay, St. Vincents Sound and the Gulf of Mexico, this island was given its name by Franciscan missionaries. Their mission of Cape San Vincente remembered the Spanish martyr of the fourth century. Dr. R. V. Pierce, a wealthy patent medicine manufacturer, developed a famous preserve of exotic game here.

S A L E M • *Taylor County*
Settlers here became numerous enough to justify a post office in 1878. Jerusalem was called the "city of Salem" or the "city of Peace."

S A L E R N O • *Martin County*
This place has undergone five changes of name. The first was Aberdeen for the home in Scotland of some early settlers; then, Alicia for Ida Alice Shourds, the second wife of Henry M. Flagler, builder of the Florida East Coast Railway; next, Mulford for B. W. Mulford, a developer; then, Salerno for the Italian seaport; and now, Port Salerno.

S A L O F K A • *Osceola County*
Near the site of a sugar plantation owned by Hamilton Disston in the 1880s and later a station on the Florida East Coast Railway. The name was taken from the Seminole *islafka*, "knife."

S A L U B R I T Y • *Gadsden County*
With a name meaning "favorable to or promoting health," this community was to be found in 1828 at the Ocklockonee River on the post road between Tallahassee and Quincy. Salubrity, or Salubria as it was sometimes spelled, passed out of postal existence in 1845.

S A M J O N E S O L D T O W N • *Hendry County*
This legend appeared on highway and sectional maps: "Ruins of Sam Jones Old Town." But Nixon Smiley went there in 1967 and reported: "The map maker who put this site on the Florida road map was a practical joker." There isn't a road within three miles, continued Smiley, "and nobody's lived here since 1861. That was the year when Sam Jones, a tough old Miccosukee veteran of the Seminole Wars, died." Smiley, author of *Florida: Land of Images* (1972) and other books, came here the easiest way, afoot, following then 80-year-old Josie Billie across prairies and through the cypress. "But there's nothing to indicate that the place was ever a town." Smiley wrote. "The site is on an island which is covered by tall pines and a solid mass of head-high saw palmettos. If you could get through the palmettos you might kick up a pottery shred or two, but nothing more." Josie Billie took Smiley to the spot where Sam Jones died and also to his grave, a mile beyond. A small monument, erected in 1951 by George Espenlaub of Clewiston, marks the site beneath the branches of an old live oak. The marker states: "In memory of Tuscanatofee, called Sam Jones, Valiant Seminole Leader." Smiley reports

Jones also was known as Arpeika, but the palefaces knew him as Sam Jones-be-dammed. He was with Wildcat and Alligator when they and 150 other Seminoles stood off 1,000 men under Col. Zachary Taylor in the Battle of Okeechobee on Christmas Day, 1837.

SAMOSET • *Manatee County*
Probably named for the Algonquin chief Osamoset, whose name is said to mean "he who walks over much." The town was established sometime before 1931.

SAMPALA LAKE • *Madison County*
The mission of San Pablo or San Pedro stood near here, and the lake's name may be a corruption in pronunciation either by Indians or Americans.

SAMSULA • *Volusia County*
Once known as Briggsville for a Capt. Briggs, the town changed its name in 1919 to honor Lloyd Samsula, a World War I soldier.

SAN ANTONIO • *Pasco County*
Founded in the early 1880s by Judge Edmund F. Dunne, a former chief justice of Arizona. Family tradition says that Dunne had once lost his way in the Arizona desert while prospecting for silver, and prayed to his patron saint for rescue, vowing that he would give the name of San Antonio to a settlement he contemplated founding in Florida. The place in Florida which he finally selected had been called Clear Lake. In fulfillment of his promise, he founded a settlement there and renamed it San Antonio. He later donated a 40-acre tract on which the Holy Name Academy, a Catholic girls' school, was built in 1890.

SAN BLAS • *Bay and Gulf counties*
The community in Bay County and the cape in Gulf County are said to have been derived from St. Blase, also spelled Blaize and Blasius, for the martyred Bishop of Sebaste in Armenia. Cape St. Blaize appears on a 1735 map.

SANDERSON • *Baker County*
Believed named for John P. Sanderson, prominent citizen of Jacksonville who represented Florida in the provisional Congress of the Confederate States. The site was used by both Union and Confederate soldiers as a camp during the campaign of 1864. *See also* Greenville.

SANDY FORD • *Madison County*
An early name of the present Greenville. Sandy Ford's post office opened on February 24, 1854.

SANFORD • *Seminole County*
This town grew from Fort Mellon, named for a U.S. Army officer killed in the Seminole War. The fort, established in 1837, stood about a mile east of the present city. In 1871, some 12,000 acres were purchased by Henry Sanford, a former U.S. minister to Belgium who bore an honorary generalship from the state of Minnesota, acquired during the Civil War. Sanford named the new town after himself.

SANIBEL • *Lee County*
Elinore M. Dormer, in her *The Sea Shell Islands*, says the name is a garbled version of a Spanish name, the end product of a mistake repeated several times. The official Spanish Army map of 1768 shows Puerto de S. Nibel.

SANITARIA • *Polk County*
A forerunner of Auburndale, a few miles west, for the railroad decided to build its station where Auburndale now stands instead of at Sanitaria. Sanitaria was in the postal register from 1883 to 1887.

SAN JUAN DE GUACARA •
The name applied to the Suwannee River on the Romans Map of 1774. *See also* Suwannee.

SAN JUAN DEL PUERTO • *Duval County*
Founded on Fort George Island by the Franciscan Order of Friars Minor in the latter part of the sixteenth century, this mission was in operation for more than 100 years. It was here that Father Francisco Pareja wrote books on the Timucuan Indians. In time, the mission gave its name, St. John of the Port, to the river. Jonathan Dickinson, the Philadelphia Quaker, passed through here in 1696 and recorded that he found in the center of the island "the town of St. Wan's, a large town and many people; they have a friar and a worship-house. The people are very industrious, having plenty of hogs and fowls, and large crops of corn." The mission was destroyed in 1701 during a raid from South Carolina, then a British colony.

SANLANDO • *Seminole County*
A town advertising itself as midway between Sanford and Orlando.

SAN MATEO • *Putnam County*
See Rollestown.

SAN NICOLAS • *Duval County*
This village and adjacent Fort San Nicolas were built by the Spanish in 1739 in what now is the south side of the river in Jacksonville. However, the present-day area is called St. Nicholas.

SAN PEDRO • *Madison County*
Carlton Smith, the historian of Madison County, reports the territorial legislative council created Madison on December 26, 1827, and designated San Pedro as the county seat. San Pedro was situated on the Bellamy Road about ten miles south of the town of Madison at the junction of S.R. 360 and S.R. 14. In the mid-1600s, San Pedro de Potohiriba, a Spanish mission, had been established in this vicinity.

SANS SOUCI • *Pasco County*
Peter O. Knight gave the name Sans Souci, or "carefree" in French, to his residence, grove, and ranch. A prominent attorney, Knight founded the Tampa Electric Company in 1899. He was influential in legislative affairs.

SANTA FE • *Alachua County*
The community is across the county from the lake of the same name, Holy Faith, but both appear on maps from the 1830s.

SANTA FE • *Bradford County*
Went through a number of changes of name before disappearing from the map. It appeared first in 1843 as Casonville, and changed to Santa Fe in 1845. In 1851, Santa Fe gave way to Collins, then changed back to Santa Fe in 1853. In 1858, it became Cherry Hill, then changed back to Santa Fe in 1872. It lost its standing as a post office in 1884.

SANTA FE RIVER •
See Discords, River of, and High Springs.

SANTA MARIA • *Escambia County*
The colony established on Pensacola Bay in 1559 by Don Tristan de Luna and abandoned in 1561 after a storm destroyed the fleet. This settlement antedated by six years the founding of St. Augustine, the oldest permanent community.

SANTA MARIA ISLAND • *Nassau County*
The name of Amelia Island before Gen. James Oglethorpe, founder of Georgia, set out along the coast in 1736 and gave English names to the islands as far south as the St. Johns River. Amelia Island took its name from Princess Amelia, daughter of King George II. A Spanish post had stood here since 1686 when the island first was called Santa Maria.

SANTA ROSA COUNTY •
The twenty-first county, established February 18, 1842. Named for Santa Rosa Island, which in turn was named for St. Rosa de Viterbo, a Catholic saint.

SAPP • *Baker County*
Founded in 1902 and likely named for M. A. Sapp, described as a pioneer in the blueberry industry.

SARASOTA COUNTY •
The sixtieth county, established May 14, 1921. The origin of the name of this county is shrouded in dispute and legend. The Spaniards are said by one version to have named it to designate it "a place for dancing," referring to the celebrations held by the Indians on or near the shore of the bay here, but there are no words in modern Spanish to give this meaning to the name. A legend, more colorful but more obviously fabricated, ascribes the name to a beautiful daughter of DeSoto, the great Spanish explorer—Sara Sota. An Indian prince is said to have allowed himself to be taken prisoner by the Spaniards so that he could be near her; when he fell sick she nursed him back to health, only to fall sick herself and die. The Indian prince and a hundred of his braves buried her beneath the waters of the bay, then chopped their canoes with their tomahawks and sank to death themselves. Eighteenth-century maps show the name variously as Sarasote, Sarazota, and Sara Zota.

SARASOTA • *Sarasota County*
Founded on July 27, 1886, by Scottish and American settlers and named for the county. On December 23, 1885, a number of Scottish families came ashore here to settle land they had purchased for their homes in a new

country. They met wilderness and hardship instead of the established town promised them. Many returned in disappointment to Scotland. The remaining colonists joined with American settlers to develop a town.

SARAXOLA INLET • *Sarasota County*
When James Grant Forbes navigated the waters of the southwest Florida coast in 1803, Saraxola Inlet was among the places he mentioned. This was the present Sarasota Pass.

SATELLITE BEACH • *Brevard County*
One of the communities that sprang up near the missile-launching center of Cape Canaveral, and derived its name from this activity.

SATSUMA • *Jackson County*
Named for the satsuma oranges growing here.

SATSUMA • *Putnam County*
Known variously as Satsuma and Satsuma Heights, the town was established in 1882 by three developers, Messrs. Whitney, Gold, and Hodges, who purchased one of the Hernandez grants of some 10,000 acres. The name came from the satsuma orange, a variety originating in the former Japanese province of the same name.

SAULSVILLE • *Volusia County*
A trail in the 1850s led through the scrub to Old Enterprise on the St. Johns River. Along its route was the home of George Sauls, afterwards called Saulsville and later Osteen. *See also* Osteen.

SAUNDERS • *Bay County*
Named for a family of early settlers.

SAWDUST • *Gadsden County*
An area of small farms before the Civil War. A post office by that name was opened in 1895 and discontinued in 1909.

SAXTON • *Bradford County*
Took its name from a family of early settlers.

SCANLON • *Taylor County*
Named in 1920 for the Brooks-Scanlon Lumber Company.

SCOTTS FERRY • *Jackson County*
Memorializes a Lt. Scott, whose party was massacred by Indians in the early 1800s.

SCOTTSMOOR • *Brevard County*
Vermonters named Scott and Moore coined a Scottish-sounding name for a development in 1925 which outlasted the great land boom.

SCRATCHANKLE • *Palm Beach County*
Will (1964) relates how John Tyner, Fred Reynolds, and Claude Santee settled on Lake Okeechobee around 1912. "Their location was called Tynersville, though it was better known as Scratchankle."

SCRATCH ANKLE • *Santa Rosa County*
In telling of the smuggling here to avoid the official import-export center at Spanish Pensacola in the early 1800s, King (1972) said "a lively and healthy trade went on during those years through Milton, often in those days spoken of as 'Scratch Ankle' since many of the surreptitious landings made here were at points where the briars came down to the water's edge."

SEA HORSE ISLAND • *Levy County*
One of the islands of the Cedar group. Seahorses often were caught in the nets of shrimp and sponge fishermen.

SEA RANCH LAKES • *Broward County*
Named for a hotel, the Sea Ranch Hotel, a landmark across the highway from the town site. There are also two artificial lakes in the village.

SEBASTIAN • *Indian River County*
Named for Saint Sebastian, a Roman soldier martyred as a Christian about 288.

SEBRING • *Highlands County*
In 1912, this town was founded by and named for George Eugene Sebring, a pottery manufacturer of Sebring, Ohio. Family members scoff at the legend that he intentionally patterned the city plan after that of Heliopolis, the ancient Syrian city with its Temple of the Sun at the center and the streets radiating. It is the county seat of Highlands County.

Boarding the Orange Blossom Special at the Sebring railroad depot.

SECOTAN • *Taylor County*
Possibly a transplant from North Carolina, where an Algonquin tribe of that name lived. The name is said to mean "burnt place."

SEFFNER • *Hillsborough County*
Because the first name, Lenna City, could become confused with Lemon City in Dade County, a change was required before the post office was established in 1884. It was called Seffner after the first postmaster, F. P. Seffner.

SEMINOLE COUNTY •

The fiftieth county, established April 25, 1913, and given the name of the Indian tribe. There is a tendency among non-Indians to think of Florida's Indians as Seminoles. Actually, there are two groups, the Seminole and the Miccosukee. They are separated by language. The Miccosukees speak a dialect of the Hitchiti, once the most powerful Indian group in south Georgia. The Seminoles speak a dialect of the Creek, originating in Alabama. Simpson (1956) traces the development of the most recent aboriginal inhabitants of Florida. He says the name was applied by the Creeks to the emigrant Muskogean Indians who settled in Florida during the eighteenth and early nineteenth centuries, after the original aboriginal population had been exterminated. Perhaps the earliest Indians to begin the repopulation of Florida were the Yamassees, originally residents of coastal Georgia, whom the Carolinians had obliged to remove to South Carolina to get them beyond Spanish influence. During the so-called Yamassee War of 1715, these fled to Florida nearly en masse. The next immigrants, a band of Oconee under Ahaya or Cowkeeper, were auxiliaries of Oglethorpe in his 1740 attack on St. Augustine. They did not return to reside among the Lower Creeks, but settled in Alachua. They, rather than the Yamassee, are usually considered to be the group to whom the term Seminole was originally applied. Immigration, largely from the Lower Creeks, continued over the greater part of the following 100 years. Settlements appeared along the course of the Apalachicola River, and in the area between that river and the Suwannee River, while the presence of a few further south in the peninsula is known. It is unlikely that all of this movement was stimulated by prospects for a more comfortable living in Florida, and it is probable that it stemmed from internal friction in various communities, often the consequences of partisanship favoring British or Spanish interests, or from resentment toward the policies followed by the U.S. government, in particular after 1814. As a consequence of the deserted condition of Florida, the names given to its natural features by the Timucuans, the Apalachians, and the Calusas were forgotten, unless preserved in the literature of European languages, and became supplanted by names derived from the languages of these immigrants, from Creek and from Hitchiti. The derivation of the word Seminole is uncertain. Probably most authorities incline to the view that the name is a corruption of the Creek *ishti semoli,* "wild men," an epithet applied by the Creeks to these separatists. The Upper Creeks designated them as *aulockawan* in recognition of their place of residence. While the number of these immigrants may have included some who were guilty of infractions of tribal regulations, there does not appear to be any implication in the name that these people were regarded as outlaws. It has also been suggested that the word is an Indian corruption of the Spanish word *cimarron,* which although primarily meaning "wild or unruly," was also applied to runaway slaves or beasts.

SEMINOLE • *Pinellas, Duval and Bay counties*
In addition to Seminole County, there is Seminole in Pinellas County, Seminole Beach in Duval County, and Seminole Hills in Bay County.

SENECA • *Lake and Broward counties*
Twice used as a Florida place name. Seneca in Lake County was given its name by an early settler from Seneca, N.Y. Seneca, Lake County, is described in *History of Lake County* (1929) as having been big enough in the 1880s to support a brass band of 14 pieces. Seneca, so the story goes, "was a very prosperous town before the Big Freeze, so wealthy in fact that it didn't 'consider a dollar bill anything, fives and tens were all that talked.' A settler who came after the Big Freeze was told that it was the 'wrath of Divine Providence that had wiped out the town' because of its wealth." Seneca in Broward County was a station on the Seaboard Coast Line, which no longer shows on the maps by that name. Likely it, too, was a New York transplant.

SEVILLE • *Volusia County*
Established in 1879 and named for the ancient Spanish city, which in turn had been named Sephala, marshy plain, by its founders, the Phoenicians. The fertile hammocks of this region produce the small, wild Seville orange, said to have been imported and planted by the Spaniards, but it is not clear whether the town was named for the fruit or vice versa.

SEWALLS POINT • *Martin County*
Known first in the 1880s as Waveland, the name was changed in 1891 to Sewalls Point, likely for a family residing here.

SHADEVILLE • *Wakulla County*
Origin of the name is not known, but the area furnishes some of the finest tomatoes raised in the vicinity of Tallahassee.

SHADY GROVE • *Taylor County*
Settled in the 1860s and called Shady Grove for the old oaks, the town changed its name to Luther in 1894 and then back to Shady Grove in 1909.

SHADY REST • *Gadsden County*
Again, the oaks suggested a pleasant place, especially in combination with Rest.

SHAKERAG •
See Melrose.

SHALIMAR • *Okaloosa County*
Said to have been named by one of the daughters of James E. Plew, probably after the river in Kashmir described in the popular song, "Pale Hands I Pressed." Plew, who was from Chicago, bought up the holdings of John Perrine. The land included most of Valparaiso and Niceville and all of Shalimar. Plew started a winery here just after the repeal of Prohibition. The grapes came from the old Bunte farm near Crestview, and the product was called Shalimar wine.

SHAMROCK • *Dixie County*
Named for a big lumber company whose mill was here, and long a favorite pause for motorists on the gulf coast highway.

SHARPES • *Brevard County*
From the name of settlers here in the 1890s.

SHAWANO • *Palm Beach County*
Located on the Hillsboro Canal seven miles below the Palm Beach–Belle Glade road. Also known as Brown's Farm, a name taken from the enterprise of the Brown Company, of Portland, Maine, paper manufacturers who made a vegetable cooking fat as a by-product. With only a dozen voters in the 1950s, it was always the first precinct to report in Florida elections.

SHELL POINT • *Wakulla County*
Shells remaining from an Indian village here gave this place its name.There was a post office here in 1831.

SHELTON • *Dixie County*
Horseshoe was known as Shelton for a while in the early 1900s. Then the name was changed back to Horseshoe and again in 1948 to Horseshoe Beach.

SHILOH • *Brevard County*
In the 1880s, George C. Kuhl wanted to name this community for his sister Anna, but postal authorities suggested the possibility of conflict with another place so he selected Shiloh, a Biblical name applied to many communities, usually because of a church having stood there first.

SHINGLE CREEK • *Osceola County*
From a shingle and lath mill operated by the Prescott family in the 1880s.

SIESTA KEY • *Sarasota County*
On Siesta Key in the Gulf, *siesta* (Spanish for "rest") suggests midday naps or a generally relaxed atmosphere.

SILVER BLUFF • *Dade County*
Named for the banks along south Bayshore Drive, Miami. It is one of the towns, along with Lemon City, Allapattah, and Coconut Grove, that were swallowed up by Miami in an annexation vote on September 2, 1925.

SILVER SPRINGS • *Marion County*
Took its name from the celebrated springs, Florida's largest, whose crystal clearness inspired the name. A town has been here since 1852.

SIMMONS • *Taylor County*
When the post office was established in 1898, the postmaster, Thomas Simmons, gave the place his name.

SINK CREEK • *Jackson County*
A creek disappears underground here, to reappear a quarter of a mile away.

SLAUGHTER • *Pasco County*
This name could be regarded as a reminder of the Dade Massacre (*see also* Dade City) which occurred some ten miles, away, but actually Slaughter was the name of one of the families which settled here about 1880, primarily for turpentine farming. From April 13 to December 19, 1898, there was a post office for a Slaughter in Madison County. Again, this was a family name.

SLAUGHTER, PLACE OF • *St. Johns County*
See Matanzas.

SLAVIA • *Seminole County*
The Slavia Colony Company settled Yugoslavians from Cleveland on 1,200 acres of land here in 1912.

SMITH CREEK • *Wakulla County*
Settlers from Georgia and North Carolina began coming into this area in 1845, although a post office did not materialize until 1872.

SNEADS • *Jackson County*
A community has been here since the 1880s. The name is said to be that of a pioneer dentist.

SOAK RUM • *Hillsborough County*
Robinson (1928) remarks upon the transition in the spelling of the names of places. "Perhaps as interesting as any is the gradual change of the name of a settlement in the southeastern part of the present Hillsborough County," writes Robinson. "It first appears about 1850 by the name Soak Rum, then Soccrum and now Socrum."

SOCRUM • *Polk County*
The Socrum settlement in Polk County is one of the two oldest, reports Heatherington (1928), with Fort Meade being the other. They date from 1850. There is no record of the origin of the name of Polk's Socrum.

SOLONA • *Charlotte County*
The people who named this town wanted to honor the sun, Old Sol.

SOPCHOPPY • *Wakulla County*
From the Creek *sokhe*, "twisted," and *chapke*, "long." The town, established in 1853, is on the Sopchoppy River, which is, indeed, long and twisted. Read (1934) disagrees, saying Sopchoppy is Seminole-Creek for *lokchapi*, "(red) oak," a combination of *lokcha*, "acorn," and *api*, "stem."

SORRENTO • *Lake County*
When the first settlers came about 1875, they could not agree on a name for the place. "The settlers were enjoying the Italian novel, *Agnes of Sorrento*, at that time and since Sorrento is a city in Italy that is noted for its oranges, that name was among those offered. It was finally decided to place them all in a hat and have a blindfolded person draw the chosen name. Sorrento was the one that was drawn" (Kennedy, 1929).

SOUTH •
Prefixed to the names of numerous satellite communities. See the name of the parent community.

SOUTH BAY • *Palm Beach County*
Named for the southern arm of Lake Okeechobee, at a corner of which it is situated.

The Sopchoppy post office in Sally Lewis' store.

SOUTH FLOMATON • *Escambia County*
An offshoot of Flomaton, Escambia County, Ala. The communities are sepa-rated by the Florida-Alabama boundary. Al Burt, writing in *The Miami Herald* for October 14, 1973, reports Flomaton was created about 1850 and first named Reuterville, after the man who built the railroad to Pensacola. Later, continues Burt, Flomaton was called Whiting, for an early settler; then Pensacola Junction. The resultant mail confusion was settled momentarily by taking a fourth name: Floma, from the first three letters of Florida and the last two of Alabama. But the post office rejected Floma, finding it sounded too much like Florala, another border town to the east. So the townspeople decided upon Flomaton.

SOUTH MERE • *Brevard County*
On the boundary of Seminole and Brevard counties. *Mere* means "boundary" in British dialect or in Greek, "part." Take your choice.

SOUTH MIAMI • *Dade County*
Until the land boom of the 1920s, this place was called Larkins after a pio-neer family whose descendants and friends still take a dim view of the change.

SOUTH PALM BEACH • *Palm Beach County*
Of Palm Beach County's 37 incorporated communities, 11 have populations in excess of 10,000. Thirteen communities have Palm Beach in variations of their names. In addition, there are the names Atlantis, Briny Breezes, Juno adjoined by Jupiter, and Tequesta.

SOUTH PASADENA • *Pinellas County*
A satellite of St. Petersburg with Pasadena Avenue furnishing the South for a subdivision which has become home for several thousand people.

SOUTHPORT • *Bay County*
Established in 1893 as Anderson, the name was changed in 1907 to Southport to advertise its availability as a shipping point.

SPARR • *Marion County*
Postmaster M. S. Sparr gave his name to the place in 1882.

SPRINGFIELD • *Bay County*
The founding fathers are said to have settled upon Springfield because the name, popular in other states, had not been used in Florida.

SPRING GARDEN • *Volusia County*
Maj. George H. Norris laid out the hamlet in 1872, using the name by which the area had been known since Spanish land grant days. It also was called Garden Springs, but now is known as De Leon Springs.

SPRING HILL • *Polk County*
Prior to 1881, Medulla was known as Spring Hill.

SPRING HILL • *Volusia County*
There was an election in 1869 to determine whether Spring Hill should be the county seat instead of Enterprise. Spring Hill received 74 votes and Enterprise 21, but the county commissioners were not impressed and the seat remained at Enterprise for another 18 years. Spring Hill was near the present site of DeLand, which had not yet been established then.

SPRUCE CREEK • *Volusia County*
Near the present Port Orange and named for the spruce trees growing on the banks of a creek.

SPUDS • *St. Johns County*
Recognizes the potato farming here.

STAGEPOND • *Citrus County*
It seems obvious that the stagecoaches paused here.

STANTON • *Marion County*
When E. Stanton Perrin founded this community in 1881, the place was given his middle name.

STAR • *Jackson County*
Named in 1903 from the fact that the settlement was on a "star" route of the post office.

STARKE • *Bradford County*
Two versions of the naming of this town ascribe the name to two different people. The *Bradford County Telegraph*, in a 75th anniversary edition of November 12, 1954, said: "Since the earliest residents of the little village included more people from South Carolina than any other state it is not surprising that the town was called Starke in honor of Madison Starke Perry, governor of Florida from 1857 to 1861. Governor Perry was born in South Carolina in 1814 and his mother was a member of the prominent Starke family of that state." The other version says the town was named for Thomas

Starke's volunteer firemen checking the hoses, 1910s.

Starke, also of South Carolina, who in 1854, with 50 black women slaves, purchased the land around DeLeon Springs in Volusia County. The town of Starke was established prior to 1867, and is the county seat of Bradford County.

STARKE LAKE • *Orange County*
Dr. J. D. Starke camped at a lake here in the 1870s and 1880s. First the lake was given his name and then a settlement which grew up at the lake. Now the place is known as Ocoee.

STARR • *Suwannee County*
A locomotive engineer named Starr lived on the Live Oak, Perry and Gulf Railway.

STEELE CITY • *Jackson County*
Named for A. B. Steele, builder in 1895 of the Atlanta & St. Andrews Bay Railway.

STEINHATCHEE •
First there was a community by this name in Lafayette County and then, when the Lafayette post office was discontinued, in Taylor County. There also is a Steinhatchee River forming the boundary between Taylor and Dixie counties. From the Creek *ak*, "down," *isti*, "man," and *hatchee*, "creek," put together as dead man's creek. Deadman's Bay is at the mouth of the river.

STETSON • *Volusia County*
Named for Stetson University, which in turn took its name from John B. Stetson, the hatter and philanthropist.

A 1914 automobile/train collision near the tiny Stetson railroad depot.

STILLEPICA • *Madison County*
Seminole-Creek *stillipaika*, "moccasin."

STILTSVILLE • *Dade County*
In Biscayne Bay. There were 12 occupied houses in Stiltsville in 1922; 18 made up this little waterborne neighborhood-on-stilts in 1961. Located on the northern edge of the Biscayne National Monument, Stiltsville was reduced by Hurricane Andrew to five houses all with leases which are to expire in 1999.

STUART • *Martin County*
Named for Samuel C. Stuart, first telegraph operator and station agent, when the Florida East Coast Railway was built across the St. Lucie River in 1893. Originally, the town site was known as Potsdam. Stuart is the county seat of Martin County.

STYX RIVER • *Liberty County*
This Styx can be crossed in Liberty County, where the river—really a creek—is a tributary of the Apalachicola River. The stream first was known as Taffia Creek, which J. Clarence Simpson, writing in *Apalachee*, the journal of the Tallahassee Historical Society, in 1946, defines as corrupted from the Creek *atapha*, "dogwood."

SULPHUR SPRINGS • *Hillsborough County*
The area about the sulphur spring here has been a favorite picnicking place since the turn of the century. There was a separate community by the name here beginning in 1924, but Tampa has grown out to absorb Sulphur Springs.

S U M A T R A • *Liberty County*
Established in 1908, the town derived its name from the variety of wrapper tobacco cultivated in the area, a variety known as sumatra because it is similar to the tobacco grown in Sumatra, in Malaysia.

S U M I C A • *Polk County*
From the initials of the French mining company which owned land here.

S U M M E R F I E L D • *Marion County*
An area of rich muck soil, once the bed of ancient lakes, given a name in 1885 that emphasized the long agricultural season.

S U M M E R H A V E N • *St. Johns County*
A vacation retreat for a time in the 1890s.

S U M M E R L A N D K E Y • *Monroe County*
A reference to the climate.

S U M M I T • *Lake County*
Paul Shockley laid out a township here which was the apex, in his opinion, until the big freeze of 1897.

S U M T E R C O U N T Y •
The twenty-ninth county, established January 8, 1853. Named for Gen. Thomas Sumter (1736-1832), a native of South Carolina who was prominent in the southern campaigns of the Revolutionary War. Many South Carolinians were early settlers in this area.

S U M T E R V I L L E • *Sumter County*
Settled in 1858, Sumterville took its name from the county's namesake, Gen. Thomas Sumter.

S U N •
Another of the names identified with Florida and particularly with areas seeking to attract tourists and retirees. There is, or has been: Suniland in Dade County; Sunnyhill in Leon County; Sunny Isles in Dade County; Sunnyside in Taylor County, Sunnyside in Putnam County, Sunnyside in Clay County, and Sunnyside in Bay County, a total of four Sunnysides; Sunrise in Broward County; and Sunset Hill in Lake County.

S U N B E A M • *Duval County*
Once known as Nine Mile Springs on the King's Highway when first settled in 1796 by Lewis Schofield. Renamed Sunbeam in 1915.

S U N B E A M • *Orange County*
Another Sunbeam, in Orange County, existed for a brief time beginning in 1903.

S U N C I T Y • *Hillsborough County*
When Ross was caught up in the boom of the 1920s, its name was changed to Sun City and a motion picture studio was built in hopes of enticing the film industry. Sun City was a relic of the boom for many years, but revival signs appeared in the 1960s.

SUNRISE • *Broward County*

This community reversed the usual order of a day, going from Sunset to Sunrise. According to Mayor John Lomelo, Jr., in 1974, the community originally was planned as a retirement area and was called Sunset. The developers quickly found retirees did not like to be reminded they might be in the sunset of life; hence, the switch in 1961 to Sunrise Golf Village, the Golf emphasizing the two golf courses bordering the community. In 1971, the village was incorporated as the city of Sunrise.

SUNSHINE BEACH • *Pinellas County*

On Treasure Island, northwest of St. Petersburg. Formerly called Sunset Beach, but when it was incorporated in 1937 its present name was adopted. Another portion of Treasure Island had at first been called Coney Island when it was platted in 1920, but there were protests about the amusement-park associations of the name, so the town adopted the name of Sunset Beach, which had been abandoned by the other town.

SUNSHINE SKYWAY • *Pinellas and Manatee counties*

The architecture critic of *The New York Times*, Paul Goldberger, described Florida's Sunshine Skyway as startlingly beautiful, almost a religious experience. The 1,260-foot main span of the 8.1-mile causeway across Tampa Bay, which opened to traffic in 1987, soars "over the water with a lyrical and tensile strength."

The Sunshine Skyway bridge was designed by Figg & Muller of Tallahassee, an engineering firm specializing in concrete bridge design. It replaced a pair of steel-truss bridges, one of which collapsed in 1980 when it was rammed by a freighter on a foggy night, killing 35 people.

The state and federal governments considered repairing the bridge, which was only nine years old at the time; a companion span was 26 years old. But it was decided to replace both spans with a larger and safer bridge instead.

"For roughly $220 million they got not only a bridge that is both large and safe—they also got a structure that from an esthetic standpoint may rank as the most impressive piece of large-scale bridge design in this country in half a century," wrote critic Goldberger. "Not since the George Washington, Bronx-Whitestone and Golden Gate Bridges, the high points of suspension bridge design in the 1930s, has a major bridge been as compelling a visual presence as this one."

SURFSIDE • *Dade County*

A community alongside the Atlantic north of Miami Beach, originally named as a subdivision.

SUTHERLAND • *Pinellas County*

Said to have been named for the Duke of Sutherland; replaced by Palm Harbor. In 1886, the Sutherland Improvement Company built two hotels, stores, and other buildings. The duke, cousin of Queen Victoria, is said to have purchased 30 acres on Lake Butler.

SUWANNEE COUNTY •

The thirty-fifth county, established December 21, 1858. One of the few counties in the United States whose name has been immortalized in song: Stephen Collins Foster wrote in "Old Folks at Home" about "Way down upon the Swanee River." The river that Foster spelled Swanee has become a world symbol of love for family and home. Etymologists disagree on the origin of Suwannee. Utley (1908) says the name comes from a Cherokee Indian word *sawani*, "echo river." Gannett (1947) agrees. Brinton (1859) suggests it may have been a corruption of the Spanish *San Juan*. He mentions a Shawnee tradition that their tribe originated on this river and claims that the name may be a corruption of

Stephen Foster never saw the Suwannee River even though he made it famous in his song "Old Folks at Home."

Shawanese. Simpson (1956) says Suwannee seems to be identical with the name of a village in Gwinnett County, Ga., that stands on the site of a former Cherokee town called Suwani. According to Read (1834), the Cherokees claim their village is from Creek origin. If this is true, the derivation of the name is probably from the Creek *suwani*, "echo." Simpson mentions that good echoes are a feature of this stream. He continues, saying that the stream is probably the one called River of the Deer by De Soto. During the seventeenth century, a Franciscan mission called San Juan de Guacara was located somewhere along the left bank. This name for the river persisted despite the destruction of the mission and the change of flags. An English surveyor named Romans in 1774 called the river the River St. Juan de Duacara vulge Little Sequana. Sequana appears to be an Indian attempt to pronounce San Juan.

SWEETWATER • *Dade County*

Called by one of the popularly accepted English translations of Miami, this community was founded by a troupe of Russian midgets stranded along the Tamiami Trail between Miami and Naples when one car ran out of gasoline. The troupe liked the desolation so much that they returned in the 1930s to build a new town. For a while, the town government was best known for the lack of officials who could speak English. Sweetwater's boom largely has come from Cuban and Nicaraguan exiles.

SWIMMING PEN • *Pinellas County*

A community on the Old Tampa Bay side of the Pinellas peninsula. When the time came to establish a post office in 1875, the feeling was that a more dignified name should be found. Bayview was agreed upon.

SWITZERLAND • *St. Johns County*
Francis P. Fatio was born near Vevey, Switzerland, and when he settled here during the period of British ownership of Florida, he transplanted the name of his native land. Switzerland's post office opened in 1881.

SYCAMORE • *Gadsden County*
Randall Johnson came here in 1822, the first immigrant to settle in what today is known as the Sycamore community. Stanley (1948) relates how Johnson built a stockade around his log home. The pioneer stuck his sycamore riding switch into the damp earth within the stockade. It took root, lived, and grew into a Gadsden landmark from which a community, a church, and a post office derived the name Sycamore.

TAFT • *Orange County*
Formerly Smithville, for M. M. Smith, who operated a turpentine camp here. Then Prosper Colony was started in 1909. Six thousand acres were platted for a town, to be surrounded by small farms. After a long advertising campaign, a contest was conducted to name the town. The winner honored William H. Taft, 27th president of the United States.

TAHITI • *Martin County*
A remembrance of the South Seas came briefly to Martin County in 1890 when settlers applied Tahiti to their area. But the name was gone by 1893 and not replaced. Pasco County today has an unincorporated community known as Tahitian Gardens.

TAINTSVILLE • *Seminole County*
The *Florida Times-Union* for December 16, 1971, reported the Seminole County Commission had sanctioned the name Taintsville for a formerly nameless community between Oviedo and Chuluota. The delegation spokesman, Theodore Peterson, was quoted as having told the commision: "We are tired of telling people that we live behind the fire tower on the road that doesn't have a name." He also said the community "tain't in Oviedo and tain't in Chuluota."

TALLAHASSEE • *Leon County*
Virtually every authority agrees that the name of the capital city of Florida is derived from a Creek Indian word meaning "old town." And an old town it is indeed, if you count the residence of the Indians and the Spaniards. The first date we know definitely is 1539, when De Soto met here with the Apalachee tribes, who controlled the fields and streams in this area. How long before that the Indians had been using this spot as a center of activity we have no way of knowing. About 1633, the Spanish mission of San Luis was established a few miles northwest of the present city of Tallahassee. The spot was chosen for the capital of Florida on March 4, 1824, while Florida was still a territory, and the town began to be occupied in 1825-1826 by people

from Georgia, North Carolina, and Virginia. Legend says the name and spelling were finally chosen by Octavia Walton, daughter of a territorial governor of Florida and granddaughter of a signer of the Declaration of Independence. In addition to being the capital of Florida, Tallahassee is the county seat of Leon County.

TALLAVAST • *Manatee County*
Came into being in 1910 as Cates City but changed to Tallavast in 1919. The meaning is not known.

TALLULAH • *Lafayette County*
This lovely name was allowed to lapse after only a year's use in 1880-1881.

TALOFA • *Putnam County*
Derived from the Seminole-Creek *talofa*, meaning "town, tribe or settlement."

TALUGA RIVER • *Liberty County*
Corrupted from the Seminole *talaka chapko*, "cow peas."

TAMARAC • *Broward County*
In 1963 named by Kenneth E. Behring, the original developer, for the tamarack, a tree of the larch family not ordinarily found here. As the story goes, a tamarack tree was discovered here and it was taken as an omen that transplanted people also would flourish. A metal sculpture of a tamarack branch has been placed in the community's country club and the representation of a branch also shows in the city seal.

TAMIAMI TRAIL •
"The Trail" opened a highway between Tampa and Miami, and took its name from the first three letters of Tampa and the last four of Miami. The idea of this cross-state highway through the Everglades was ramrodded by a number of people along the route, William Stuart Hill of *The Miami Herald* being among the first in 1914. Tebeau (1957) reports "it was E. P. Dickey who formally suggested the name of 'Tamiami Trail' at this first meeting of the State Road Department. The name was such a natural that it was almost immediately accepted. The *American Eagle* (at Estero) at first objected that it sounded 'like a bunch of tin cans tied to a dog's tail and clattering over cobblestones,' and queried, 'Why not call the Jacksonville to Miami Dixie Highway "Jackiami Joypath" and the road through Arcadia to the east coast "Pair-o-Dice Loop"?'" The *Tampa Tribune* was among the objectors, describing the name as impossible, difficult and unfair because "it includes the whole name of Miami and only two letters of the name of Tampa." The Tamiami Trail was officially opened on April 25, 1928, nearly 13 years after the first dirt was turned for its construction.

TAMPA • *Hillsborough County*
As with so many names of Indian origin, tracers of the name of this important Florida west coast city have a choice among three unrelated suggestions as to meaning. One is "near it" or "close to it;" another is "split wood for quick fires," while the third, by Tampa historian D. B. McKay, found the source in a fifteenth-century Spanish city. The first has the support of the

greater number of authorities, but the second is supported by the chief bibliographer of the Library of Congress as well as the Greater Tampa Chamber of Commerce. The "near" presumably referred to the closeness of the original Indian village to what is now Tampa Bay. The split wood is said to have been used because of the quantities of driftwood found along the shore. The bay was first known as Espiritu Santo or "holy spirit," and was entered in 1528 by Narváez, who found the Indian village. Tampa historian Karl H. Grismer (1950) says Hernando de Escalante Fontaneda, a Spanish lad of 13 when shipwrecked off the Florida coast in 1545, was responsible for preserving Tampa's ancient name. Friendly Indians gave Fontaneda hospitality and the opportunity to travel in the Florida peninsula for 17 years before he returned to Spain. He learned the languages of four tribes and compiled a list of 22 towns within the Caloosa territory of south Florida, "and the name 'Tanpa' led all the rest. He spelled the word with an 'n' instead of an 'm'. Contemporary writers and mapmakers who saw Fontaneda's *Memoir* apparently liked 'Tampa' better than 'Tanpa' and when they picked up the word and used it, they gave it more euphonic spelling" (Grismer, 1950). Fontaneda did not give a meaning for the name. Dr. John R. Swanton of the Smithsonian Institution, an authority on the languages of the primitive Indians of the southeastern United States, says there is little hope an authentic interpretation ever can be ascertained unless a Caloosa vocabulary is discovered. Present-day Tampa grew from Fort Brooke, named in the spring of 1824 for its commanding officer, Col. George Mercer Brooke. "The farm and fishing village which grew up outside the military reservation also was called Fort Brooke but eventually was known by the Indian name of Tampa" (Dunn, 1972). Settlers objected to the military name and adopted the name Tampa Bay for their first post office in 1831. It was soon decided that the Bay could be dropped. The city is the county seat of Hillsborough County.

Nine tons of the Sunday edition of The Tampa Tribune, 1921.

TANGERINE • *Orange County*
Named in 1881 for the citrus fruit.

TANG-O-MAR BEACH • *Walton County*
On the Gulf, where there is indeed a flavor of the sea.

TANTI • *Okeechobee County*
For the redheaded schoolteacher Tanti Huckabee of South Carolina, whose contributions to this community in its early days were forgotten when a railroad official was sent down, as the *Palm Beach Weekly* News reported on December 21, 1911, to lay out "the future great city." Tanti obviously was not a sufficiently dignified name to fit those dimensions but Okeechobee City would, although some old-timers continued to call the community for the teacher.

TARPON SPRINGS • *Pinellas County*
Established in 1876 by South Carolinian A. W. Ormond, who brought with him his daughter Mary and built his cabin near Spring Bayou, inland on the Anclote River. Mary Ormond, later Mrs. Joshua Boyer, is credited by her husband with naming the community "because of the great numbers of tarpon fish that frequent the springs." After Hamilton Disston bought the area for 25 cents per acre, Ormond re-bought his property and welcomed Disston agent A.P.K. Safford, former surveyor general of Nevada and governor of the territory of Arizona. With Safford came his sister Mary Jane Safford, a physician, perhaps the first woman to practice medicine in Florida. They all helped to incorporate the city in 1887, years before Clearwater or St. Petersburg.

Sponges and coral for sale at the Tarpon Springs Sea Curiosities store, 1928.

TASMANIA • *Glades County*
The name selected in 1916 when a new generation wanted to shed the old name, Fisheating Creek. Tasmania remained on maps although Nixon Smiley reported in 1973 that not a single relic remained. Writing in *The Miami Herald*, Smiley reported other replacement names for the community were rejected by the Post Office Department because they already were in use. "Call it Tasmania," said a retired sea captain, "I'll bet there ain't no name like that in the postal guide." So they did.

TATE'S HELL • *Liberty and Franklin counties*
Cebe Tate, a 45-year-old cattleman, decided in 1875 to go into the dense swamp near Sumatra in search of cows which had disappeared from the area. In the ten days that followed, Tate combated underbrush and thorny vines which shredded his clothing. Thirst forced him to drink stagnant black swamp water and hunger required him to eat bamboo bugs and green roots. He stumbled into a clearing, practically naked, a ten-day beard covering his cut and bruised face, and his hair turned from brown to white. Bill Snyder, a writer who explored the swamp, wrote that Tate approached a startled man on the outskirts of Carrabelle. "Where am I?" gasped Tate. "You're in Carrabelle, partner," responded the stranger. "Where you coming' from?" Tate answered, "I've been in Hell! I've been in Hell for ten days and nights." Appropriately, the swamp has been known since as Tate's Hell.

TAVARES • *Lake County*
Established around 1880 by Maj. Alexander St. Clair Abrams, and named by him for a Spanish ancestor of his. It is the county seat of Lake County.

TAVERNIER • *Monroe County*
A protected anchorage here has attracted mariners since small boats began sailing in the vicinity some two centuries ago. How the key got its name is a matter of conjecture. Earl Adams, a former newsman who in later years served as clerk of the Circuit Court at Key West, is quoted as having said an enterprising saloonkeeper had a place near the site of the modern settlement of Tavernier. To attract trade, he stuck a sign in the mangroves. It misspelled the message "tavern near" and the misspelling has been preserved.

Less fanciful is the belief the name may be a corruption of Spanish *Cayo Tabona*, or "Horsefly Key," given to a small island on the seaward side of Tavernier harbor (Stevenson, 1970). Commencing in the 1760s, Bahamian turtle catchers and woodcutters added wrecking to their occupations. With the original savages gone from the Keys, the Bahamians, known also as Conchs, would anchor in summer off Tabona to wait for sailing ships to wreck. Conchs would then rescue the shipwrecked crews and passengers and salvage the cargoes (Brookfield and Griswold, 1949).

TAYLOR COUNTY •
The thirty-fourth county, established December 23, 1856. Named for Zachary Taylor, twelfth president of the United States and commander of the U.S. Army forces in Florida during a part of the Second Seminole War.

TAYLORVILLE • *Lake County*
Settled in 1899, it became Groveland in 1912. *See also* Groveland.

TEENJAY • *Alachua County*
From the Tampa & Jacksonville Railroad: the "T" and "J."

TELOGIA • *Liberty County*
Another version of the Seminole *taluga,* "cow peas." *See also* Taluga.

TEMPLE TERRACE • *Hillsborough County*
These 1,500 acres of land were bought from Mrs. Potter Palmer of Chicago in 1921 by a group of Tampa financiers and laid out in groves of temple oranges. The community took its name from the variety of orange, whose trees bear glossy, dark-green leaves and brilliant golden fruit.

TENILE • *Escambia County*
For a family of settlers from South Carolina.

TEQUESTA • *Palm Beach County*
The obsolete aboriginal name for Biscayne Bay. Tekesta Indians formerly lived on its shores. The Spaniards called the entire coastal region south of Cape Canaveral the Province of Tequesta.

TERRA CEIA • *Manatee County*
Hernando De Soto, in May 1539, landed somewhere in Tampa Bay. A U.S. commission, headed by John R. Swanton of the Smithsonian Institution, concluded De Soto landed at Shaw Point and made Terra Ceia Island his headquarters during the six weeks he remained in the vicinity. Bickel (1942) states, "We know the Mangrove Coast Indians were sun worshipers. The fine, high temple mound at Terra Ceia Island shows the long ramp coming up from the west to the top of the pyramid where the temple, facing eastward, once stood. De Soto's soldiers destroyed it in 1539." Terra Ceia is translated as "heavenly land."

TEXAN • *Alachua County*
There was a Texan in Florida from 1896 until 1898. Who the Texan was is not known.

THIGPEN • *Duval County*
Thigpen's name was changed to Baldwin to recognize Dr. A. S. Baldwin's efforts in the 1850s in causing the building of the first railroad out of Jacksonville.

THLAPACHATCHEE CREEK • *Osceola County*
Known now as Shingle Creek, the Indian name of this stream flowing into Lake Tohopekaliga meant "fallen enemy creek."

THOMAS CITY • *Jefferson County*
Although it remains on the map, the postal register shows the name changed to Wacissa in 1899.

THONOTOSASSA • *Hillsborough County*
A lake and town named from Seminole-Creek *thlonoto,* "flint," *sasse,* "is

there," likely from the quarries in the vicinity where flint was extracted for making arrow and spear heads.

TICE • *Lee County*
Early in the 1900s, Chauncey O. Tice and an uncle, former Chief Justice W. W. Tice of Kentucky, who at that time lived in Fort Myers, decided to start a grove. They bought acreage between the Atlantic Coast Line and the Caloosahatchee River, about three miles east of Fort Myers. Later, C. O. Tice bought out his uncle's interest. He built his own packinghouse, on which he one day found a sign saying "TICE." It had been put there by the railroad people, who wanted to use his packinghouse for a station. Later a new station was built nearby, and the same name continued to be used.

TIGER • *Nassau County*
Once there was a Tiger in Nassau County, perhaps named by a Princeton alumnus, but no longer on the map.

TIGER BAY • *Polk County*
Not the political club in Miami nor the one in Tallahassee but a community in the phosphate region of Polk County which had a post office from October 24, 1899, to March 31, 1922.

TILDENVILLE • *Orange County*
Named for Luther Fuller Tilden, who was born in Vermont, lived in Illinois, and came to Orange County in 1875, buying land fronting on Lake Apopka where Tildenville developed.

TILLMAN • *Brevard County*
A land development company in 1910-1912 created here the Florida Indian River Catholic Colony, with some 100 farm families from the Midwest. Kjerulff (1972) reports the farmers were frustrated because they were unfamiliar with the soil here. By 1916, many of the Catholic farmers either had quit the area or found employment in fishing and other work. Tillman was renamed Palm Bay in 1925.

TITIE CREEK • *Okaloosa County*
Named for the shrub or small tree, a variety of which has glossy leaves and fragrant white flowers.

TITUSVILLE • *Brevard County*
Established just after the Civil War by Col. Henry T. Titus, who had been a fierce antagonist of John Brown in the struggle over Kansas before the war. The locality had been known as Sand Point, but Titus, who was postmaster and something of an autocrat, changed the name to perpetuate his own.

TOCOI • *St. Johns County*
From the Indian name for "water lily," it was the rival of nearby Picolata on the St. Johns River for passenger and freight traffic between the river and St. Augustine. Shortly after the Civil War, a crude combination mule-drawn and steam railway was built, causing the decline of Picolata. In turn, Tocoi's day passed when a railroad was built between Jacksonville and St. Augustine. During the Spanish occupation there was a Franciscan mission at Tocoi.

TOHOPEKALIGA, LAKE • *Osceola County*
Two lakes in Osceola County have this name, one distinguished from the other by the prefix East. Residents usually refer to the lakes as Toe-hope. The name is derived from the Creek *tohopke*, "fort," and *a-laiki*, "site." Moore-Willson (1935) reports that a century ago the islands within the main lake were Indian forts or stockades for defense against U. S. soldiers. "Erroneously," writes Mrs. Moore-Willson, an authority on the Seminole vocabulary, "the meaning of the lake is given as 'sleeping tiger,' this having been so frequently used by publicity venders, and while this meaning is seemingly appropriate, because of the frequent squalls, the correct meaning is Fort Site."

TOHOPKEE • *Osceola County*
Seminole-Creek *tohopki*, "fort."

TOMOKA CREEK • *Volusia County*
Simpson (1956) says this word is a corruption of Timucua, the name of a powerful tribe of Florida Indians at the time of Spanish exploration of the peninsula. The area of Tomoka Creek is believed to have been the last stand of the fragment of Timucuans who survived the English-instigated raids by the Creeks during the eighteenth century. The Spanish called the village here Pueblo de Atimucas, and the stream was named Rio de Timucas.

TORONTO • *Orange County*
Some Canadian settlers brought with them the name of the capital of the province of Ontario.

TORREYA STATE PARK • *Liberty County*
This park advertises the torreya tree, a rare variety of cedar found growing naturally only on the east bank of the Apalachicola River.

TORTUGAS ISLANDS • *Monroe County*
See Dry Tortugas.

TOTOSAHATCHEE CREEK • *Orange County*
This stream enters the St. Johns River just south of the world-renown post office of Christmas. The stream's name is Seminole-Creek *totlosi*, "chicken," and *hatchi*, "creek."

TOWNSEND • *Lafayette County*
Settled at the turn of the century and named for a pioneer family.

TRABUE • *Charlotte County*
See Punta Gorda.

TRAILER ESTATES • *Manatee County*
A mobile home development where residents own their own mobile home sites or estates.

TRAILS •
Dr. Mark F. Boyd concluded there was every reason to believe the communities of each aboriginal tribe in Florida were in relatively free communication

with each other, not only over the network of natural waterways but also by footpaths. Writing in *Florida Highways* for June 1951, Dr. Boyd suggested there also was abundant evidence that in peaceful interludes there was communication between the tribes. "One reason for the comparatively rapid penetration of the interior (of Florida) by the earliest Europeans," wrote Dr. Boyd, "was their conduction over these paths by friendly guides during periods of amity, or by those who had been reluctantly impressed during hostile incursions." The Indian trails usually followed the natural ridges, avoiding swamps and other impediments to travel.

TRAPNELL • *Hillsborough County*
An agricultural community between Spring Head and Turkey Creek. Among the first settlers in the 1850s and 1860s were Nathaniel Sparkman and J. W. Hawkins, influential in the progress of eastern Hillsborough County. Among the families were the Trapnells, whose name was given the place.

TREASURE ISLAND • *Pinellas County*
A. B. Archibald, early Gulf Beach developer, gave the name of Treasure Island to this island southwest of St. Petersburg, and the community took its name from this island.

TRENTON • *Gilchrist County*
Named after Trenton, Tenn., by Ben Boyd, who at age 18 had run away from home after a fistfight at a racetrack. He first settled in Lafayette County, Fla. He married a girl named Sarah Sapp from near Mayo; shortly thereafter, they moved to what is now Trenton but then was known as Joppa. Boyd served in the Confederate Army, and some time between 1875 and 1885, having established a sawmill at Joppa, he renamed the town after his Tennessee home. Trenton is the county seat of Gilchrist County.

TRILBY • *Pasco County*
Began as McLeod in 1885, changed to Macon six weeks later, then became Trilby in 1901. At the turn of the century, many people were reading George Dumaurier's novel *Trilby*. Not only was the town's name changed to Trilby but streets were given names from among the book's characters. There was a Svengali Square and Little Billee Street.

TROPIC • *Brevard County*
The perfect promotional name! Short, combining the imagery of salubrious weather and luxuriant foliage. Tropic was founded in the 1880s. Along with Fairyland, Georgiana, Indianola, and Audubon, it was one of the communities on the Scenic Drive or Tropical Trail of Merritt Island.

TSALA APOPKA, LAKE • *Citrus County*
This series of lakes adjacent to the west bank of the Withlacoochee River has a name which signifies trout eating place, from the Creek *tsala*, "trout or bass," and *apopka*, "place for eating."

TURKEY CREEK • *Brevard County*
The large number of wild turkeys here resulted in the name.

A log cabin at Turkey Creek, 1900s.

TURKEY CREEK • *Hillsborough County*
In the first days of the settlement, so the story goes, an arbor here was used as a place of worship. However, wild turkeys insisted upon roosting at the arbor, forcing the settlers to find another place.

TURKEY LAKE • *Orange County*
Before groves were planted here, there was an oak thicket on the ridges and wild berries in the low flat woods, each an attraction to the turkeys.

TURKEY SCRATCH • *Jefferson County*
In the early days, before inhabitants became self-conscious about the names of their communities, there was a settlement in Jefferson County known as Turkey Scratch. A resident of Turkey Scratch suggested to the people of Lick Skillet that another name would be more suitable for their settlement. Lick Skillet was changed to Lamont and Turkey Scratch to Panola.

TURNBULL • *Brevard County*
The name of this community and of a creek in St. Johns County are reminders of Dr. Andrew Turnbull, a Scottish physician who in 1767 brought 1,500 colonists to the British Florida area that has become New Smyrna. About 1,200 were from the Spanish Island of Minorca in the western Mediterranean. The others were Italians and Greeks. The British government provided a sloop of war, a money bounty of 4,500 pounds, and more than 100,000 acres of land. The colonists accomplished much in the Florida wilderness in the nine years of the settlement's life. Canals were built to drain the land and roads were laid out. Some of the canals and roads still are used. Many of the settlers moved in 1776 to St. Augustine, where descendants still live.

TUSCAWILLA • *Alachua County*
Settlements named Tuscawilla once existed in Alachua, Leon, and Seminole counties, but the names have disappeared from the map except for a lake in Alachua County. Read (1934) suggests the name was derived from either the Choctaw or Chickasaw *taska*, "warrior," and *weli*, "plunderer."

TUTTLE CAUSEWAY, JULIA • *Dade County*
With groves to the north devastated by the twin freezes of 1894 and 1895, orange trees adjacent to old Fort Dallas at Miami still were flourishing. As evidence the cold had not killed the foliage of Miami, a widow sent a few flowers, some say orange blossoms, wrapped in damp cotton, to Henry M. Flagler, together with an offer to share land in what has become downtown Miami. The ingenuity of Julia De Forest Sturtevant Tuttle spurred Flagler to extend his railroad and hotel interests to Miami. Today, Mrs. Tuttle is remembered by a causeway linking Miami and Miami Beach.

TWO EGG • *Jackson County*
A sign on U.S. 90 delights tourists. It points the way to a place called Two Egg. The story goes that Will Williams, a black man with 16 children, didn't have enough money to give each of them an allowance, so as each became old enough to barter at the local store the child was given a chicken. Traveling salesmen who overheard the children exchanging two eggs for candy began calling the community, formerly called Allison, "Two-egg Crossing."

TYNDALL AIR FORCE BASE • *Panama City*
Named on June 13, 1941, for Lt. Frank B. Tyndall, a World War I ace who was killed in line of duty near Mooresville, N.C., on July 28, 1930. Lt. Tyndall was born at Sewalls Point near Fort Pierce, Fla., on September 28, 1894. He entered combat with the AEF Air Corps in 1918 and took part in the St. Mihiel and Meuse-Argonne offensives. He was credited officially with four victories over German pilots and was flight commander of his squadron.

UCETA YARD • *Hillsborough County*
The story goes that Uceta was the name of a Timucuan Indian leader whose village, given the Spanish spelling of Ucita or Ocita, was the first invaded by Hernando De Soto after his landing in Tampa Bay in 1539. Why the name, with slightly different spelling, would have been applied to a railroad junction is beyond surmise. Possibly the name really is an acronym for some quite modern words.

ULETA • *Dade County*
Seems to have been absorbed by Miami's metropolitan sprawl, but once was known as Snake Creek. Residents wanted a change, and took the name from a motion picture of the South Seas filmed here.

UMATILLA • *Lake County*
The name was apparently imported clear across the country from Oregon. The town was established in 1862. The name was suggested by William A. Whitcome, formerly of Cincinnati, who had been in correspondence with some people in Umatilla, Ore., where Umatilla is also the name of a county. It is also the name of a waterfall in Washington State. The name is an Indian word thought to mean "water rippling over sand."

UNCLE JACK • *Nassau County*
Another of the picturesque names which have passed out of existence, at least on the map. Uncle Jack had its post office from September 1887 to July 1889.

UNION COUNTY •
The sixty-first county, established May 20, 1921. Originally, the name of the county was to have been New River, thereby reestablishing a county name which had existed from December 21, 1858, until December 6, 1861, when New River was changed to Bradford to honor a fallen soldier. *See also* Bradford. However, the bill's sponsor in 1921 amended it to replace New River with Union. Union was separated from Bradford, and a reason for the name may be found in the bill sponsor's statement, as quoted in the *Florida Times-Union* for May 6, 1921, that the counties "were united this time in asking for the divorce though the two parts of the (Bradford) county have never before been able to get together on this proposition." This explanation of the use of "Union" seems more logical than the lofty reasons used through the years, one of which was "for the Union of the United States."

UNION • *Walton County*
Settled about the time of Reconstruction, this name may have resulted from the readmission of Florida to the Union.

UNION PARK • *Orange County*
A postal branch of Orlando.

UNIVERSITY PARK • *Palm Beach County*
Recognizes the presence nearby of Florida Atlantic University at Boca Raton.

UPCOHALL • *Lee County*
William P. Pearde, who settled here at the turn of the century, gave the community a name reminiscent of his former home, Upton Hall, in Devonshire, England.

UPSALA • *Seminole County*
See New Upsala.

USEPPA ISLAND • *Lee County*
Gasparilla's island. Joseffa was his favorite wife, so the story goes, and Useppa was the local pronounciation of her name. *See also* Gasparilla Island.

USHER • *Levy County*
A family name in this vicinity.

UTOPIA • *Holmes County*
Utopia in Holmes County lasted only four months on the postal register for 1882. The name means a place of ideal perfection.

UTOPIA • *Okeechobee County*
Will (1964) relates that one of the first settlements on the lake was started by Clifford Clements in 1897, eight miles southeast of Taylor Creek on the north shore. "At first he hunted there," recalls Will, "but others joined him later to trot lines and set pound nets in the lake. Clements called his place Utopia. The settlement grew to be a cluster of palmetto shacks with a two-story store and a school, both presided over by Clements. Of course it had a post office, too, but when catfishing expired, so also did Utopia." Thus, alas, Utopia can no longer be found in Florida.

VALKARIA • *Brevard County*
Ernest Svedalius, a Swede who settled here in 1886, gave the place a name reminiscent of his homeland, the Valkyries of Scandinavian mythology with a Latin ending.

VALLOMBROSA • *Washington County*
Editor E. W. Carswell says Vallombrosa presumably was named for Italy's Vallombrosa because of the scenic view "strikingly similar to that seen from this imposing hill in western Florida." James Bright of North Carolina and his son-in-law, N. H. Mitchell, settled here in territorial Florida. (Mitchell was a distant kinsman of Florida Rep. Sam Mitchell, who lives at Vernon, near the site of Vallombrosa.) Bright had been a member of the Florida Legislative Council and held other public offices. He died in 1840, and Mitchell moved to Hancock County, Miss. Carswell writes that without the leadership of its founders, the Vallombrosa community withered. The "mellifluous Italian place name" soon became only a fading memory and the place now is called New Hope.

VALPARAISO • *Okaloosa County*
Named for the city in Indiana, although that in turn had come from that of the famous Chilean port. The word means "valley of paradise." It was chosen for this community by John Perrine, who came here from Valparaiso, Ind., about 1918.

VALRICO • *Hillsborough County*
When Valrico, meaning "valley of gold," was founded in 1890, the community prided itself on having a name not shared with any other place in the country. Settled before the Civil War, the region previously had been known as Long Pond.

V E N I C E • *Sarasota County*
Named in 1888 by Franklin Higel, who felt that the blue waters of the bays, rivers, and Gulf gave the place a resemblance to the famous Italian city. Long ago, the area was known as Horse and Chaise to boatmen who saw likeness to a carriage in a distinctive clump of trees on the shore.

The Venice Arcade building about 1950.

V E N U S • *Highlands County*
On S.R. 17, just above the southern boundary of Highlands County, is to be found the Roman goddess of love and beauty, Venus. In this embodiment she is a hamlet of turpentine and agricultural workers. Here again we do not know who gave this name of all loveliness to this obscure little settlement, but the wife of Vulcan, the mother of Cupid, the mistress of Adonis brightens the scene here as she does wherever she appears throughout the world. Nearby is Old Venus.

V E R N O N • *Washington County*
Since the county is Washington, and this community was once the county seat, it likely was named for Mount Vernon. However, there are those who say the name was derived from a place in France.

V E R O B E A C H • *Indian River County*
Named for Vero Gifford, the wife of John T. Gifford, a former sheriff of Royalton, Vt. (Smiley, 1972). Gifford moved his family to Florida in 1888, settling on the west side of the Indian River. Gifford received permission in 1891 to establish a post office and selected his wife's name for the place. The Beach was added later. Vero Beach is the county seat of Indian River County.

VETERAN • *Pinellas County*
See Gulfport *or* Disston City.

VICKSBURG • *Bay County*
Named not as a reminder of a great siege for a city on the Mississippi during the Civil War, but from a collaboration by two turpentine distillers, Messrs. Vickers and McKenzie. Mr. Vickers gave part of his name while Mr. McKenzie added the "burg."

VICTOR • *Pinellas County*
Named for the nearby plant of the Victor Chemical Company.

VIKING • *St. Lucie County*
A group of Scandinavians settled here in the 1890s.

VILAS • *Liberty County*
After starting as Vilas in 1918, the town changed its name to Wilma in 1947.

VILLANO BEACH • *St. Johns County*
A popular beach area just north of St. Augustine. The source of the name is not known.

VILLA TASSO • *Walton County*
Villa means "a country residence or estate." In combination with a person's name, it usually means "house of." In this case, it would have been "House of Tasso" but likely used as a guest house. There was a Villa City in Lake County from 1886 until 1901, and a Villa Franca in Charlotte County from 1890 until 1891.

VINELAND • *Orange County*
First Englewood, then Orange City, the name was changed to Vineland in 1918 when three brothers planted a small vineyard as a real estate promotion.

VIOLA, VIOLET, VIRGIN • *Lake, Okaloosa, and Gulf counties*
Viola in Lake County, Violet in Okaloosa County, and Virgin in Gulf County no longer exist. Virgin likely was named for the stand of first-growth timber being cut in this area at the turn of the century.

VIRGINIA GARDENS • *Dade County*
Resurrects the name of an older, lost Virginia Gardens whose residents were scattered when their property was taken for an airport.

VISTA • *Levy County*
Vista, likely meaning a view of the Suwannee River, remained on the postal register from 1900 until 1932.

VISCAYA (Deering Residence) • *Dade County*
Villa Viscaya, the like of which most Americans had not seen this side of Europe, in 1914 had an immense effect on the growth and development of Miami. Stonecutters were imported from Italy, gardeners and other technicians from Scotland and other places in addition to the more than 1,000 Miamians. It was constructed as a winter residence by James Deering, vice

president of International Harvester Company. Deering had no idea of Viscaya when he started but, bored with the accumulated millions of dollars, succumbed to the blandishments of an international decorator, Paul Chalfin, who persuaded Deering he really wanted more than the two-story, simple residence beside Biscayne Bay that he had in mind. Instead, Deering found he had an Italian palazzo, which was eventually acquired by Dade County and opened to the public as a museum.

VITIS • *Pasco County*
No clue to the origin of this name.

VOLCO • *Volusia County*
On a branch line of the Florida East Coast Railway, the name appears to be a contraction of Volusia County.

VOLUSIA COUNTY •
The thirtieth county, established December 29, 1854. Named for a landing called Volusia on the St. Johns River near Lake George. But how the landing got its name no one now can say for sure. There is a tradition that the name is one of Indian origin, but Simpson (1956) does not include Volusia. The other tradition is that a Frenchman or Belgian named Veluche, pronounced Voolooshay, owned a trading post at the landing during the English period. It is claimed that Veluche was anglicized into Volusia. Gold (1927) says whether the story is true or not, "there is no record either in the Spanish, Territorial or County titles of any land being owned at any time in that vicinity or in the county for that matter, under the name 'Veluche' or any name that resembles it. If such a man held title to land under the English regime, there would be no way of ascertaining the fact, as all English titles were denied."

WABASSO • *Indian River County*
Settlers here from Ossabaw, Ga., spelled the name of their hometown backward.

WACAHOOTA • *Alachua County*
From the Creek *wakka*, "cow," and *hute*, "house," and meaning "cow pen."

WACASASSA • *Levy County*
A river and a bay, from the Creek *wakka*, "cow or cattle," and *sase*, "there are," or cow range.

WACHOOTEE • *Marion County*
A variation of Wacahoota.

WACISSA • *Jefferson County*
A river and hamlet, the meaning of whose name is lost. Well remembered, however, is the fact that Achille Murat, nephew of Napoleon Bonaparte and

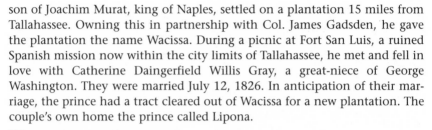

son of Joachim Murat, king of Naples, settled on a plantation 15 miles from Tallahassee. Owning this in partnership with Col. James Gadsden, he gave the plantation the name Wacissa. During a picnic at Fort San Luis, a ruined Spanish mission now within the city limits of Tallahassee, he met and fell in love with Catherine Daingerfield Willis Gray, a great-niece of George Washington. They were married July 12, 1826. In anticipation of their marriage, the prince had a tract cleared out of Wacissa for a new plantation. The couple's own home the prince called Lipona.

WACO • *Madison County*
Read (1934) says this could be the Seminole *wako*, "little blue heron," or a transplant of the Texas place name, which is a shortened form of *tawakoni*, "river bend among red sand hills."

WAGNER • *Seminole County*
On the postal register from 1911 until 1925; named by the Atlantic Coast Line Railway for one of its employees.

WAHNETA • *Polk County*
Probably the phonetic spelling of Juanita. At any rate, Wahneta Farms was developed by the Inland Realty Company, which was spearheaded by William G. Brorein of Tampa. The post office was organized in 1901.

WAKULLA COUNTY •
The twenty-third county, established March 11, 1843. The name also is applied to the famous Wakulla Springs, to a river which unites with the St. Marks River and falls into Apalachee Bay, and to a community. Simpson (1956) says there "is no factual basis for the interpretation of this name as meaning 'mystery.' This is entirely fanciful." However, there remains a mystery as to what Wakulla means. Simpson comments: "Since Wakulla was probably a Timucuan word, it is unlikely that its meaning will ever be known. It may contain the word *kala* which signified a 'spring of water' in some Indian dialects." Read (1934) suggests Wakulla comes from the Creek word *wahkola*, meaning "loon," two species of which winter in Florida.

WALDO • *Alachua County*
Named about 1856 for Dr. Benjamin Waldo, a physician and member of the legislature who was born in South Carolina in 1816 and died in Marion County in 1871.

WALNUT HILL • *Escambia County*
While the post office was established in 1888, there has been a settlement here known as Walnut Hill since 1823. The walnut trees gave the area its name.

WALTON COUNTY •
The eighth county, established December 29, 1824. Named for Col. George Walton, secretary of the Territory of West Florida during the governorship of Andrew Jackson, 1821-1822, and of the combined territory, 1822-1826. He was the son of George Walton, governor of Georgia and signer of the Declaration of Independence. Col. Walton's daughter Octavia suggested the name Tallahassee for the new capital.

WANEE • *Gilchrist County*
A contraction of Suwannee, as the settlement originally was known.

WARD RIDGE • *Gulf County*
Created by the legislature in 1953, and named in honor of Dr. Albert Ward, who died that year.

WARREN BRIDGE, FULLER • *Duval County*
Fuller Warren was a resident of Jacksonville when he was elected governor in 1948. During his term, 1949-1953, the Jacksonville Expressway System came into being, and the naming of this bridge across the St. Johns River was in recognition of Gov. Warren's energies on behalf of the system. Warren was born in Blountstown on October 3, 1905. He was a member of the 1927 House of Representatives from Calhoun County at the age of 21. He served three terms in the Jacksonville City Council, and was elected to the 1939 House of Representatives from Duval County. Gov. Warren's sponsorship resulted in cattle being outlawed from Florida highways, the enactment of a "taste-test" for citrus, preliminary planning for Florida's turnpike, and the start of construction of the Sunshine Skyway over Tampa Bay. The Warren Bridge is 3,667 feet long and has a vertical clearance of 37 feet.

WARRINGTON • *Escambia County*
Named for Commodore Lewis Warrington of the U. S. Navy and established during the 1840s when the Pensacola Navy Yard was first being built. About 1929, the village was moved to make way for expansion of the government facilities, and the new settlement on the banks of Bayou Grande was called New Warrington. Officially, however, New is not part of the name.

WASHINGTON COUNTY •
The twelfth county, established December 9, 1825, and named for George Washington. Chipley is the county seat.

WATERTOWN • *Columbia County*
Thought to have been settled in 1895, and probably named for Watertown, N.Y.

WAUCHULA • *Hardee County*
The name of this seat of Hardee County is spelled Wauchuta on the map published with Norton's *Guidebook* in 1894. Simpson (1956) says this spelling allows two logical interpretations. Wauchula could be derived from the Creek *wakka*, "cow," and *hute*, "house," or it could be a contraction of the Creek *wewa*, "water," and *hute*, "house." Still another guess is *watula*, "sand hill crane."

WAUKEENAH • *Jefferson County*
Col. John G. Gamble in 1827 named a plantation in honor of a Spanish lady from Pensacola who was a guest. Her name was Joachina, the English pronunciation of which approximates Waukeenah. Col. Gamble's land grant was known as Welaunee, near the Marion Cross Roads where, according to McRory and Barrows (1935), the Tallahassee Road crossed a local north-south road. Among the other plantations in the area were William Nuttall's El Destino, Prince Achille Murat's Lipona, Kidder Meade Moore's Pinetucky, and Judge Randall's Belmont.

WAUSAU • *Washington County*
Mary Lloyd Grantham wrote in 1972 that Wausau received its name from
John Glen, a Scot who first settled in Wausau, Wis., and then, traveling
south, found such a resemblance in this area that he transplanted both him-
self and the name of his first American home. The original name is from a
Wisconsin Indian word meaning "far or distant."

WAVELAND • *Martin and St. Lucie counties*
The state's sectional map shows Wavelands a few miles apart on the coast in
Martin and St. Lucie counties. Only one shows up in the postal register, in
Martin County, for eleven years ending in 1891.

WAVERLY • *Polk County*
W. D. Campbell and his family from Waverly, N.Y., were the first settlers here
in 1882. For a while the place was called Buffalo Ford, but the name was
changed to Waverly. After the big freeze of 1894-1895, the settlement fell on
hard times, and its name reverted to Buffalo Ford, but when the railroad
came through, Waverly was revived.

WAYLAND • *Lake County*
Settled in 1886. The name combines Waycross, Ga., and Lakeland, Fla., for a
railroad which then served those points.

WEBSTER • *Sumter County*
Settlers of this community in the 1850s first chose Orange Home for a name.
The postmaster, G. F. Hays, learned there was another Orange Home, so he
chose Webster in honor of Daniel Webster.

WEEDON ISLAND • *Pinellas County*
If you drive north on Fourth Street in St. Petersburg, take a right at 83rd
Avenue and keep bearing right, reports *The St. Petersburg Times*, all of a sudden you are on a peninsula called Weedon Island. In 1975, this area was St.
Petersburg's last big chunk of undeveloped waterfront. The land got its name
in 1898 when Dr. Leslie W. Weedon settled in Tampa, took a fancy to the
peninsula, planted an orange grove and established his vacation retreat there.
The island, or peninsula, was bought in 1975 from the Ed Wright estate for a
fine state park at St. Petersburg's front door.

WEEKI WACHEE SPRINGS • *Hernando County*
From the Creek words *wekiwa*, meaning "spring," and *chee*, meaning "little."

WEEOKAYKAYKA, LAKE • *Volusia County*
An obsolete Indian name for what now is known as Lake George, a lake
formed by expansion of the St. Johns River. The Indian name is a combination of the Creek *wewa*, "water," and *haiyayaka*, "clear."

WEKIVA •
A tributary of the St. Johns forming the boundary between Seminole and
Lake counties. It also is the name of a lake and of a settlement in Orange
County, and of a spring and stream near the village of Gulf Hammock in Levy
County. It also is the obsolete name for Rainbow Springs, which discharges

The Waverly Growers Coop citrus gift shop in the 1950s.

into the Withlacoochee River near Dunnellon. The name is derived from the Creek *wekiwa*, "spring of water."

WELAKA • *Putnam County*
From a combination of Indian words meaning "tide or intermittent springs." The town is on the St. Johns River, which the Seminoles called *Ylacco* or *Welaka*. Another interpretation given the word is "river of lakes," which is most applicable to the St. Johns.

WELAUNEE CREEK • *Jefferson County*
Also the name given to Col. G. Gamble's land grant in this vicinity in the 1820s. The name is from the Creek *we*, "water," and *lane*, "yellow," or yellow water.

WELCHTOWN • *Jackson County*
Named for Columbus Welch, prominent citizen, at the turn of the century.

WELCOME • *Hillsborough County*
First gained postal status in 1907, lost it in 1911, regained it in 1914, and gave up this symbol of community status in 1916. Welcome later was shown on the map as Welcome Junction, a meeting place for two branches of the Seaboard Coast Line in the phosphate country.

WELLBORN • *Suwannee County*
L. W. Wellborn laid out this town site in the 1860s.

WEST •
Some 15 places have West prefixed to another name: for example, West Miami.

WEST FARM • *Madison County*
The West brothers settled here in the 1880s.

WEST GATE • *Palm Beach County*
Founded at the western entrance to West Palm Beach, and so simply called West Gate.

WEST LAKE • *Hamilton County*
Remembers E. J. West, who settled here in 1870.

WEST PALM BEACH • *Palm Beach County*
After Henry M. Flagler decided he would extend his railroad and hotel chain to Palm Beach, he purchased several hundred acres across Lake Worth in April 1893. He laid out the town site of West Palm Beach to provide housing first of all for his workers and thereafter for commercial development. Sidney Walter Martin (1949) tells how "the workmen rowed across Lake Worth each morning to their jobs at the Royal Poinciana and then back across the lake in the afternoon." The streets of West Palm Beach were given the names of trees, fruits, and flowers common to the area: Clematis, Datura, Narcissus, Sapodilla, and Tamarind. By 1909, Palm Beach County was carved out of Dade County and the newly created county seat of West Palm Beach had outgrown its sister-city, as Martin points out, both in size and commercial importance.

WESTON • *Broward County*
Roger Hall and Walter Collins, two executives of the developer, the Arvida Corporation, selected the name in 1980 from some 100 names. "We wanted something that didn't sound like a subdivision," remembers Collins. "We didn't want a cutesy, gimmicky kind of name but a whole community name."

WESTVILLE • *Holmes County*
Once the seat of Holmes County, having wrested this honor from Cerro Gordo about 1900. There was another squabble over the seat in 1905 and Bonifay won. The story goes that people in Westville hid the county records in a swamp, but these were recovered. The resistance in Westville to giving up the county seat was said to have caused men from Bonifay to drive mules and wagons to Westville at night, take the courthouse apart, and haul the pieces to Bonifay.

WESTWOOD LAKE • *Dade County*
The Mackle Corporation chose this name to emphasize the presence of man-made lakes in the development. The "west" indicated its location in the county, and the wood was added purely for euphonious reasons.

WETAPPO CREEK • *Gulf County*
Creek *we,* "water," and *tapha,* "broad," or broad water.

WETUMPKA • *Gadsden County*
Creek *wetamke* or *wetumke,* "noisy water." Simpson (1956) suggests this must be an import, since the name does not seem appropriate in its Gadsden County setting.

Palm Beach Bottling Works in West Palm Beach, 1927.

Whitehall, Henry M. Flagler's Palm Beach home.

W EWAHITCHKA • *Gulf County*
Established in 1875 by Dr. William C. Mitchell and others, who gave it this complex Indian name believing that it meant "water eyes," because a perfect pair of eyes is formed by two oblong lakes along the town's edge. They are separated by a pronounced ridge a few feet wide which corresponds to the bridge of the nose. An aviator can easily distinguish this formation from aloft. Other interpretations of the name point to "water view" or "place where water is obtained."

W EWAHOTEE • *Orange County*
A station on the branch line of the Florida East Coast Railway which used so many modern Seminole names. But this name was taken from the Creek *wewa*, "water," and *hute*, "house," or water tank.

W HIDDON CORNER • *Hendry County*
Settled around 1875 and named for the Whiddon family.

W HITE CITY • *Gulf County*
Had the status of a post office from 1956 to 1959.

W HITE CITY • *St. Lucie County*
Settled shortly after 1893 by Danish immigrants from Chicago who became interested in citrus culture after reading a series of articles on growing oranges, written by a Danish newsman covering the Chicago World's Fair. They named the main street Midway for the thoroughfare of that name at the fair, and called the settlement White City after a Chicago amusement park.

W HITEHALL (Flagler Residence) • *Palm Beach County*
This museum is the magnificent mansion Mr. Flagler built for his wife, Mary Lily Kenan, in 1901. Sold by the heirs in 1925, the building, with a tower addition, served as a luxury hotel until 1959. The museum, with Mr. Flagler's granddaughter, Mrs. Flagler Matthews, as president, acquired the building and opened the restoration to the public in February 1960.

Today's visitors see this American palace much as it was when the Flaglers lived there, with many of the original furnishings. The rooms have been carefully restored to reflect the opulence of a bygone era.

In addition to the period rooms, there are special collections of porcelains, paintings, silver, glass, dolls, lace, costumes, and family memorabilia. Other exhibits illustrate the local history of the area and the vast enterprises of the Flagler system, particularly the building of the Florida East Coast Railway.

Henry Morrison Flagler, 1830-1913, was founder of the Standard Oil Company with John D. Rockefeller. He became interested in Florida in the 1880s and by the time of his death had singlehandedly developed the entire east coast of the state, built a railroad from Jacksonville to Key West and established St. Augustine, Daytona Beach, Palm Beach, and Miami as famous resorts.

W HITEHOUSE • *Duval County*
First known as Ten Mile Station for its location on the railroad between Baldwin and Jacksonville. It was near here that Confederate troops found a

railway carload of hard bread abandoned by federal soldiers fleeing the bloody battleground of Olustee in February 1864. That discovery has caused the place to be known since as Cracker Swamp.

WHITE SPRINGS • *Hamilton County*
Known as Rebels' Refuge during the Civil War, because many plantation owners moved here with their families and slaves, living in safety throughout the war, out of the path of Union invasion. The modern town was founded about 1900 by Dr. R. J. Camp. The name was selected because of the clear, white spring whose water was said to contain more than 50 minerals of medicinal value.

WHITEWATER BAY • *Monroe County*
This name, not quite as picturesque as the Seminole-Creek *Wehadkathecco*, means the same.

WHITNEY • *Lake County*
John M. Robertson homesteaded here in 1856, but the settlement was given its name by State Treasurer John C. Luning to honor a railroad official. Luning owned an orange grove here.

WHITTIER • *Osceola County*
A family name for a settlement believed to be the oldest in the county, perhaps earlier than 1875. Local legend says this is one of the Florida counties whose vote helped elect Rutherford B. Hays in the contested presidential contest of 1876. In the precinct here, a cowboy hat served as a ballot box.

WILBUR-BY-THE-SEA • *Volusia County*
Founded by J. W. Wilbur in 1915. It lies between the Atlantic Ocean and the Halifax River.

WILDCAT • *Madison County*
An offshoot of the Harmony Community.

WILDERNESS • *Clay County*
When this area was settled in 1875, it likely was a wilderness, although its first name was Thomasville. It no longer shows on the sectional map.

WILDWOOD • *Sumter County*
Named long before there was any town. A telegraph construction engineer ran out of wire at this point, so he notified his headquarters, heading his dispatch Wildwood. The town was established in 1877.

WILLACOOCHEE • *Gadsden and St. Johns counties*
A creek in Gadsden County and a landing on the east coast waterway in St. Johns County. From Creek *we*, "water," *lako*, "big," and *uchi*, "little," or little big water.

WILLIAMSBURG • *Jefferson County*
The first name of Aucilla. Settlers came as early as 1832. Scruggs (1966) says Williamsburg was so called because so many male settlers bore that name, including William Norcu, who ran the saloon and general store; Dr. William

Emery, the physician and pharmacist; and William Kersey, the blacksmith. The post office spelled the name Williamsburgh. When the railroad was built, its stop for this area was known as Station Number Four, because it was the fourth station east of Tallahassee.

WILLISTON • *Levy County*
Established prior to 1885 by J. M. Willis, who named it after himself.

WILSON • *Brevard County*
Between the Atlantic Ocean and Indian River, Wilson recalls James Wilson, who homesteaded here around 1912.

WILTON MANORS • *Broward County*
Developed during the 1920s by E. J. Willingham. Presumably he devised a name which in part perpetuated his own.

WIMAUMA • *Hillsborough County*
Formed from the first letters of the names of Wilma, Maud, and Mary, daughters of the first postmaster here, Capt. Davis.

WIMICO • *Gulf and Franklin counties*
A lake in Gulf County and of a tributary stream in Gulf and Franklin counties. Creek *we*, "water," and *micco*, "chief," signifying chief lake.

WINDER LAKE • *Brevard County*
Said to have been named for an officer in the Seminole Wars.

WINDERMERE • *Orange County*
Platted in 1887 by engineers of the Florida Midland Railroad. Named by John Dawe in remembrance of the lake country of England, where he had grown up.

WINDLEY KEY • *Monroe County*
This island, once one of a group known as the Umbrella Keys, took its name from a settler. Here in 1935 was situated one of the camps of World War I veterans devastated by the wind and water of the Labor Day hurricane.

WINDLEY • *Polk County*
Named for the Winn family, which settled here.

WINSTON • *Polk County*
Named for the Winn family, which settled here.

WINTER BEACH • *Indian River County*
First known as Woodley, then Quay, the community adopted its present name in 1925 during the land boom, when many communities took names which advertised their assets for the northern homeseeker.

WINTER GARDEN • *Orange County*
Established by Henry Harrel of Alachua in 1857, and formerly called Beulah. In 1908 the name Winter Garden was chosen because of the perennial blossoms and greenery and the mild temperature in winter.

WINTER HAVEN • *Polk County*
Platted in 1884-1885 and named by P. D. Eyclesheimer because it was con-

The Winter Haven post office, 1924.

sidered a haven from the severities of winter. Also known as the City of a Hundred Lakes.

WINTER PARK • *Orange County*
First settled by David Mizell of Alachua County in 1836. There is said to have been a town here called Lakeview, founded in 1858 and rechristened Osceola in 1870. In 1882, Loring A. Chase and Oliver E. Chapman laid out a new 600-acre town site very much along the lines of New England towns where they had come from, and gave the town its present name because it is a veritable park in winter.

WINTER SPRINGS • *Seminole County*
An old community where one day a spring appeared.

WISCON • *Hernando County*
Founded by C. C. Peck in 1882, the place is said to have taken its name from Wisconsin, home state of many of the early settlers.

WITHLA • *Polk County*
An abbreviation of Withlacoochee. *See also* Withlacoochee.

WITHLACOOCHEE •
Two rivers with the same name. One is a tributary of the Suwannee flowing through southern Georgia, then 23 miles in Florida to unite with the Suwannee near Ellaville in Madison County. The other flows in south-central Florida to empty into Withlacoochee Bay and the Gulf of Mexico at Port Inglis. Its length is variously reported from 86 miles to 157 miles. The name is taken from the Creek *we*, "water," *thlako*, "big," and *chee*, "little," or little big water.

WOODLAWN BEACH • *Santa Rosa County*
A pleasant combination of woods and green grass to create a desirable image.

WOODMERE • *Sarasota County*
Woods by the sea. First known as Manasota, a combination of Manatee and Sarasota.

WOODS • *Liberty County*
Named not for the trees here but for a family. Settled in 1897.

WOODS JUNCTION • *Pasco County*
Several railroad lines meet here.

WOODVILLE • *Leon County*
Down the St. Marks highway from Tallahassee, Woodville has had a post office since 1888 and settlers for perhaps a half century earlier. Probably so called because it was a wood stop for steam railroad engines.

WORTHINGTON SPRINGS • *Union County*
Established in 1825 and named for William G. D. Worthington of Maryland, secretary and acting governor of the Territory of East Florida.

YALAHA • *Lake County*
The permanent settlers—there had been some living here as early as 1847—decided in 1869 or 1870 that a name was needed, so they selected Yalaha, which they understood to be Indian for yellow orange.

YAMATO • *Palm Beach County*
Fifty Japanese colonists settled here around 1907, changing the name from Wyman to Yamato, a reminder of their homeland.

YANKEETOWN • *Levy County*
Founded early in 1923 by Judge A. F. Knotts of Gary, Ind., and a nephew, Eugene Knotts, who set up a small fishing camp and a few houses and hoped to start a community. They advertised the community under the name of Knotts. In derision of the Northerners, however, the Southerners who lived in this vicinity—especially Hugh Coleman, rural mail carrier—called the place Yankeetown. When the town was incorporated by an act of the 1925 legislature, Yankeetown was adopted. The word Yankee, according to the *Random House Dictionary*, originated in the Dutch *Jan Kees* (John Cheese), a nickname the Dutch of colonial New York called the English settlers in Connecticut. A subdivision adjacent to Yankeetown has been named Crackertown.

YBOR CITY • *Hillsborough County*
The cigar-making industry moved to Ybor City, on the outskirts of Tampa, with Vicente Martinez-Ybor and Ignacio Haya the first cigar factory owners to move there. The migration from Cuba to Key West and Tampa had

The railroad depot for the Japanese community of Yamato, about 1910.

occurred after the outbreak of the Ten Years War for Cuba's independence from Spain in 1868. Labor unrest in Havana and a fire in Key West accelerated the move to Tampa, whose Board of Trade supplied the $4,000 difference between what Martinez-Ybor would pay and what the owner of the land, John T. Lesley, wanted for the tract. Martinez-Ybor gave his name to 40 acres on the outskirts of Tampa which he acquired to house workers for his cigar factory. Dr. L. Glenn Westfall, professor of history at Hillsborough Community College, reports that 176 two- and three-room houses had been built by the end of 1886 at a cost of $750 to $900. A steam-engine street car began running between Ybor City and downtown Tampa. Tampa shortly enveloped Ybor City, which Leland Hawes of the *Tampa Tribune* reports never attained legal status.

YEEHAW • *Indian River County*
Another of the stations on the Florida East Coast's abandoned Okeechobee branch. This one also had a modern Indian name, a corruption of Creek *yaha*, "wolf."

YELLOW BLUFFS • *Pinellas County*
Grew to be a settlement on the Gulf in 1875. In 1878, the name was changed to Bay St. Joseph and in 1889 to Ozona, which stuck.

YELLOW BLUFFS • *Sarasota County*
On U.S. 41 at Eleventh Street in Sarasota; so called because of its outcroppings of yellow limestone. This was the home of Sarasota's first inhabitants, prehistoric and Calusa Indians. Yellow Bluffs later became the home of William

H. Whitaker, Sarasota's first known white settler. It was also the embarkation point for Judah P. Benjamin, member of the Confederate Cabinet, who fled the United States for England while pursued at the end of the Civil War.

YELVINGTON • *St. Johns County*
Named for a family of early settlers. The post office was across the line in Putnam County.

YOUMANS • *Hillsborough County*
Near Plant City and said to have been named in 1899 by the Atlantic Coast Line for a railroad employee.

YOUNGSTOWN • *Bay County*
Named for T. B. Young, who came here from Georgia as a pioneer naval stores operator in the early 1900s. Formerly known as Lawrence.

YUKON • *Duval County*
Imported from northwest Canada, the name in the Athapascan dialect means "the river." Yukon was established by the Atlantic Coast Line, likely for the convenience of the nearby A. M. Read plantation. Its post office was opened in 1893.

YULEE • *Nassau County*
Once known as Hart's Road, but named Yulee in 1893 in honor of David Levy Yulee. *See also* Levy County.

Z

ELLWOOD • *Orange County*
Named for Col. T. Elwood Zell of Philadelphia, publisher of *Zell's Cyclopedia*, who spent the winters of 1875 and 1876 here with his brother-in-law and business associate, John A. Williamson, and then built his own home. He called his home Zellwood and the community adopted the name in his honor.

ZEPHYRHILLS • *Pasco County*
Originally called Abbott's Station but renamed in 1915. Its name calls attention to the cooling breezes that blow over the hills in this section.

ZION • *Palm Beach County*
Zion's post office was kept in a House of Refuge, one of several built by the Treasury Department along the coast between Cape Canaveral and Cape Florida for the rescue and sustenance of the shipwrecked. The postal register shows Zion in existence from 1888 to 1892. The *Random House Dictionary* says one meaning of Zion is "heaven as the final gathering place of true believers."

ZOLFO SPRINGS • *Hardee County*
Named for the large number of sulphur springs in this area. Zolfo is the Italian word for sulphur; the name was applied by Italian laborers in the vicinity.

Zolfo Springs' main street, November 1925.

ZONA • *Broward County*
The first name of the present Davie, because many of its original settlers had just come to the Everglades from the Panama Canal Zone.

ZUBER • *Marion County*
Named for a family of longtime residents.

BIBLIOGRAPHY

Among the books, manuscripts and other sources used by the compiler were these:

Barbour, George M. *Florida For Tourists, Invalids and Settlers.* New York: Appleton, 1883.

Barbour, Ralph Henry. *Let's Go To Florida.* New York: Dodd, Mead & Company, 1926.

Bellamy, Jeanne. "The Everglades: Unlike Anything Else," *The Florida Handbook 1973-1974.* Tallahassee, Fla.: Peninsular Publishing Company, 1973.

Bickel, Karl A. *The Mangrove Coast.* New York: Coward-McCann, Inc., 1942

Bishop, E. W. *Florida Lakes.* Tallahassee, Fla.: Florida Division of Water Resources, 1967.

Blackman, Ethan V. *Miami and Dade County, Florida.* Washington, D.C.: Victor Rainbolt, 1921.

Blackman, William Fremont. *History of Orange County, Florida.* DeLand, Fla.: E. O. Painter Printing Company, 1927.

Boyd, Mark F. "Historic Sites in and Around the Jim Woodruff Reservoir Area, Florida-Georgia." *Bureau of American Ethnology Bulletin 169.* Washington, D.C.: U.S. Government Printing Office, 1958.

_____."Early Highways of Florida," *Florida Highways.* Tallahassee, Fla.: Florida State Road Department, June 1951.

Bradbury, Alford G., and Hallock, E. Story. *A Chronology of Florida Post Offices,* Handbook No. 2. Vero Beach, Fla.: The Florida Federation of Stamp Clubs, 1962.

_____. *A Chronology of Florida Post Offices,* Handbook No. 2., Addenda No. 1. Vero Beach, Fla.: The Florida Federation of Stamp Clubs, 1966.

Brinton, Daniel Garrison. *Notes on the Floridian Peninsula: Its Literary History, Indian Tribes and Antiquities.* Philadelphia: Joseph Sabin, 1859.

Brookfield, Charles M., and Griswold, Oliver. *They All Called It Tropical.* Miami: The Data Press, 1949.

Brooks, T. J. *Foreword, Seventh Census of Florida.* Tallahassee, Fla.: State Department of Agriculture, 1945.

Browne, Jefferson B. *Key West, The Old and the New.* St. Augustine, Fla.: The Record Company, 1912.

Bryant, Elam J. *Early History of Lithia.* Lithia, Fla.: Bryant, 1981.

Buchholz, F. W. *History of Alachua County.* St. Augustine, Fla.: The Record Company, 1929.

Cantrell, Elizabeth A. (Aultman). *When Kissimmee Was Young*. Kissimmee, Fla.: Philathea Class, First Christian Church, 1948.

Cash, W. T. "Newport as a Business Center," *Apalachee*. Tallahasssee, Fla.: Tallahassee Historical Society, 1944.

Cohen, Isidor. *Historical Sketches and Sidelights of Miami, Florida*. Miami: Privately printed, 1925.

Compiled General Laws Of Florida. Atlanta: The Harrison Company, 1929.

Cooke, C. Wythe. "Scenery of Florida Interpreted by a Geologist." *Geological Bulletin No. 17*. Tallahassee, Fla.: State of Florida Department of Conservation, 1939.

Covington, James W. *The Story of Southwestern Florida*. New York: Lewis Historical Publishing Company, Inc., 1957.

Dau, Frederick W. *Florida Old and New*. New York: G. P. Putnam's Sons, 1934.

Davis, Mary Lamar. "Tallahassee Through Territorial Days," *Apalachee*. Tallahassee, Fla.: Tallahassee Historical Society, 1944.

Dickison, Mary Elizabeth. *Dickison and His Men*. Louisville, Ky.: Courier-Journal Job Printing Company, 1890.

Dictionary of American Biography. Edited by Allen Johnson. New York: Scribners, 1964.

Dodd, Dorothy. "Florida in the War, 1861-1865," *The Florida Handbook 1959-1960*. Tallahassee, Fla.: Peninsular Publishing, 1959.

Douglas, Marjory Stoneman. *The Everglades: River of Grass*. Revised Ed. Sarasota, Fla.: Pineapple Press, 1988.

_____. *Florida the Long Frontier*. New York: Harper & Row, 1967.

Dovell, J. E. *Florida: Historic, Dramatic, Contemporary*. New York: Lewis Historical Publishing, 1952.

Dunn, Hampton. *Re-Discover Florida*. Miami: Hurricane House, 1969.

Eidge, Frank, "Mr. Perky's Bat Tower Stands as Lone Monument," *Tallahassee Democrat*, February 8, 1973.

Fairbanks, George Rainsford. *Florida: Its History and Romance*. Jacksonville, Fla.: Drew Company, 1904.

Federal Writers Project, WPA. *Florida: A Guide to the Southernmost State*. New York: Oxford University Press, 1939.

_____. *Florida Place Names*. Unpublished manuscript.

_____. *A Guide to Key West*. New York: Hastings House, 1949.

Fleming, Francis Phillip, editor, and Rerick, Roland H. *Memoirs of Florida*. Atlanta: The Southern Historical Association, 1902.

Florida Lakes, Part III Gazetteer. Tallahassee, Fla.: Florida Board of Conservation, Division of Water Resources, 1969.

Florida State Advertising Commission, unpublished replies to 1950 questionnaire on place name origin sent to Chambers of Commerce and postmasters.

Fontaneda, Hernando de Escalante. *Memoirs*. Washington, D.C.: 1854 (original Spanish text); Coral Gables, Fla.: Glade House, 1944 (English language translation).

Forbes, James Grant. *Sketches Historical and Topographical of the Floridas; More Particularly of East Florida.* Gainesville, Fla.: University of Florida Press, 1964 (facsimile reprint of 1821 edition).

Forshay, David A. *Lure of the Sun: A Story of Beach County.* Lake Worth, Fla.: First Federal Savings & Loan Association of Lake Worth, 1967.

Franklin County . . . Its Resources, Advantages, Possibilities. Apalachicola, Fla.: Promotional literature, 1901.

Fritz, Florence. *Unknown Florida.* Coral Gables, Fla.: University of Miami Press, 1963.

Fuller, Walter P. *This Was Florida's Boom.* St. Petersburg, Fla.: Times Publishing Company, 1954.

Gannett, Henry. *American Names.* Washington, D.C.: Public Affairs Press, 1947.

Gazetteer of Florida Streams. Tallahassee, Fla.: Florida Board of Conservation, Division of Water Resources,1966.

Gold, Pleasant Daniel. *History of Duval County, Florida.* St. Augustine, Fla.: The Record Company, 1928.

_____. *History of Volusia County, Florida.* DeLand, Fla.: The E. O. Painter Printing Company, 1927.

Gore, Eldon H. *History of Orlando.* Orlando, Fla.: Eldon H. Gore, 1949 and 1951.

Grismer, Karl H. *The Story of Sarasota.* Sarasota, Fla.: M. E. Russell, 1946.

_____. *The Story of St. Petersburg.* St. Petersburg, Fla.: P. K. Smith, 1948.

Guide to Florida's Historic Markers. Tallahassee, Fla.: Florida Department of State, Division of Archives, History and Records Management, 1972.

Hanna, Alfred J. *A Prince in Their Midst.* Norman, Okla.: University of Oklahoma Press, 1946.

Hanna, Alfred J., and Hanna, Kathryn Abbey. *Florida's Golden Sands.* Indianapolis, Ind.: Bobbs-Merrill Company, 1950.

_____. *Lake Okeechobee: Wellspring of the Everglades.* Indianapolis, Ind.: Bobbs-Merrill Company, 1948.

Hanna, Kathryn Abbey. "The Story of the Lafayette Lands in Florida," *Florida Historical Quarterly.* January, 1932.

Heatherington, M. F. *History of Polk County, Florida.* St. Augustine, Fla.: The Record Company, 1928.

Heitman, Francis Bernard. *Historical Register and Dictionary of the United States Army from its Organization, September 29, 1789, to March 2, 1903.* Vol. 2. Washington, D.C.: Government Printing Office, 1903.

Hollingsworth, Tracy. *History of Dade County.* Miami, Fla.: Miami Post, 1936.

Horgan, James J.; Hall, Alice F.; and Herrmann, Edward J. *The Historic Places of Pasco County.* Dade City, Fla.: Pasco County Historical Preservation Committee, 1992.

Johnson, Malcolm. "Old Street Names are Index to History of Tallahassee,"

Tallahassee Democrat. August 24, 1973.

Jones, Eloise Knight. *Ocala Cavalcade.* Ocala, Fla.: S. F. McCready, 1946.

Kennedy, William T. *History of Lake County, Florida.* St. Augustine, Fla.: The Record Company, 1929.

King, M. Luther. *History of Santa Rosa County: A King's Country.* Milton, Fla.: Mrs. M. L. King, 1972.

Kjerulff, Georgiana Greene. *Tales of Old Brevard.* Melbourne, Fla.: Florida Institute of Technology Press, 1972.

Lowery, Woodbury. *Spanish Settlements Within the Present Limits of the United States.* New York: Putnam, 1905.

Madison County Jaycees Official Program. Madison, 1963.

Martin, Sidney Walter. *Florida's Flagler.* Athens, Ga.: The University of Georgia Press, 1949.

Mayo, Nathan. *Sixth Census of the State of Florida.* Winter Park, Fla.: The Orange Press, 1936.

McDuffee, Lillie B. *The Lures of Manatee.* Atlanta: Foote and Davies, Inc., 1961.

McNeely, Ed, and McFadyen, Al R. *Century in the Sun.* Orlando, Fla.: Robinsons, 1961.

McRory, Mary Oakley, and Barrows, Edith Clarke. *History of Jefferson County, Florida.* Monticello, Fla.: Kiwanis Club, 1935.

Moore-Willson, Minnie. *History of Osceola County: Florida Frontier Life.* Orlando, Fla.: The Inland Press, 1935.

Moore-Willson, Minnie. *Seminoles of Florida,* 8th edition. Kissimmee, Fla.: Kingsport (Tenn.) Press, 1928.

Morris, Allen. *The Florida Handbook.* Tallahassee, Fla.: Peninsular Publishing Company [biennially, 1947-1995].

Motte, Jacob R. *Journey Into Wilderness.* Gainesville, Fla.: University of Florida Press, 1953.

Muir, Helen. *Miami, U.S.A.* New York: Henry Holt and Company, 1953.

Norton, Charles Ledyard. *A Handbook of Florida.* New York: Longmans, Green & Company, 1891.

Peeples, Vernon E. *"Trabue, Alias Punta Gorda,"* Florida Historical Quarterly. Vol. 46, 1967.

Perkerson, Medora Field. *White Columns of Georgia.* New York: Rinehart, 1952.

Pickett, Mrs. Harold Major; Rice, Kenneth L.; and Seplman, Henry M., III. *Florida Postal History and Postal Markings During the Stampless Period.* Handbook No. 1. Palm Beach, Fla.: Palm Beach Stamp Club, 1957.

Plowden, Jean. *History of Hardee County.* Wauchula, Fla.: The Florida Advocate, 1929.

Random House Dictionary of the English Language. New York: Random House, Inc., 1967.

Read, William A. *Florida Place Names of Indian Origin and Seminole Personal Names.* Baton Rouge, La.: Louisiana State University Press, 1934.

_____. *Indian Place Names in Alabama.* Baton Rouge, La.: Louisana State University Press, 1937.

Redford, Polly. *Billion-Dollar Sandbar: A Biography of Miami Beach.* New York: E. P. Dutton and Company, Inc., 1970.

Rerick, Rowland H. *Memoirs of Florida.* Atlanta: The Southern Historical Association, 1902.

Rhodes, Harrison Garfield, and Dumont, Mary Wolfe. *A Guide to Florida for Tourists, Sportsmen and Settlers.* New York: Dodd, Mead & Company, 1912.

Robinson, Ernest L. *History of Hillsborough County, Florida.* St. Augustine, Fla.: The Record Company, 1928.

Rogers, William W. *Outposts of The Gulf, Saint George Island and Apalachicola from Early Exploration to World War II.* Pensacola, Fla.: University of West Florida Press, 1986.

Scruggs, Mrs. Oliver. *History of Aucilla.* Unpublished manuscript, 1966.

Sectional Map of Florida, Florida Department of Agriculture. DePew, N.Y.: J. W. Clement Company, 1963.

Shofner, Jerrell H. *Nor is it over yet.* Gainesville, Fla.: University Presses of Florida, 1974.

Simpson, J. Clarence. *Florida Place-Names of Indian Derivation.* Edited by Mark F. Boyd. Florida State Board of Conservation Special Publication No. 1. Tallahassee, Fla.: 1956.

_____. "Middle Florida Place Names," *Apalachee.* Tallahassee, Fla.: Tallahassee Historical Society, 1946.

Smiley, Nixon. "Cape Area Retains Bit of Scenic Old Florida," *The Miami Herald,* June 24, 1973.

_____. *Florida, Land of Images.* Miami: E. A. Seemann, 1972.

_____."Only Sam Could Find Sam Jones Old Town," *The Miami Herald,* August 13, 1967.

_____."You'll find Interest, Bumps on Glades Road To Tasmania," *The Miami Herald,* May 7, 1973.

_____. "Yulee Had Harem in His Heritage," *The Miami Herald,* December 11, 1968.

Smith, Elizabeth F. *Wakulla County Pioneers 1827-1967.* Crawfordville, Fla.: The Magnolia Monthly Press, 1968.

Snodgrass, Dena. "The St. Johns: River of Five Names," *The Florida Handbook 1967-1968.* Tallahassee, Fla.: Peninsular Publishing Company, 1967.

Stanley, J. Randall. *History of Gadsden County.* Quincy, Fla.: Gadsden County Times, 1948.

Stevenson, George B. *Keyguide to Key West and the Florida Keys.* Tavernier, Fla.: 1970.

Stewart, George R. *American Place-Names.* New York: Oxford University Press, 1970.

_____. *Names of the Land.* Boston: Houghton Mifflin, 1958.

Straub, William L. *History of Pinellas County, Florida.* St. Augustine, Fla.: The Record Company, 1929.

Swanton, John R. *Early History of the Creek Indians and Their Neighbors.* Washington, D.C.: U.S. Government Printing Office, 1922.

_____. *Final Report of the United States De Soto Expedition Commission.* Washington, D.C.: U.S. Government Printing Office, 1939.

Tebeau, Charlton W. *Florida's Last Frontier/The History of Collier County.* Coral Gables, Fla.: University of Miami Press, 1966.

_____. *A History of Florida.* Coral Gables, Fla.: University of Miami Press, 1971.

_____. *They Lived in the Park.* Coral Gables, Fla.: University of Miami Press, 1963.

Utley, George W. "Origin of the County Names of Florida," *Florida Historical Quarterly.* Vol. 1, No. 3. October 1908.

Webb, Wanton S. *Webb's Historical, Industrial, and Biographical Florida.* New York: Webb & Company, 1885.

Whitfield, J.B. *Florida Statutes, 1941.* Vol. III. Tallahassee, Fla.: State of Florida, 1946.

Will, Lawrence E. *Cracker History of Okeechobee.* St. Petersburg, Fla.: Great Outdoors Publishing Company, 1964.

_____. *A Dredgeman of Cape Sable.* St. Petersburg, Fla.: Great Outdoors Publishing Company, 1967.

_____. *Okeechobee Boats & Skippers.* St. Petersburg, Fla.: Great Outdoors Publishing Company, 1965.

INDEX

NOTE: *Illustrations are indicated by italics. The main entry for each county is indicated by boldface.*

Woodlawn Beach, 258
Woodley (*see* Winter Beach)
Woodmere, 258
Woodrow (*see* Bayshore)
Woods, 258
Woods Junction, 258
Woodville, 171, 258
Worthington Springs, 258
Wyman (*see* Yamato)

Y

Yalaha, 258
Yamato, 258, *259*
Yankeetown, 59, 258
Ybor City, 258-259
Yeehaw, 259
Yellow Bluff (*see* Ozona)
Yellow Bluffs, 259-260
Yelvington, 260
Youmans, 260
Youngstown, 260
Yukon, 260
Yulee, 148, 260

Z

Zellwood, 260
Zephyrhills, 260
Zion, 260
Zolfo Springs, xiv, 260
Zona, 261 (*see also* Davie)
Zuber, 261

ACKNOWLEDGMENTS

I am indebted to many people for their help. First, as always, is Dr. Dorothy Dodd, the late state librarian. Next, Patty Paul, Mary Ann Cleveland, and Cynthia Wise of the Florida State Library.

Miss Dena Snodgrass shared her vast store of Florida facts.

Others I would like to thank, in alphabetical order, are: Judge Charles C. Anderson of Monticello; Mrs. Carol Jo Beaty of Tallahassee; Miss Jeanne Bellamy (Mrs. John T. Bills) of Miami; Mrs. Ada Bilbrey of Duette; Rep. R. Ed. Blackburn, Jr., Tallahassee; Mrs. James D. Bruton, Jr., of Plant City; Daniel B. Cameron, Jr., of Palm Bay; Mr. and Mrs. Harold Chapman of Tallahassee; C. L. Clark of Tallahassee; James A. Clendinen, *The Tampa Tribune*; Hampton Dunn of Tampa; Rep. Vince Fechtel of Leesburg; Dr. C. A. Gauld, Miami-Dade Community College; William L. Gibson of Orlando; Alice F. Hall of Pasco County; J. Ralph Hamlin of Tallahassee; Leland Hawes of *The Tampa Tribune*; Rep. Mary Ellen Hawkins of Naples; Edward J. Herrmann of Pasco County; T. E. Holcom of Lakeland; Homer Hooks of Lakeland; James J. Horgan of Pasco County; Mrs. Nell Hutchins of Fort Walton Beach; Rep. Holmes Melton of Mayo; Rep. Jerry G. Melvin of Fort Walton Beach; Rep. Tom McPherson of Fort Lauderdale, Lucy Morgan of the *St. Petersburg Times*; Emmet B. Peter, Jr., of the *Orlando Sentinel*; Rep. Curtis Peterson of Eaton Park; Rep. Ted Randell of Fort Myers; W. D. Roberts of Collier County; Rep. Jane Robinson of Cocoa; Mrs. M. G. Shuman of Duette; Nixon Smiley, Miami columnist and author; Mrs. Elizabeth F. Smith of the *Magnolia Monthly*, Crawfordville; William R. Spear of the *Fort Myers News Press*; Mrs. Bonita Swann of Wauchula; Sen. Pat Thomas of Quincy; George L. Thurston of Tallahassee; Rep. Fred N. Tittle, Jr., of Tavernier; Mrs. Juanita S. Tucker, postmistress of Christmas; Mrs. Peg Twichell of Tamarac; and Dr. Robert O. Vernon and Marvin Witt, of Tallahassee.

The many people who helped in the early years of my research are acknowledged in the *Florida Handbook*, 1955 edition, pages 39–41.

I f you enjoyed reading this book, here are some other books from Pineapple Press on related topics. For a complete catalog, write to Pineapple Press, P.O. Box 3899, Sarasota, FL 34230, or call (800) 746-3275.

History/Biography/Folklore

African Americans in Florida by Maxine D. Jones and Kevin M. McCarthy. Profiles of African American writers, politicians, educators, sportsmen, and others in brief essays covering over four centuries. Suitable for school-age readers. Teacher's manual available.

Classic Cracker by Ronald W. Haase. A study of Florida's wood-frame vernacular architecture that traces the historical development of the regional building style as well as the life and times of the people who employed it.

The Florida Chronicles, Vol. I: Dreamers, Schemers, and Scalawags by Stuart B. McIver. Engaging character sketches of unusual characters who made Florida their home: includes storytellers, tycoons, movie makers, and more.

The Florida Chronicles, Vol. II: Murder in the Tropics by Stuart B.McIver. A diverse collection of bizarre and sometimes unbelievable true crime from Florida's history.

Florida's First People by Robin Brown. A fascinating account of the Paleoindians of Florida using modern archaeological techniques and replications of primitive technologies.

Florida Portrait by Jerrell Shofner. A beautiful volume of words and pictures that traces the history of Florida from the Paleoindians to the rampant growth of the twentieth century.

The Florida Reader edited by Maurice O'Sullivan and Jack Lane. A historical and literary anthology of visions of paradise from a diverse gathering of voices, including Ralph Waldo Emerson, Marjorie Kinnan Rawlings, and Harry Crews.

Florida's Past (3 volumes) by Gene Burnett. A popular collection of essays about the people and events that shaped the state.

Legends of the Seminoles by Betty Mae Jumper with Peter Gallagher. Tales told around the campfires to Seminole children, now written down for the first time. Each story illustrated with an original painting by Guy LaBree.

Thirty Florida Shipwrecks by Kevin M. McCarthy. The best shipwreck stories, from young Fontaneda, wrecked in 1545 and held captive by Indians for 17 years, to the Coast Guard Cutter Bibb, sunk off Key Largo in 1978. Illustrated by William Trotter.

Twenty Florida Pirates by Kevin M. McCarthy. Tales of the most notorious Florida pirates, from the 1500s to the present day. Illustrations by William Trotter.